The New C

THE NEW CRUSADES, THE NEW HOLY LAND

Conflict in the Southern Baptist Convention, 1969–1991

David T. Morgan

The University of Alabama Press

Tuscaloosa

Library of Congress Cataloging-in-Publication Data

Morgan, David T.
The new crusades, the new Holy Land : conflict in the Southern
Baptist Convention, 1969-1991/David T. Morgan.
p.   cm.
Includes bibliographical references and index.
ISBN 0-8173-0804-0 (alk. paper)
1. Southern Baptist Convention—History—20th century.
2. Baptists—United States—History—20th century.   3. Church
controversies—Baptists—History—20th century.   4. Southern Baptist
Convention—Doctrines.   5. Baptists—Doctrines.   6. Fundamentalism—
United States—History.   7. United States—Church history—20th
century.   I. Title
BX6462.3.M67 1996
286'. 132' 09045—dc20   95-12245

*To Judy, Cindi, Brian, my mother,
and Willene—the dearest people in my life*

Preface

AMERICA'S LARGEST Protestant denomination, the Southern Baptist Convention, experienced deep divisions and vast change between the late 1960s and the beginning years of the 1990s. Serious controversy shook the denomination's foundations to a limited degree in the 1970s and profoundly during the 1980s. This book is designed to provide a detailed and well documented history of the conflict that troubled the SBC from 1969 to 1991 and reached its greatest intensity in the 1980s. It is demonstrated that the struggle was both a crusade for truth and a bid for power. The many battles of those years were in some ways reminiscent of the great Crusades of the middle ages, for the latter-day crusaders regarded the Southern Baptist Convention as a holy land to be redeemed, not from Muslim infidels but from what, to their way of thinking, were the forces of theological "liberalism."

In the year 1095 Pope Urban II, speaking at Clermont in France, called for a crusade against the Muslims who had conquered the Christian Holy Land in Palestine and had deprived Christians of the right to visit the places where Christ had walked and where he had died. The response to the pope's call was amazing. Great lords and lowly peasants, as well as many from the social ranks in between, joined the crusading army and headed eastward to redeem the Holy Land by force. Over the next two centuries there were at least seven papally approved expeditions to the Holy Land, but only the first Crusade was genuinely successful. Some of the others accomplished little, while one was diverted to Constantinople and resulted in Christians fighting Christians. Those who answered the call to the first Crusade were able to recapture much of the Holy Land and to establish their Latin Kingdom of Jerusalem, but those who came after them struggled to hold it. Near the end of the thirteenth century the Muslims retook Palestine.

Far away from France and much farther away from the land where Christianity originated, a new crusade was launched for the holy land of the Southern Baptist Convention in 1969. Not an influential pope but a small-town Baptist preacher who held views that he called "conservative" but others termed "fundamentalist" started a movement to redeem the SBC, which, in his mind, had been captured by "liberals." That preacher was M. O. Owens, Jr., of Gastonia, North Carolina. His call, unlike Urban II's, was not answered by countless multitudes and abundant financial support. After struggling to launch his crusade in North Carolina and to expand it to cover the nation, Owens was forced to give up the enterprise for lack of adequate means. By the time he did so, two others stepped forward in 1978 and 1979 and called for a second crusade to achieve the same objective that Owens's crusade had failed to attain. The two men were Paul Pressler, a layman and an appeals court judge from Houston, Texas, and Paige Patterson, a preacher and academician from Dallas.

Like Owens, the two Texans were fundamentalists who preferred to be called conservatives and who believed that the denomination's leaders had compromised theological truth, especially the tenet of an "inerrant" Bible, and had allowed "liberalism" to undermine the foundations of the SBC. Pressler, Patterson, and other fundamentalist crusaders who joined them were able to convince a majority (ranging from just over 50 percent up to 60 percent at times) of the messengers to the annual Conventions beginning in 1979 that the denomination had veered from the path of theological truth. They insisted that the Convention had to be put back on the course originally set by the SBC's founders who, they contended, had stood forthrightly for an infallible Bible.

Many Southern Baptists, though they were obviously in the minority, denied that there was any widespread liberalism in the denomination. They argued that theological diversity was the traditional Baptist way and that the fundamentalists sought to control the SBC by secular political means. Although labeled as liberals by the fundamentalists, the "traditionalists" eventually came to be known as moderates. The moderates resisted as best they could—albeit without success—the fundamentalist crusaders' "war" against the perceived forces of denominational "liberalism."

In the pages that follow it is argued that the "conservative resurgence" (as the fundamentalists called it) and the "takeover" of the Southern Baptist Convention (as the moderates called it) was in fact both a crusade for truth, at least in the minds of the fundamentalist crusaders, *and* a bid for power through the use of secular political means. The moderates denied the former, and the fundamentalists seldom admitted the latter. Moderates called what happened a "takeover," while fundamentalists called it a "take back." Neither side ever recognized the validity of the opposing side's claims, and that is why the conflict became so bitter and divisive and led in 1990 and 1991 to the emergence of a moderate quasi-denomination, called the Cooperative Baptist Fellowship, within the SBC.

It is also argued here that there was a direct and significant link between the Owens crusade, which failed, and the Pressler-Patterson crusade, which succeeded. Judge Pressler, who had talked of doing something about liberalism in the SBC since the early 1960s, was only minimally active until he was spurred into a leadership role in 1977 by William A. (Bill) Powell, Sr., a key figure in the

Owens movement. There was no difference between the views of Pressler and Patterson and those of Owens and Powell. All of them sought to establish as a cardinal doctrine of Southern Baptists that the Bible was the "infallible and inerrant word of God." They were convinced that Christianity and the SBC rose or fell on this theological tenet, and they were determined to have the SBC affirm forthrightly and officially that the Bible was the final authority for all Christians.

What the fundamentalist crusaders came to realize was that they could not achieve their objective of establishing theological truth without changing the power structure of the denomination and that could not be done apart from using political means and gaining political power. They had to win control over the appointment of the trustees who governed denominational agencies and that meant employing politics to elect fundamentalist candidates to the presidency of the SBC. How that was done is described at some length in this book.

In a real sense the second crusade was a continuation and extension of the first, but it succeeded, where the first had failed, because Pressler and Patterson could muster adequate financial support and because they were able to forge a political coalition of rural and big city churches. Pastors of the urban superchurches who had halfheartedly backed the efforts of M. O. Owens, a small-town preacher, were persuaded by Pressler and Patterson to give vital and visible support. Both of the Texans had impressive Southern Baptist credentials, and Judge Pressler was independently wealthy, too. The leaders of the second crusade knew how to organize and, more importantly, had the wherewithal to carry out their designs. By 1990, when the SBC met in New Orleans, the fundamentalist crusaders had triumphed and were clearly in the ascendancy in the denomination.

The convention in New Orleans marked the final political triumph of the fundamentalist crusaders following more than two decades of bitter conflict under the banner of an "inerrant" Bible. After that annual meeting serious moderate resistance ceased, and the fundamentalist victors consolidated their power during the second half of 1990 and throughout 1991. Hence, by the end of the latter year, the controversy was settled in favor of the fundamentalists.

Since the purpose of the book is to focus primarily on the conflict—its origins, development, and outcome—only cursory attention is given to the years of fundamentalist domination following 1991. The general developments of the post-1991 period are highlighted in an epilogue, but no effort has been made to offer details and thorough documentation of the fundamentalists in power. Exploring the aftermath of the "new crusades" is best left for a subsequent study.

Acknowledgments

Every author is helped along in his work by many people, and this one is indebted to a long list of kind and generous men and women. Bill Sumners, archivist at the Southern Baptist Historical Library and Archives in Nashville, pointed me toward sources time and again, sources that proved crucial in the research and writing of this work. Mrs. Pat Brown, the former librarian at SBHLA, was most kind in making necessary books available to me for my use at home when I had to leave Nashville before finishing my research. Mrs. Elizabeth Wells and her staff in Special Collections at the Samford University Library assisted me many times.

Participants in the conflict, from both the fundamentalist and moderate sides, were generous in sharing their thoughts and materials with me. I owe a special debt of gratitude to M. O. Owens, Jr., Paige Patterson, Paul Pressler, and Gerald Primm. Each of them provided me with material which was absolutely essential to my work. Alan Neely has my heartfelt thanks for giving me an interview and pointing me toward valuable sources when I first embarked upon the project. Fisher Humphreys shared materials with me and constantly encouraged me in my work, for which I thank him sincerely. W. W. Finlator was another generous contributor of thoughts and material. I appreciate the information and encouragement he provided. I am deeply grateful to Glen Holt, William E. Hull, Mrs. Anne Neil, James A. Pate, Mrs. Betty Powell, and Frank Turner, my friend since adolescence, for the interviews they gave me. Bert Card and Lee Porter were kind enough to share information with me in telephone interviews, and I thank both of them. But for the help of all of these good people my study would have suffered serious deficiencies.

Helping in other ways were some wonderful people at the university where I teach. I thank Robert McChesney, my president, for the encouragement and support he gave me. He demonstrated a strong interest in what I was writing, taking time to read a considerable part of it. Justin Fuller, my friend and colleague for over twenty years, read the manuscript and offered many helpful suggestions. Mrs. Judy Morris, who keeps our department from sliding over the precipice into chaos at the beginning and end of each semester, assisted me invaluably in getting the computer glitches (which I inadvertently keyed in) out of the manuscript and making it presentable to the publisher. The Research and Special Projects Committee of the University of Montevallo awarded me several research grants without which I could not have carried out the research. I was also awarded a grant by the Southern Baptist Historical Commission. That grant was of great assistance, and I deeply appreciate it.

There are no doubt many others whom I should thank. If, because of slipping memory, I have failed to include someone, I apologize. I am most grateful to everyone who helped in any way. I have not forgotten two very important people in all of this—my publisher, Malcolm MacDonald, for his interest, encouragement, and support, and my wife, Judy, who made so many of those trips to Nashville with me, endured my neglect of her while I worked on the project, and waited anxiously with me to hear from the publisher about the manuscript's fate. To both I am forever grateful, along with all the others, mentioned and unmentioned, who kindly lent me a helping hand.

Abbreviations

ABP	Associated Baptist Press
ATS	Association of Theological Schools
BCE	Baptist Center for Ethics
BCMP	Baptist Cooperative Mission Program
BFM	Baptist Faith and Message
BFMF	Baptist Faith and Message Fellowship
BGCT	Baptist General Convention of Texas
BJC, BJCPA	Baptist Joint Committee, Baptist Joint Committee on Public Affairs
BP	Baptist Press
BSSB	Baptist Sunday School Board
CBF	Cooperative Baptist Fellowship
CLC	Christian Life Commission
CP	Cooperative Program
EC	Executive Committee
FMB	Foreign Mission Board
HMB	Home Mission Board
NRPR	New Religious Political Right
PAC	Public Affairs Committee
RLC	Religious Liberty Commission
SACS	Southern Association of Colleges and Schools
SBA	Southern Baptist Alliance
SBC	Southern Baptist Convention
SBHLA	Southern Baptist Historical Library and Archives
SSB	Sunday School Board [same as Baptist Sunday School Board]
SBWIM	Southern Baptist Women in Ministry
TC	Triennial Convention
WMU	Woman's Missionary Union

The New Crusades, the New Holy Land

1

SBC Origins and Development to 1979

An Overview

THE ROOTS OF all modern-day Baptists, including Southern Baptists, were nurtured in the soil of seventeenth-century England, where English General and Particular Baptists sprang to life. Thomas Helwys, who had spent time in Holland, was imprisoned in England for his advocacy of religious freedom. His followers, who believed in a "general atonement" as taught by the Dutch theologian Jacob Arminius, multiplied and became known as General Baptists. By the 1630s English independents who believed that Christ's death was for the "elect" formed congregations and became known as Particular Baptists. They were thoroughgoing Calvinists. By the end of the seventeenth century the Generals and the Particulars had formed their respective general assemblies and associations. Both adopted confessions of faith and both saw members from their churches emigrate to England's American colonies.

In the colonies the Particular Baptists began to flourish under the new name of "Regular" Baptists, while the General Baptists failed to thrive. During the 1750s a new group of Baptists, a by-product of the Great Awakening, emerged and became known as Separate Baptists. Like evangelist George Whitefield, their spiritual father, the Separates were very evangelistic. About the time the Separates were filtering into the backcountry of the southern colonies, during the mid-1750s, many of the General Baptists were absorbed by the Regular Baptists.

A generation later, after the American Revolution, negotiations were undertaken by various Baptists to see if a merger was possible. Eventually the different groups united and took the name of United Baptists. In 1814 they organized on the national level by forming at Philadelphia the General Missionary Convention of the Baptist Denomination, usually called the Triennial Convention. The TC was primarily a foreign missionary society, but it soon organized home mission work, Sunday schools, publication work, state conventions, and educational institutions. Not all Baptists appreciated these efforts. Disgruntled antimissionary Baptists created tensions during the 1820s and 1830s and ultimately broke away to form the Primitive Baptists, whose hyper-Calvinist views led them to see no need for missions. As they saw it, God was more than able to save those he elected without the help of the TC or any other human agency.[1]

Trouble emerged in the TC during the early 1840s when it refused to appoint slaveholders as missionaries. Baptists from the South pulled out in 1845, forming the Southern Baptist Convention at a meeting in Augusta, Georgia. The division was mainly over slavery, not theology, thus prompting historian Walter Shurden to conclude that "the blunt historical fact is that we formed the Southern Baptist Convention in defense of the southern way of life."[2]

Shurden has correctly observed that Southern Baptists are a mix of four distinct traditions. Two of the traditions predate the American Revolution. They were the Charleston tradition and the Sandy Creek tradition. Charleston, South Carolina, was the center of the Regular Baptist tradition in the South. Among the principal founders and developers of this tradition were Oliver Hart and Richard Furman, both prominent South Carolina Baptist ministers. Rooted in Calvinism, they emphasized ministerial order.

At Sandy Creek in North Carolina the Separate Baptists in 1755 launched their campaign to convert the inhabitants of the Carolina, Virginia, and Georgia backcountry. Their leaders were Shubal Stearns and his brother-in-law Daniel Marshall. Revivalism, emotionalism, and pietism were the earmarks of these zealous Baptists. Every Sunday was a revival, as sinners were admonished to repent publicly and demonstrably. Oftentimes energized converts announced that they had received a call from God to preach.

During the years after the formation of the Southern Baptist Convention two new traditions emerged and gained considerable support. There was the Georgia tradition founded by W. B. Johnson, an early SBC president, and I. T. Tichenor, director of Home Missions. They advocated "cooperative denominationalism" to promote foreign and home missions and downplayed theological uniformity. And they gloried in the southern way of life.

The final tradition was established in Tennessee by James R. Graves, who first stirred the waters of controversy in the new denomination. Graves sought to ground the identity of Southern Baptists in a false history through his high church beliefs that came to be labeled Landmarkism. He proclaimed local church successionism, and the "exclusive validity of Baptist churches," meaning that the only true churches were local ones that could trace their lineage back through the ages to the church in Jerusalem founded by the apostles in the first century.

From these four traditions Southern Baptists acquired order from Charleston, ardor from Sandy Creek, "Southerness" from Georgia, and from Tennessee an "ecclesiological identity resulting in narrow sectarianism." Since Shurden first pointed out these four traditions around 1980, other students of Baptist history, especially H. Leon McBeth and Albert McClellan, have contended that there are also the Texas and Virginia traditions, but to the author the characteristics of the latter two had already been manifested in the four noted by Shurden.[3] Strains of Shurden's four traditions were readily apparent among Southern Baptists during the controversy that erupted first in 1969. Moderates lauded the Georgia tradition of "cooperative denominationalism" and the Charleston tradition of order, while the fundamentalists adhered to the narrow theological perspective and fervent evangelism of the Sandy Creek tradition. Relatively few Southern Baptists, even among fundamentalists, openly admitted to following the Landmarkist tradition.

As the SBC grew after 1845 it became a composite of the four traditions noted above, but the Landmark movement encountered strong opposition. Graves, the father of the movement, taught that the local church was the kingdom of God on earth and that the only true church was the one that followed the New Testament to the letter—especially in the matter of baptism. Baptists, according to Graves and his followers, could trace their lineage unbroken from New Testament times to the present. Baptism had to be performed by Baptists, only members of a local Baptist church could take communion in that particular church, and Baptists should not invite to their pulpits non-Baptists nor recognize non-Baptist churches as true churches, asserted the Landmarkers.

This extremely narrow view was unacceptable to many Baptists who believed that the SBC should be open to people of divergent views, as long as their views were within the general realm of what Baptists had believed for over two centuries. In their minds Landmarkism was rigidly creedal and diminished the role of the denomination and individual believers. Although the vast majority of Southern Baptists were committed to local church autonomy, most were convinced that each church could better fulfill its mission by working with other churches as a denomination and that each believer was his or her own priest in the matter of interpreting the Scriptures. Controversy raged during the 1850s, and for a half century Landmarkers remained in the SBC as a vocal minority. In 1905 *some* left the SBC to form a separate Landmark body, but many who held Landmark views remained in the SBC. The fact that some Southern Baptist churches until contemporary times condemned "alien immersion" (i.e., baptism administered by non-Baptists) and practiced "close communion" (i.e., permitted communion to be given in a church only to that church's members) offered clear evidence that Landmarkism's influence lingered in the SBC.[4]

That the narrow perspective of the extreme Landmarkers was out of harmony with the Southern Baptist mainstream is indicated by an action taken at the annual meeting of the Southern Baptist Convention held in Birmingham,

Alabama, in 1891. At that meeting a committee on forming the Sunday School Board made its report, the last paragraph of which declared:

> In conclusion, your committee, in its long and earnest consideration of this whole matter in all its environments, have been compelled to take account of the well known fact that there are widely divergent views held among us by brethren equally earnest, consecrated and devoted to the best interest of the Master's Kingdom. It is therefore recommended that the fullest freedom of choice be accorded to everyone as to what literature he will use or support, and that no brother be disparaged in the slightest degree on account of what he may do in the exercise of his right as Christ's freeman.

The report was approved with only a few dissenting votes.[5] Undoubtedly Landmarkers saw little to appreciate in such a statement or in the fact that it was overwhelmingly approved.

The flames ignited in the SBC by the Landmark controversy had scarcely died out when the Convention was rocked by another disturbance—the fundamentalist/modernist controversy of the 1920s. Fundamentalism resembled Landmarkism in that both were ultraconservative in theology and vicious in their attacks against denominational agencies. Moreover, both fought to control denominational organizations and spawned dissident factions that abandoned the Convention when they could not have their way. But, as in the case of the Landmarkers, plenty of Southern Baptists who were fundamentalists remained in the SBC.

Fundamentalism was not peculiar to Southern Baptists. In fact, it manifested itself first among northern Baptists and northern Presbyterians. Cutting across denominational lines, fundamentalism is the militant, ultraconservative wing of Christianity. As George Marsden and Ernest Sandeen, two leading authorities on the subject, have demonstrated, fundamentalism grew out of several nineteenth-century movements, including British and American millenarianism, dispensationalism, and the "Princeton theology" exhibited in the views of such teachers as Charles Hodge and Benjamin B. Warfield of the theological seminary at Princeton University.

Fundamentalism made its first deep impression on American life and society during the early 1920s when it put forth stout opposition to the idea of biological evolution, the historical critical study of the Bible, and liberal or "modernist" theology. Fundamentalists set out to prevent the teaching of evolution in the public schools and to take over several Protestant denominations.[6]

Adherents to fundamentalism tended to be creedalists and separatists and found it difficult to live in harmony with those who did not endorse all of their beliefs. Words like *accommodation* and *diversity* were not in their vocabulary. As a consequence they found themselves ill-at-ease in a denomination. It has been observed that fundamentalism is more than a set of theological beliefs; it is an attitude—a frame of mind. In most cases it is an inflexible frame of mind.[7]

Modern fundamentalism's theological tenets were set forth in a series of twelve small volumes published between 1910 and 1915 and entitled *The Fundamentals: A Testimony to the Truth*. Various American and Canadian scholars contributed articles to this work. Among those who did were three Southern Baptist seminary professors and one former Southern Baptist pastor, Amzi Clarence Dixon, who also was one of the work's three editors. About one third of the articles in the twelve volumes were devoted to defending the authority and verbal inspiration of the Bible. Other articles dealt with the deity of Christ, the virgin birth, the substitutionary atonement, the bodily resurrection of Christ, and Christ's imminent and visible return.

The twelve volumes were sent to hundreds of theological students and clergymen all across the United States. Paying the postage were two wealthy brothers, Milton and Lyman Stewart, who were from California. Reportedly three million pieces of literature were sent at their expense.[8]

Among Baptists the most visible advocates of fundamentalism were Northern Baptists, but one Southern Baptist pastor, J. Frank Norris of Fort Worth, Texas, was as vocal in asserting fundamentalist views as were the Northern Baptist stalwarts William B. Riley and John Roach Straton. In good fundamentalist fashion Norris championed the theory of a verbally inspired, infallible Bible, claiming that God had spoken directly to his penmen in their native language and that they became "vessels or channels" through which divine thought came.

While other Southern Baptists believed in the inspiration of the Bible, not all were prepared to accept the notion that the authors had put their pens to paper only to have God move their hands for them. The meaning of the word *inspiration* became the source of a long and bitter debate. Norris was such a fierce advocate of a fully inspired and inerrant Bible, along with some of the other "fundamentals," that he alienated a majority of Southern Baptists. He virtually declared war on the SBC, labeling the denomination's leaders as "the Sanhedrin," and he attacked George W. Truett, popular pastor of Dallas's First Baptist Church, calling him such names as "the infallible Baptist Pope" and "the Holy Father." By 1924 a majority of Texas Baptists were fed up with Norris. He and his church were voted out of the Baptist General Convention of Texas. Six years later Norris and his church, First Baptist of Fort Worth, pulled out of the SBC.[9]

Fundamentalists such as Norris attacked all liberal views, and to them a liberal view was one that was out of harmony with *The Fundamentals*. Any view of the Scriptures that did not claim absolute inerrancy for them was regarded as liberal or "modernist." The so-called modernists did not turn the other cheek. Instead they launched a counteroffensive, and their leader was the popular liberal Baptist preacher Harry Emerson Fosdick, minister of the Park Avenue Baptist Church in New York City.

During the bitter but short-lived controversy between fundamentalists and modernists, two issues produced inflamed rhetoric from both sides. One, of course, was the issue of biblical inspiration. The other was the theory of biological evolution. To a fundamentalist it was not possible to believe both the Bible and Charles Darwin. Fundamentalists, including Norris, charged that Darwinism had been embraced by professors in Baptist institutions of higher learning. Enough pressure was brought to bear through various state conventions that professors in at least five Baptist schools were forced to resign, but the fundamentalists failed in their efforts to unseat the denomination's foremost Darwinist, William Louis Poteat, biology professor and president of Wake Forest College in North Carolina. The school's alumni rushed courageously and successfully to Poteat's defense.[10]

By the end of the 1920s the worst of the fundamentalist/modernist "holy war" was over. The Scopes trial and Sinclair Lewis's *Elmer Gantry* did much to turn fundamentalism into a laughingstock in the eyes of the American public. Lewis's popular novel, which was made into a Hollywood movie over thirty years later (1960), told the story of a man expelled from seminary for seducing the dean's daughter. Several years later, however, that man—Gantry—achieved some acclaim as a fundamentalist preacher, only to be ruined by revelations of his past indiscretions. Also damaging to fundamentalism was the fatal shooting of one Dexter E. Chipps by J. Frank Norris in 1926. Chipps, a wealthy friend of Fort Worth's mayor, went to Norris's office to challenge statements the fundamentalist preacher had made about corruption in the city's government. According to Norris, an argument that ensued between the two men turned violent, and he had to shoot Chipps in self-defense. The jury agreed and Norris went free, but many expressed doubt about the verdict, since Chipps was not armed and had been shot three times. The incident cost fundamentalism a great deal of support.

Although fundamentalists suffered significant setbacks, some of the SBC's leaders recognized that a considerable number of Southern Baptists sympathized with at least some fundamentalist tenets, and those leaders went in search of a compromise that would keep as many Southern Baptists in the SBC fold as possible. Norris had numerous supporters. If he left the Convention (as he did, finally, in 1930), good riddance, but there was no need to lose others who might leave, too, if no attempt was made to accommodate their views.

Thanks to E. Y. Mullins, president of Southern Baptist Theological Seminary, and George W. McDaniel, president of the SBC and pastor of Richmond's First Baptist Church, the fundamentalist/modernist controversy was defused at the 1925 annual meeting of the SBC. L. R. Scarborough, president of Southwestern Baptist Theological Seminary, was also instrumental in promoting the compromise that satisfied all sides—at least for the time being. The compromise took the form of a statement of faith called the Baptist Faith and Message of 1925. Some strongly opposed adopting it on the grounds that Baptists were a noncreedal people. Even so the statement was approved, and Southern Baptists who believed that the denomination should declare its doctrinal position were placated. Those who objected to creeds found the statement ambiguous enough to merit their acquiescence.[11]

As it turned out, enough Southern Baptists were satisfied with the 1925 statement of faith to keep the Convention together, although the peace that prevailed was an uneasy one and threatened to break down from time to time. Southern Baptist fundamentalists were somewhat discredited and less vocal, but they remained in the denomination ever alert for a cause that would enable them to promote their agenda successfully. SBC leaders made it easy for fundamentalists to remain by emphasizing "the voluntary principle," which asserted the right of every Southern Baptist member and church to do as they pleased. In 1928 the SBC's Executive Committee declared in a report that the SBC was "not an ecclesiastical body composed of churches, nor a federal body composed of state conventions." Instead churches chose to cooperate with the SBC in an effort "to extend Christ's kingdom," but "always on a purely voluntary basis, and without surrendering in any way or degree their right of self-determination." In a word, all churches were "autonomous."[12]

Fundamentalist-inclined Southern Baptists doubtlessly viewed the voluntary principle as a mixed blessing. On the one hand it allowed them and their local churches to do as they pleased without interference from any larger body, but on the other it allowed the "modernists," or "liberals," the same privilege, and to fundamentalists the liberals were wrong and had no right to call themselves true Southern Baptists. Yet, the voluntary principle continued to hold Southern Baptists together, while Baptists and Presbyterians in the North split over fundamentalism.

During the 1930s and 1940s, advocates of fundamentalism, failing to gain control of their denominations, began to establish an informal network outside the structures of the older Protestant bodies, a network of Bible institutes, liberal arts colleges, summer assemblies, radio programs, foreign mission agencies, and publication outlets. While most of these institutions and agencies were independent, they often had ties with and were supported by people in several denominations—especially Baptists and Presbyterians. There were Bible schools like Moody Bible Institute (founded much earlier but promoted by fundamentalists as a sound institution) and the Bible Institute of Los Angeles (BIOLA), and other schools like Wheaton College in Illinois, Bob Jones University (founded in Florida but moved to Tennessee and then South Carolina), and Fuller Theological Seminary in California.

Also spreading the fundamentalist message were scores of Bible conferences held regularly at various places, the best known of them being the one that met at Winona Lake, Indiana. National radio programs like Charles E. Fuller's "Old Fashioned Revival Hour," M. R. DeHaan's "Radio Bible Class," and Billy Graham's "Hour of Decision" had countless fundamentalist listeners and supporters. Youth for Christ, which was founded in the 1940s, was begun by fundamentalists. John R. Rice's *Sword of the Lord*, a paper he began publishing in 1934, was only one of many publications that enjoyed a considerable circulation among fundamentalists.

In 1942 some of the more flexible and inclusive fundamentalists organized the National Association of Evangelicals, an organization that the hardliners criticized and refused to join. Remaining somewhat out of favor with the national public during most of the 1940s and 1950s, the forces of fundamentalism asserted themselves again in the 1960s and 1970s when decisions from the United States Supreme Court striking down compulsory prayer and Bible reading in the public schools and permitting abortion nationwide threatened, in their minds, to rip apart the moral fabric of America.[13]

Southern Baptist fundamentalists became more vocal and active after the Supreme Court rendered the decisions *Engel v. Vitale* (1962) and *Abington Township v. Schempp* (1963), which excluded school-sponsored Bible reading and prayer from the public schools. Also, a particularly bitter controversy erupted in 1963 over what fundamentalists regarded as a "liberal" book on Genesis, called *The Message of Genesis*. That book's author, Ralph Elliott of Midwestern Baptist Theological Seminary, was forced to resign following a lengthy flap over his interpretation of the Genesis account.

Doctrinal donnybrooks were nothing new to Southern Baptists. They predated the 1920s' feud over fundamentalism, going back to the last quarter of the nineteenth century. Crawford H. Toy, a German-trained Old Testament scholar, had been pressured into leaving Southern Seminary in 1879 because he championed the historical and textual criticism of the Bible. In 1898 William H. Whitsitt, a church historian at Southern and the president of that institution, felt compelled to resign after his views on the origins of Baptists caused Landmarkers in the SBC to stir up serious trouble for the seminary. The Elliott controversy was the most serious involving a Southern Baptist seminary since Whitsitt had stepped down at Southern. Out of it came the adoption of the second Southern Baptist statement of faith in less than forty years—the famous Baptist Faith and Message Statement of 1963.

To defuse the crisis over the Elliott book and placate Southern Baptist fundamentalists, Porter Routh, executive secretary-treasurer of the Convention's Executive Committee, urged Herschel Hobbs, pastor of the First Baptist Church of Oklahoma City and newly elected SBC president, to appoint a committee to revise the 1925 statement of faith. It was done, and at the 1963 SBC meeting in Kansas City the new Baptist Faith and Message Statement was adopted. It offered a more forthright declaration regarding the nature of the Scriptures, proclaiming that the Bible was "truth, without any mixture of error," that Jesus Christ was the criterion by which the Bible was to be interpreted, and that all confessions of faith were merely "guides in interpretation." For the time being the fundamentalists were satisfied, as were Southern Baptists who preferred more flexibility in their approach to the Scriptures and more distance between themselves and creedal statements.[14]

No one could foresee in 1963 that the new Baptist Faith and Message Statement would not stem the tide of controversy but instead would destroy the dikes that held the tide back. In less than ten years, rallying around it, Southern Baptist fundamentalists would organize for the purpose of purging the denomination of "liberalism." W. A. Criswell, pastor of First Baptist Dallas and an avowed fundamentalist, was elected president of the SBC in 1968. Although Criswell took no direct steps to alter the course of the Convention during his two years as president, the fact that he was elected twice encouraged fundamentalists, giving them hope that the SBC could be turned in a direction which would be pleasing to them. Energized by this hope, North Carolina Baptists, led by M. O. Owens, Jr., began in the late 1960s to rally fundamentalists to stand up for an inerrant Bible and to destroy liberalism in the SBC.

The Owens movement was given impetus in 1969 when a new controversy was provoked by the Sunday School Board's publication of *The Broadman Commentary*. In particular, objections were raised to the commentary on Genesis written by G. Henton Davies, a British Baptist. Davies suggested that Abraham probably misunderstood God's command to sacrifice his son Isaac. The publication of this volume became a bitterly contested issue at the 1970 and 1971 annual meetings of the SBC, and the Convention voted to ban further distribution of the Genesis commentary and to have it rewritten. Pleas by Sunday School Board officials for a more open-minded approach went unheeded, and the volume was rewritten by Clyde T. Francisco, a Southern Baptist seminary professor. At a meeting in Atlanta in 1973, two years after the dispute over *The Broadman*

Commentary came to a head, Owens led in forming the Baptist Faith and Message Fellowship, which soon published a newspaper called *The Southern Baptist Journal* and urged all Southern Baptists who "believed the Bible" to unite and save the SBC from the forces of liberalism.[15]

Before the decade of the 1970s was over the BFMF suffered from internal dissension, and it never obtained sufficient funds to carry out its objectives. When it began to falter, Paige Patterson, who was then president of the Criswell Center for Biblical Studies (later called Criswell College), and Paul Pressler, then a Houston appeals court judge, took charge of the fundamentalist crusade to redeem the SBC holy land. These two men first met in New Orleans in March 1967 when Patterson was a graduate student at New Orleans Baptist Theological Seminary. At that meeting they talked about changing the course of the SBC, but they did not actively pursue a plan for doing so until several years later.[16] Thus, the movement which Southern Baptist fundamentalists would later call the "conservative resurgence" began with M. O. Owens, Jr., and was carried on by Paul Pressler and Paige Patterson and brought to fruition by them. Another key figure was William A. (Bill) Powell, Sr., who helped found the Baptist Faith and Message Fellowship and became editor of *The Southern Baptist Journal*, the BFMF's organ for spreading its message. What these men did and how and why they did it are questions that will be explored in the next chapter, but now it is necessary to present a thumbnail sketch of the SBC as it appeared immediately before the famous 1979 meeting at Houston that marked the beginning of drastic changes in that historic body.

By 1979 the Southern Baptist Convention, already the largest Protestant denomination in America, consisted of more than 35,000 member churches and over 13,000,000 individual members, although only 9,600,000 were "resident members." Collectively the 35,000 churches and the SBC owned property valued at close to $10 billion, and the denomination's total receipts were running over $2 billion annually. This enormous growth from a tiny, regional denomination to the country's largest Protestant body followed a gradual upward climb until the establishment of a financial apparatus called the Cooperative Program during the late 1920s and the 1930s. The year 1925 is often cited as the beginning of the CP, but actually it evolved over a fourteen-year period, its development being hindered by the Great Depression. By 1939 the CP was well established and was heralded by the Executive Committee that year as "the greatest step forward in Kingdom finance Southern Baptists have ever taken."

At that juncture SBC leaders were advocating a fifty-fifty split of CP funds between the state conventions and the SBC as the "ideal" distribution, but the division turned out to be closer to 62 percent for state programs and 38 percent for the work of the national body. The CP was enormously successful for many years, carrying the SBC to undreamed-of heights, as local churches sent a portion of their budgets to their respective state conventions, which took their share of 62 percent and forwarded the remaining 38 percent to SBC headquarters in Nashville. There the EC distributed the money among SBC agencies according to the budget adopted by the Convention at its annual meeting. Even Ellen Rosenberg, whose work is highly critical of Southern Baptists and often ridicules them, has called the CP "an ingenious plan." During the controversy that commenced in 1979 the program became a source of bitter contention between fundamentalists and moderates. The former wanted to cut off funds to denominational agencies they considered corrupted by liberalism, while the latter insisted on supporting all SBC agencies.[17]

The mission of this large denomination, according to Article II of the SBC's constitution, is to "provide a general organization for Baptists in the United States and its territories for the promotion of Christian missions at home and abroad and any other objects such as Christian education, benevolent enterprises, and social services which it may deem proper and advisable for the furtherance of the Kingdom of God." For the purpose of accomplishing its mission, the Convention created an organization that grew gradually to mammoth proportions through the years. At the time the Pressler-Patterson crusade was launched in 1979 there were four general boards (the Annuity Board, the Foreign Mission Board, the Home Mission Board, and the Sunday School Board), eight institutions (Golden Gate, Midwestern, New Orleans, Southeastern, Southern, and Southwestern Theological seminaries, plus the Seminary Extension Department and the Southern Baptist Foundation), and seven commissions (American Baptist Seminary Commission, Brotherhood, Christian Life, Education, Historical, Radio and Television, and Stewardship). There were also special committees and standing committees, and the SBC had a working relationship with four associated organizations—the American Bible Society, the Baptist Joint Committee on Public Affairs, the Baptist World Alliance, and the Woman's Missionary Union. The largest of the SBC agencies was the Sunday School Board, the world's biggest publisher of religious literature. Less well known than the highly visible boards was the Executive Committee, which conducted the business of the SBC between its annual meetings and which wielded a powerful influence in the denomination. The EC was a large committee consisting of representatives from the various states that had state conventions.[18]

Each annual meeting of the SBC was unique, since 35,000 churches elected new messengers each year. Every church was constitutionally allotted between one and ten messengers on the basis of size or financial contributions to the Convention's work. No church, not even the largest, was allotted more than ten. All SBC agencies were governed by trustees. The trustees were elected at the annual

Convention by the entire body of messengers from a slate of nominees presented by the Committee on Boards (renamed the Committee on Nominations in 1987). The Committee on Boards was chosen from a list of nominees presented to the Convention by the Committee on Committees, which was named by the president of the Convention about nine months after his election and before the next annual meeting. Hence the key to controlling the Convention was to win the presidency again and again and, through the appointive power of the president, secure the election of fundamentalist trustees to the various Convention agencies. Since there were approximately a thousand trustees, all serving staggered terms, placing a majority of trustees in the different agencies had to be a long-term project. Bill Powell was the architect of this strategy. He explained it to Pressler who, along with Patterson, eventually set out to implement it over a period of ten years.[19]

One reason the Pressler-Patterson coalition was successful in winning control of the SBC was that the SBC was so used to controversies. It had been spawned by a controversy, and it had weathered two other big ones through the years. The Landmarkers were held at bay for decades, and the fundamentalists' onslaught was blunted in the 1920s. There had also been the agitation of the 1970s caused by the unsuccessful but persistent efforts of M. O. Owens and Bill Powell. As the decade of the 1980s opened, following the election of Memphis fundamentalist pastor Adrian Rogers to the SBC presidency, many Convention leaders erroneously assumed that the new challenge to the old principles of accommodation and diversity would pass, just as had the challenges of the Landmarkers a century earlier and of the fundamentalists during the 1920s. The fundamentalists themselves were skeptical of succeeding. Even Paige Patterson, who knew the history of the SBC well, was not confident of victory until James Draper defeated Duke McCall for president at the New Orleans convention in 1982. Pressler, on the other hand, was confident. "The judge always thought we would win," Patterson told the author during an interview in late 1992.[20]

2

The First Crusade

A Scarcity of Funds and Followers, 1969–1979

IN SEARCHING FOR an understanding of the controversy that tore the SBC asunder between 1979 and 1991 it is necessary to keep in mind that conservatism had been present in the SBC from its inception. Sometimes, as in the cases of the Landmarkers and the fundamentalists, conservatism took on a radical complexion. Undoubtedly, a clear majority of Southern Baptists from 1845 to 1979 were conservative in their theological perspective, but Landmarkers and fundamentalists were more than conservative. They were basically reactionary, meaning that they reacted negatively to new ideas and cultural changes and longed to return to the pristine purity of some imagined time when the church was absolutely true to the "faith once delivered to the saints." In the case of the Landmarkers, the emphasis was on baptism and successionism, while the fundamentalists focused their attention on the Bible, which they insisted was an inerrant and infallible book handed down by God to guide true believers and to warn the wicked. Both the Landmarkers in the nineteenth century and the fundamentalists of the 1920s created disturbances in the SBC, but neither prevailed in their efforts to turn the Convention in the direction they were convinced it should go. Even so, their influence never went away entirely, and in the case of the fundamentalists they remained in the denomination, waiting for the chance to make their views heard and, if possible, to change the direction of the Convention.

The opportunity to act presented itself to the fundamentalists in the 1960s and 1970s when the United States began to abandon—at least in the fundamentalists' minds—its Judeo-Christian heritage and when prominent SBC leaders, particularly those who held high-paying jobs in Nashville as employees of the Convention, seemed to compromise with the "liberalism" that was gaining momentum in the country. For example, numerous fundamentalists were convinced that leaders like Foy Valentine, director of the Christian Life Commission, should be condemning abortion outright, not holding conferences to discuss it. Conservatives accused the United States Supreme Court and Democratic presidents John F. Kennedy and Lyndon B. Johnson of destroying the nation by chipping away at its Christian foundation. Both Kennedy and Johnson, after all, promoted a civil rights policy that would give all Americans equality, regardless of race, *religion*, or sex, and the Supreme Court had the audacity to outlaw Bible reading and prayer in the public schools.

Capitalizing on the groundswell of conservative clamoring against such new directions were President Richard Nixon, until the Watergate scandal ruined him, and later Ronald Reagan, who, while president, set a course that, he said, would take the nation back to its original economic, moral, political, and religious principles. Fundamentalists, including Southern Baptist fundamentalists, cheered Reagan on by voting for him in large numbers. This conservative climate of public opinion helped make possible what happened to the SBC at Houston in 1979 and during the years which followed, but the foundation was laid between 1969 and 1979 by four men, two of whom have been given ample credit and two who have received little or none.

With regard to the "conservative resurgence" in the SBC, most who have studied it are content to say that Paul Pressler and Paige Patterson were the instigators, for their efforts achieved lasting results. On the other hand, thorough historians who want to find the roots of the "conservative resurgence" (or the "fundamentalist takeover"—depending upon one's perspective) should not overlook or dismiss the work of M. O. Owens, Jr., and Bill Powell just because they could never gain a large enough following or acquire sufficient resources to achieve their objectives. At the least, they must be given credit for laying the foundation upon which Pressler and Patterson built their successful movement. Owens and Powell led the first crusade. Though it failed, it made it easier for the second to succeed. This chapter investigates the link between the two crusades, thus giving insight into the background of the events which occurred at the 1979 convention in Houston.

All four of the men who sought to reclaim the SBC holy land from the "liberals" had impressive Southern Baptist credentials. Milum Oswell Owens, Jr., always called M. O. by himself and others, was born at New Holland, South Carolina, on September 4, 1913. His father, M. O., Sr., was also a Baptist minister. Both father and son were educated at Furman University and Southern Baptist Theological Seminary. The younger Owens was graduated *cum laude* from Furman in 1933; in 1939 he received his Th.M. degree from Southern Seminary, and in 1976 he was awarded a D.Min. degree from Luther Rice Seminary in Jacksonville, Florida. Between 1939 and his retirement in 1981 Owens held pastorates in South Carolina, Florida, and North Carolina. In 1964 he led in founding the Parkwood Baptist Church in Gastonia, North Carolina, retiring from that pulpit in 1981. He also had a one-year stint as a missionary in Belgium, and he preached in Israel, Chile, Australia, and Alaska, in addition to Belgium and his regular pulpits. Throughout his long career Owens held significant posts in the SBC, the South Carolina Baptist Convention, and especially the North Carolina Baptist Convention, and he wrote some Training Union literature for the Baptist Sunday School Board. Owens, obviously a man of unbounded energy, also became involved in a number of "conservative" causes, not the least of which was the Baptist Faith and Message Fellowship, founded in 1973 under his leadership.[1] The founding of the BFMF turned out to be the first step in the fundamentalist march to Houston six years later, and much more will be said about it below.

Although first off the mark, Owens was not destined to lead the SBC to the fundamentalist finish line. Paul Pressler and Paige Patterson did that, and both of them had Southern Baptist credentials as impressive as those of Owens. Pressler, a Texan, came from a long line of Baptist preachers and lawyers. A Houston native, he was born there June 4, 1930, to Herman Paul Pressler, Jr., and Elsie Townes Pressler. Herman Paul Pressler III was the son of parents with considerable means, enabling him to attend Phillips Exeter Academy in New Hampshire, Princeton University, and finally the University of Texas Law School. When young Pressler left the flatlands of Texas to climb the peaks of academia in the North, he encountered "liberalism" in the churches he attended. He came to despise what he called the "negative impact" it had on "culture and society" and on the "presentation of the gospel." In the early 1960s he was moved to combat "liberalism" by writing a pamphlet to warn Southern Baptists against it and by helping found the Evangelical Christian Education Foundation, which agreed to assist New Orleans Baptist Theological Seminary financially, as long as the seminary adhered to certain doctrinal principles. Pressler served in the Texas legislature and was later appointed judge of the state appellate court in Houston. For years he was a member of the Second Baptist Church in Houston until the late 1960s, when it became too liberal to suit him any longer. At that point he joined the First Baptist Church of the same city. Though a layman, Judge Pressler preached by invitation to a number of churches on a regular basis.[2]

In searching for allies to help him slay the dragon of liberalism the judge heard about and sought out Paige Patterson who, at the time they first met in 1967, was a doctoral candidate at New Orleans Seminary. The judge described the first time he met Patterson as follows: "My wife and I knocked on Paige and Dorothy Patterson's door at the New Orleans Seminary on either March 9th or 10th, 1967. We were attending a layman's conference in New Orleans. My wife keeps her daily calendar and those dates have been confirmed by the calendar." Pressler and Patterson soon became better acquainted at the Cafe DuMonde over coffee and beignets.[3]

Like Pressler, Patterson was a Texan from a family of prominent Southern Baptists. He was born Leighton Paige Patterson in Fort Worth on October 19, 1942, the son of Thomas Armour (T. A.) and Roberta Turner ("Honey") Patterson. His father was a well-known pastor in Beaumont and, for fourteen years, executive director of the Baptist General Convention of Texas. The younger Patterson attended Hardin-Simmons University in Abilene, where he soon came to be labeled a "maverick" because of frequent confrontations over his fundamentalist beliefs. After his college days at Abilene he went on to New Orleans Seminary, where he earned both undergraduate and graduate degrees, finishing his doctorate in 1973. Following a stint as pastor in Arkansas, he eventually became president of what ultimately was known as Criswell College in Dallas. Articulate, highly intelligent, and very well educated, Patterson was quite able to explain theological subtleties for the "conservative" cause. He became the movement's theological spokesman, while Pressler served as chief organizer and political strategist, but the judge implemented a strategy first devised by another, namely Bill Powell.[4]

None of these men preferred, or even liked, being called fundamentalists. They favored being designated *conservatives,* arguing that *fundamentalist* had become a pejorative term applied to Shiite Muslims and people of still other religions outside Christianity. And yet both Owens and Patterson admitted in interviews with the author that *fundamentalists* with a small *f* was an appropriate designation for those who held their views. There can be little doubt that all of them adhered to beliefs that were clearly fundamentalist in nature, and so the author refers to them as *fundamentalists* without compunction. Also, the author has no qualms about referring to the people on the other side of the SBC controversy as *moderates,* even though the fundamentalists labeled them "liberals." They held views that, for the most part, were traditional and conservative, but they were less doctrinaire and far more flexible than the fundamentalists, allowing believers to be their own priests when interpreting the Bible.[5] Hence, in this study the two warring sides will be designated consistently as *fundamentalists* and *moderates.*

When Pressler and Patterson met and talked on that first occasion in New Orleans, they did not establish any plan for changing the SBC. They simply agreed between themselves that someone should do something. Judge Pressler later insisted that over the next ten years he was not visibly active in trying to alter the direction of the Convention. He summed up what happened after the

Cafe DuMonde meeting of March 1967: "Between 1967 and 1977, Dr. Patterson and I fellowshiped from time to time. He had me preach for him in Arkansas. I had my youth group in Houston, served as judge and did many other things, but action in the Convention was only tangential. I did communicate with M. O. Owens and others in North Carolina and was concerned about the fact that nothing was being done in the Convention."[6]

The judge claimed that he was minimally involved in fundamentalist efforts before 1977. His words to the author were as follows:

> Before meeting with Dr. Patterson, friends of mine and I had been solicited to give money to the endowment for New Orleans Seminary. We responded by setting up a foundation called The Evangelical Christian Education Foundation. This foundation was to support New Orleans Seminary so long and only so long as the seminary adhered to certain basic doctrinal positions in the opinion of the self-perpetuating independent board of trustees of the foundation. I think my communication with M. O. was to get a list of people that might be willing to contribute to that foundation. We aided students at New Orleans Seminary with scholarships and we gave several thousand dollars to the seminary in a conditional grant to help their endowment. There was no communication system envisioned at that time and therefore it was not sought for that purpose. You cannot document my activities during that period of time because they were so minimal that there was nothing to document. It was about 1976 or 1977 that Bill Powell of the Baptist Faith and Message Fellowship contacted me and he encouraged me to get involved. It was about the same time that some students from Baylor who had been in our youth group became alarmed at what they were being taught at Baylor. My activity really started about 1977.[7]

Thus, according to Judge Pressler, he played little or no part in organizing the fundamentalist forces that ultimately captured control of the SBC until two years before the famous 1979 meeting of the Convention in Houston, and there is little reason to doubt his claim. However, there is evidence that he did more than he realized. Paige Patterson's recollections of what the two men did between 1967 and 1977 were essentially the same as Pressler's, but he acknowledged that he and the judge made informal contacts and talked to people about possible action that might change the "liberal" course of the SBC, and the author knows of at least one minister whom the two men tried to "recruit" for their cause during the *early* 1970s. Also, a letter dated November 12, 1969, from Judge Pressler to M. O. Owens, indicates that the judge was a bit more active than he later admitted to being. To Owens, he wrote:

I was most delighted to receive your letter of October 16, 1969. I have heard about the Fellowship of Conservative Baptists from Brother [Robert] Tenery and am so delighted to know what is occurring in North Carolina. The liberals are well organized. We are not. We are in the majority but losing because we have not spent the time necessary to organize and assert ourselves. We have also failed to let people know the gravity of the situation and the issues with which we are confronted. I can think of nothing that I would like to work with more than a nationwide fellowship of conservative Baptists.[8]

Pressler went on to expand upon getting organized and providing leadership for the SBC as well as state conventions and local associations. He informed Owens that the Evangelical Christian Education Foundation of which he was president put out three or four newsletters each year, and the judge expressed an interest in securing the names of "your gentlemen in North Carolina who would like to be added to our mailing list."[9] The letter certainly suggests that Pressler was more than minimally involved, but he was almost certainly far less involved before 1977 than after that year.

While the judge was engaged in his limited efforts between 1967 and 1977, M. O. Owens was busy rallying fundamentalist-inclined Southern Baptist pastors in North Carolina for a crusade against what he perceived as liberalism in the SBC and particularly in the North Carolina Baptist Convention. In January 1969 the Gastonia pastor launched his movement with two hundred pastors behind him. At one of the early meetings, held at Zoar Baptist Church near Shelby in February 1969, Clark Pinnock, who was briefly on the faculty of New Orleans Seminary and who was then known for his very conservative theological stance (which he later abandoned), delivered an address entitled "The Suicide of Modern Theology and a Proposal for Its Resurrection." Approximately 150 people attended.

Almost a month before Pinnock's speech, he resigned from his seminary post at New Orleans, leaving later that year for a teaching position in Illinois. A few weeks before he spoke to the Owens group Pinnock proposed publishing a book entitled *The Crisis in Southern Baptist Theology* to expose the "liberalism" taught in Baptist seminaries. To M. O. Owens he wrote of "dismantling the Nashville Vatican before it smothers us all." Regarding the book, he said: "It must be factual and accurate so that the liberals cannot fault it. Yet it must be hard hitting so they cannot duck it either." Pinnock asked what the Owens group might think of the idea and how much money it would contribute toward producing it. He offered his services as editor of the book if the resources to produce it could be obtained.[10]

Besides being connected with the Owens group, Pinnock was also in touch with Judge Pressler. In May, while he was still teaching at New Orleans Seminary, Pinnock wrote Pressler and told him that Piedmont Bible College in Winston-Salem, North Carolina, planned "to set up the *Piedmont Baptist Seminary*" and hoped to work with "Bible believing Baptists" but independent of "the Nashville Vatican." The disgruntled professor thought this was a good idea because "the way New Orleans now is going it seems highly unlikely it will ever give sound conservative leadership."[11]

By the end of the summer Pinnock was gone from New Orleans, and he soon faded from the ranks of the Southern Baptist army that planned to conquer liberalism in the SBC. M. O. Owens, however, had just begun to fight. In May he began working with his allies to put together a slate of "conservative" officers for nomination at the North Carolina Baptist Convention's meeting later that year. He also continued to contact pastors throughout the state, urging them to join what he called the Fellowship of Conservative Baptists and to help "stem the trend of liberalism among North Carolina and Southern Baptists." Owens made the position of his group clear: "We affirm our belief that the Bible is the Word of God and is an inerrant and authoritative Word from God." Claiming that his group then numbered four hundred North Carolina pastors, he said they dared hope that they could elect "conservatives" to offices in the state convention.[12]

Within a few months of its organizing, the Owens group came under attack. William W. Bell, pastor of Proctor's Chapel Baptist Church in Rocky Mount, North Carolina, and an Owens supporter, was an early target. He received a letter from Lynwood Walters of nearby Enfield, a letter that suggested that the Fellowship of Conservative Baptists was guilty of bibliolatry. Walters said, "You indicated that Southern Baptists are 'People of the Book.' Even though I highly exalt the Bible as *man's* recorded, faith-interpretation of God's revelation in a particular history (have I lost you?), and that it also is relevant to our day, the CENTRAL fact of Christianity is not a BOOK but a PERSON. God doesn't want to live in a King James Version or in brick and mortar (church) but in human flesh. . . . The only way to prove faith is not to run to a Book, but to have it! I ask you which came first, Bible or faith?"[13]

Such barbs apparently left Owens and his cohorts undaunted as they continued to make plans for the approaching meeting of the state convention in Fayetteville. In late October, just before the meeting, he urged his allies to be sure that their churches elected messengers to the state convention and to make certain that those elected took their credentials with them. He urged them all to be there "on Tuesday when we elect the officers." To lend additional credibility to his cause, Owens noted that Greensboro pastors Gerald Primm and Jack Wilder were working with him to promote "our Conservative movement and work." The Owens forces were optimistic about the possibility of effecting changes in North Carolina in part because of what had happened at the annual meeting of the SBC in June. Contrary to custom, the "Liberal wing" had nominated W. C. Smith to run for president against W. A. Criswell, the fundamentalist incumbent who sought a second term. Usually an incumbent who chose to run for a second term was not challenged. Robert Tenery, an Owens ally, claimed that Smith's nomination was "the big test between the Liberals and the Conservatives. The Liberals had hoped to mount an attack and if not beat, to seriously challenge his [Criswell's] candidacy." Criswell's landslide victory of 7800 to 400 votes was an encouraging sign to the Owens group that they, too, might triumph in Fayetteville, and to a degree they did.[14]

The Owens supporters left Fayetteville convinced that they had made some headway in their cause. One Owens man, Forrest L. Young, saw "a magnificent victory in the election of a conservative president and first vice-president for our Baptist State Convention." Young gave Owens the credit, saying it could not have happened without the leadership of the Gastonia pastor. Robert Tenery, then pastor of Pleasant Hill Baptist Church in Elkin, wrote to both Owens and Pressler afterward, giving his impressions of what had taken place. In his letter to Owens, Tenery praised Pressler and requested that Owens send the entire "mailing list of our Conservative fellowship" to the Houstonian. He spoke of a meeting of the fellowship's supporters at Faymont Baptist Church in Fayetteville (apparently held at some point during the state convention) at which Owens "handled things well" and left "the press thoroughly confused." Tenery expressed the belief that other North Carolina Baptists would identify with them "since Fayetteville."

To Pressler, Tenery reported that the "Conservatives" did not win every battle at Fayetteville, but did "win the war" and expressed confidence that the "Conservative movement" would move forward from that time. He referred to encouraging signs from other states. He had heard that the Georgia and Texas annual meetings had been "more Conservative than usual." Moreover, it was reported that W. A. Criswell "took the ball" in Nashville recently in regard to "Liberalism among us." In his letter to Pressler, Tenery enclosed the names of "some strategic men in Alabama and Georgia."[15]

So encouraged by what happened at Fayetteville that he wanted to expand the efforts of the Owens group was Gerald Primm, pastor of Greensboro's Eller Memorial Baptist Church and probably Owens's closest friend and ally. The two men had met in Charlotte about 1957 and had been friends through the years. Primm was a great admirer of Charles H. Spurgeon, the famous British Baptist minister of the nineteenth century. In honor of Spurgeon he resolved to start a publication called *The Sword and the Trowel*, a paper with the same title as one started by Spurgeon in 1865 and published until 1968. The Greensboro pastor carried through with his plans, and his paper became the first organ of the North Carolina Fellowship of Conservative Baptists in 1969. Along with Owens, Primm became an early mover and shaker in the effort to rally fundamentalist Southern Baptists in North Carolina against the forces of "liberalism," and it was he and Robert Tenery who first suggested that the group send the call to arms to like-minded brethren in other states. In a letter to Owens dated November 29, 1969, Primm mentioned J. C. Lanning, a former North Carolina pastor who had moved to Virginia. Lanning had told Primm of a conservative group in Virginia led by Richmond pastor V. Allen Gaines. The Greensboro pastor urged Owens to add Lanning to their mailing list, for he was "a good foot man." He continued, saying that "this movement of conservatives" needed to be "coordinated all across the land." Primm envisioned a loose Southern Baptist conservative fellowship and state fellowships in each state. He believed Owens was the man to coordinate the movement and "get it going."[16]

Two weeks after writing the aforementioned letter Primm wrote another, urging Owens to take the reins of leadership and push the movement forward. He noted that the purpose of the crusade was "evangelization with a pure gospel," and he was sure that God had raised up Owens to be the "spokesman." One of the first initiatives that Primm thought the fundamentalists should undertake was the purification of Baptist schools. He noted:

> Anyone can see that if our schools continue to put out pastors who are not certain about the Word of God written we are going to continue the downgrade road! We *MUST* either change many of the personnel in the existing schools or begin a new one. Time is short! We can't wait much longer. Campbell [College] may be the place to start with massive financial help on condition that school pledge itself from top to bottom to quality education with no equivocation on the Bible as the inerrant, infallible Word of God without error of any kind in the original. I would personally like to see us pressure Mars Hill [College] into the same commitment before the new president (of that school) takes it down the road of no return![17]

Owens was just as concerned as Primm with regard to spreading the fundamentalist message and redeeming Baptist institutions that, to his way of thinking, had fallen victim to liberalism. Rounding up the troops and persuading them to do their part was not always easy, however, especially in view of the fact that Owens had to take care of his duties as a full-time pastor. He wrote countless letters admonishing other Baptists, many of them full-time pastors like himself, to attend the meetings of the fellowship and to offer their financial support. Over and over he received replies from people expressing regret for missing the last meeting. Some gave reasons; some did not. Another problem Owens faced was money. His efforts depended on donations. In many of the letters he received, the correspondents enclosed a measly dollar or two "to help with the mailing."[18] As a rule, Baptist ministers who hearkened to Owens were not wealthy, and so he never received much in the way of financial support. In the end this was one of the reasons his movement sputtered.

In spite of the obstacles Owens trudged on, and more and more Baptists joined his ranks. He soon became aware of other groups that were springing up outside North Carolina. For example, late in 1970 the Owens group made contact with a layman named J. C. Caruthers of Naples, Florida. He called himself executive director of Concerned Christians and claimed to be on the same mission as the North Carolina group. Gerald Primm sent him issues of *The Sword and the Trowel*, and Caruthers was well pleased with the views expressed in that publication. Two years later Caruthers, taking his cue from Primm's 1969 suggestion of state fellowships of conservative Southern Baptists, changed the name of his group to the Fellowship of Conservative Southern Baptists. Meanwhile, M. O. Owens had renamed his North Carolina group Baptists United for Spiritual Revival, which sponsored still another paper, *Baptists United News*, edited by Robert Tenery. In *The Sword and the Trowel*, which Primm published independently but in association with the Owens group, the Greensboro minister traced the evolution of Owens's work:

> While several voices of concern have been raised among Southern Baptists, the first organized movement of note started in North Carolina. After proceeding rather informally for over three years, the group became more concretely structured last September [1971], since then having as its name Baptists United For Spiritual Revival and as its president M. O. Owens, Jr., unofficially the leader from the first. The Steering Committee includes some of the best-known N.C. ministers, such as James DeLoach and former State Convention President A. Leroy Parker.[19]

Although it was not until September 1971 that Owens officially organized Baptists United for Spiritual Revival, he called his movement by that name as early as November 1970. He referred to himself as a "convener" and his group as "the organization through which Conservatives in North Carolina" were working. At the end of 1970 he claimed to have a mailing list of supporting pastors and laymen with eight hundred names on it. He also, at that point, referred to *The Sword and the Trowel* as the movement's organ.[20]

The year 1971 was a time of two fierce battles for Owens and his supporters. The first concerned a sermon preached by William E. Hull, Southern Seminary's dean of theology, at Crescent Hill Baptist Church in Louisville, Kentucky, in 1970. Entitled "Shall We Call the Bible Infallible?" the sermon was published in that year's December issue of *The Baptist Program*, a publication of the SBC's Executive Committee. Its appearance in an official SBC publication brought forth a torrent of criticism from fundamentalist Southern Baptists because it called into question the notion of biblical inerrancy. Hull went even further, asserting that "even if we did have a perfect text rendered in a perfect translation, we would be far from an infallible Bible because it would still have to be explained by fallible interpreters." Thus, he concluded, "it is not wise to call the Bible infallible." Hull, over two decades later in an interview with the author, said that the sermon was casual and that he never expected the furor which followed its publication.

M. O. Owens in particular was offended, and at the SBC meeting in St. Louis in 1971 he moved that the Convention respectfully request that the Executive Committee and the editor of *The Baptist Program* provide equal space so that competent conservative scholars could present the "Convention viewpoint," which, Owens maintained, was that the Bible was inerrant. The Executive Committee studied the matter, declared that the editors had presented a "balanced response to the article," and concluded that there was no good reason for "continuing the controversy in *The Baptist Program*." The matter was dropped, but it was not forgotten by Owens, who suggested in 1992 that the fundamentalists might not have pursued their crusade until it led to victory in Houston if SBC leaders had been willing to give their views a fair hearing in 1971.[21]

Owens's other major battle in 1971 was fought in North Carolina over the issue of baptism by immersion. A number of Baptist churches in the state accepted members who had been sprinkled instead of immersed. Owens saw this as a serious matter and insisted that such churches should have no voice in the affairs of the state convention. He informed fellow Baptist pastors, "we must stop the inroads of liberalism here, or not at all. If the uniqueness of immersion is taken from us, we have no reason to call ourselves Baptists." He proposed adding to the constitution of the state convention an amendment that would have limited membership to persons from churches that recognized only immersion as the biblically required form of baptism.

When he raised the immersion amendment issue on the eve of the annual meeting of the North Carolina Baptist Convention, Owens set off a bitter controversy that lasted through the following year and did not finally end until 1974. J. S. Larrimore, pastor of Monroe's First Baptist Church, wrote Owens of his opposition to the proposed amendment, calling it "a reversion to Landmarkism" and "creedal in nature." He accused Owens of starting fights and destroying unity and peace among North Carolina Baptists. Marion D. Lark, another pastor, wrote to Julian Hopkins, the state convention's former director of evangelism and an insider in the Owens group, and proclaimed his opposition: "You and others in the M. O. Owens 'group' have taken this issue of the mode of Baptism and turned it into a vehicle for trying to gain 'political power' within the structure of the Baptist State Convention." Lark vowed to help defeat the Owens amendment. Many others, however, supported the amendment. When it came to a vote at the 1971 state convention 1,245 messengers (54 percent) voted for it, while 1,028 voted against it. Since a two-thirds vote was required to amend the constitution, the amendment went down to defeat. Owens vowed to try again at the next annual meeting.[22]

Instead of discouraging Owens, the two defeats he suffered in 1971 spurred him on. Soon after losing the fight over the immersion amendment at the annual meeting of the state convention, he was contacted by J. C. Caruthers, who proposed forming the Fellowship of Conservative Southern Baptists convention-wide. He urged Owens to take charge of "Convention Politics"—in other words, to be the political leader of a new nationwide organization of "Conservative Southern Baptists." By this time Owens's supporters (most but not all of whom were from North Carolina) numbered one thousand—five hundred pastors and five hundred laymen, according to his count. Owens seemed ready to take the lead, and he had no hesitancy in admitting that his activities were political. He wrote to W. Ross Edwards, editor of *Word & Way,* the state journal of Missouri Baptists, on January 6, 1972: "It is distasteful to be engaged in what is patently 'political' action. But I have come to the conclusion that we have no choice. It is either work together to protect what we believe in, or else throw in the towel, and abandon the Convention."[23]

Owens was convinced that the dangers of liberalism were as real and ubiquitous as ever, and he saw no help to combat them coming from the large churches. To one supporter he wrote that many of the young pastors had been "brainwashed at Southeastern Seminary" and knew "very little about God's Word" and cared less. To another sympathizer he wrote that the pastors of the "First churches" were "liberal, or else afraid to take a stand." The hope of turning the SBC in a fundamentalist direction lay with "the smaller churches and the lay people." He reported to his friend Joe T. Odle, editor of the *Baptist Record* (the journal of the Mississippi Baptist Convention), that the "dilemma in North Carolina" was creating interest all across the country, that he was hearing from other areas, and that this was perhaps God's way of "helping us begin to form a fellowship of those who truly believe the Word."[24]

The year 1972 turned out to be a pivotal one for Owens and Southern Baptist fundamentalists, for at the end of that year they held the preliminary meeting that would lead to the founding of the Baptist Faith and Message Fellowship in the spring of 1973. Many fundamentalists left the 1972 SBC meeting in Philadelphia disgruntled after the fight over *The Broadman Commentary.* They were convinced that the officials at the Sunday School Board were going to go as far to accommodate "the liberals" as the Convention would tolerate. People who were disenchanted with various and sundry developments wrote to Owens, assuming he would sympathize with their discontent. While he *was* concerned with liberalism in the SBC, the Gastonia pastor still focused primarily on the problems in North Carolina, which, he believed, stemmed from Baptist institutions having fallen into the hands of liberals. He went after Wake Forest College and even the Baptist Hospital. He asserted that many professors at Wake Forest were neither Christian nor Baptist and that they attempted to "destroy the faith of our young people." Owens was appalled that the school allowed dancing on campus and unchaperoned visitation of men and women in the dormitories. He argued that the Baptist Hospital was "really no longer operated by Baptists," and he suggested that the churches that supported his movement designate their Cooperative Program funds so as to exclude both Wake Forest and the Baptist Hospital. In Owens's eyes his organization of Baptists United for Spiritual Revival was in a "life and death struggle to keep the Baptist Convention 'Baptist' and not a conglomerate of any and everything."[25]

The matter still uppermost in Owens's mind as the summer of 1972 slipped away was his immersion amendment, which he intended to present once more on the floor of the state convention in November. He continued to receive some letters supporting the amendment and others opposing it. Complicating the situation, as far as Owens was concerned, was a compromise amendment that a pastor named Thurmond Allred of Concord intended to introduce in place of the Owens amendment. The Allred amendment allowed churches that accepted nonimmersed members to send messengers to the state convention, provided that the messengers themselves had been immersed. Owens called this an unacceptable compromise and rallied his forces to defeat the Allred amendment and pass his. In the end, both amendments failed. During the heat of the battle at the convention Owens withdrew his amendment for the sake of "harmony." This action brought Owens several letters of praise, including one which said that Owens had proved himself to be a "spiritual giant—a man ten feet tall." The writer of those words claimed that he was proud to be numbered among Owens's friends.[26]

Even though Owens was primarily concerned about his own state convention through most of 1972, he took time to call preliminary meetings that soon led to the founding of the Baptist Faith and Message Fellowship. He called a meeting at Charlotte that summer. Among those who attended was Bill Powell, at that time an employee of the SBC's Home Mission Board. A great deal will soon be said about Powell, but it should be noted now that it was at the meeting in Charlotte in the summer of 1972 that he first articulated the strategy for changing the SBC—the very strategy later implemented by Paul Pressler and Paige Patterson. When the group held its second preliminary meeting in October at the First Baptist Church of Atlanta, Georgia, Powell reiterated it. That meeting was attended by twenty-five men from eleven states, and those present decided to call another meeting for the purpose of organizing the BFMF. Once more meeting at the Atlanta church, with the support of its pastor Charles Stanley, those who responded to Owens's call organized the BFMF on March 3, 1973.[27]

One of Owens's major problems was that of enlisting the *open* support of pastors from big-city churches. Although a few pastors from the big urban churches offered their support, most who sympathized with BFMF's objectives were cautious. Demonstrating the typical reticence of pastors from the "super churches" was Homer Lindsay, Jr., of Jacksonville, Florida's First Baptist Church. Owens urged Lindsay to attend what would be the BFMF's organizational meeting in Atlanta, but in January before the meeting was held Lindsay wrote: "I am thankful for your leadership and for the stand you have taken. I personally do not see myself as a fighter. . . . I am not sure that I would be of much value as a leader in this." A few weeks later Owens wrote, urging Lindsay to reconsider: "I earnestly hope you will be with us. This will be a crucial meeting. If the interest is little, then there will be little incentive or reason to continue our efforts to rally the conservative men. . . . It is imperative that men from some of the larger churches stand firm in this matter. The leadership of the Convention will pay little or no attention if the men active in this effort are pastors of the small town and rural churches. But if there are a number of the larger, more influential churches, then they must notice."[28]

Adrian Rogers, pastor of the huge Bellevue Baptist Church in Memphis, Tennessee, in like fashion to Lindsay, claimed to be sympathetic toward Owens's efforts but found it necessary to miss the "crucial" meeting. Instead he sent regrets along with his "prayers and best wishes . . . for bringing our convention closer to the Bible." Eventually Lindsay and Rogers both joined the effort, and their names, along with Charles Stanley's, were used by Owens in trying to rally additional support. Also identifying with the BFMF eventually was Jerry Vines, who in 1973 was pastor of the West Rome Baptist Church in Rome, Georgia.[29] Vines, like Rogers, was one of the fundamentalists who would be elected president of the SBC during the 1980s.

While few pastors from large urban churches joined the BFMF, many pastors from small towns and rural areas were enthusiastic about the new organization. An example was Wendell Wentz, pastor of Benton Baptist Church in the tiny town of Benton, Alabama. Wentz was eager to strap on his armor and join the battle. On the eve of the organizational meeting he wrote Owens: "I know what Liberalism will do to a man in the ministry and I have seen many of my dear friends who were as sound and solid and fundamental as a John R. Rice or Frank Norris while in college turn to Liberalism once they were enrolled in our seminaries. I hate Liberalism." He was even more excited after the organizational meeting in Atlanta, where he was put on the "Steering Committee" of the new organization. In a letter to Owens on March 13, he said, "The battle for the Bible is on in our Convention, but I am asking every pastor I know of to stand for the Faith once delivered to the saints."[30]

In spite of the enthusiasm of some, Owens must have been at least a little disappointed after the organizational meeting. He sent out six hundred letters about the March meeting, but only sixty men attended. An offering was taken, yielding only $330, but $6,000 more was pledged. This was still a meager beginning in the BFMF's endeavor to turn the gigantic SBC back "to the Bible as the revealed, infallible, and authoritative Word of God."[31] The problems of inadequate funding and lack of support from a significant number of influential Southern Baptists would plague the BFMF during its entire existence.

Still, in the early days there seemed to be plenty of room for optimism. At the founding meeting "it was learned that Conservative groups" were "springing up all over the Southern Baptist Convention composed of pastors and laymen . . . deeply disturbed about the continuing liberal bent of some Southern Baptist leaders." The BFMF was not alone, and it moved forward with its first president, M. O. Owens, Jr. Other officers elected included first vice-president Laverne Butler, pastor of Ninth and Oak Baptist Church of Louisville, Kentucky; second vice-president Bill Sutton, pastor of First Baptist Church of Pine Hills, Arkansas; and secretary-treasurer Aubert Rose, an associate minister of First Baptist Atlanta. Besides these officers, twenty-five members were elected to serve as the "Board of Directors." The organization proposed to be a strong advocate of "the doctrinal and theological positions" set forth in the Baptist Faith and Message Statement of 1963, and Owens set the tone of the fundamentalist crusade: "We do have Liberalism and Neo-Orthodoxy in our midst. For our leaders and our editors to say that Southern Baptists are all conservative is a lot of hogwash. To say 99% of Southern Baptists are conservative and believe the Bible is pure semantics. There are hundreds of neo-orthodox pastors serving Southern Baptist churches. There are hundreds of teachers in our seminaries and colleges who are rationalists and liberals. And there are many, many lay people who follow the same lines." On several earlier occasions Owens had declared that the number one "hotbed of liberalism and neo-orthodoxy/existentialism" was in North Carolina and that it was centered in Southeastern Baptist Theological Seminary.[32]

In addition to identifying its enemies as liberalism and all the institutions that promoted it, the BFMF spelled out its objectives. The members intended to establish a fellowship for pastors and lay people who were "orthodox," to encourage pastors and churches to stay in the SBC, to urge all Southern Baptists to remain true to the Baptist Faith and Message statements of 1925 and 1963, to promote meetings at which "the truth, inerrancy and authority of God's Word is fully affirmed and proclaimed," to provide an "independent Southern Baptist news and opinion medium—nationwide in coverage" that would "offer a sounding board for those who believe in the Bible as 'truth without any mixture of error,' " to support Baptist schools, colleges, and seminaries that "stand true to the Word of God," and to "call Southern Baptist pastors to stand true to the Word." Approximately six months after the BFMF was founded, it was incorporated by the state of Georgia. In the articles of incorporation the stated purpose of the organization was that of promoting the Baptist Faith and Message Statement of 1963, "with particular emphasis on Article I, (*The Scriptures*)." That article said, "The Holy Bible . . . has God for its author, salvation for its end, and truth, without any mixture of error, for its matter." The organization's bylaws declared membership "open to persons who subscribe wholeheartedly to the beliefs and purposes of the Corporation as set out in these by-laws." The bylaws also provided that a two-thirds majority of the members present at a meeting could admit or expel members and announced that there would be an annual meeting sometime between April and November.[33]

Before the BFMF was a month old, it experienced internal problems. Aubert Rose, the organization's first secretary-treasurer, resigned on March 30, saying he had never been at peace about serving. He promised to support the BFMF "financially and bodily in attendance." Rose was succeeded as secretary-treasurer by LeRoy Cooper, a pastor from East Point, Georgia. Just over a month after Rose resigned, Owens was informed that a church Rose had served in Ohio had split under his leadership because he had "holiness inclinations." In addition, Doug Chatham, who served on the new fellowship's steering committee, turned out to be a charismatic. He was ousted from Woodlawn Baptist Church in Decatur, Georgia, because he was going to have a Bible conference there and invite "known 'glossamaniacs' to speak." Owens was called upon to clarify the BFMF's position on "the holiness-pentecostal question." He and the officers of the fellowship did that on April 26, 1973, by asking Chatham to resign, for they desired "no identification at all with the charismatic movement."[34]

A host of other problems cropped up, and Owens was the man called upon to deal with them. Some BFMF supporters thought that the organization ought to leave the SBC, while others talked of not supporting the Cooperative Program, and still others stopped using the literature published by the Baptist Sunday School Board. One pastor wrote: "We no longer use Southern Baptist literature as it follows the same liberal line as the [*Broadman*] Commentary. We do not give to the Cooperative Program, because I was a graduate of Southern [Seminary] and know the heresies taught in our Seminaries." Wendell Wentz, steering committee member and one of the directors, also stopped using literature from the Sunday School Board. As these little problems came up, Owens somewhat surprisingly urged moderation. He advised one pastor to keep giving to the Cooperative Program for the time being until Owens could work out a plan to designate money in a way which would be "fair and equitable."[35]

At the same time Owens sought to urge the friends of the BFMF to act cautiously and with patience, he had to defend himself and the fellowship against severe criticism. One irate pastor from Hollywood, Florida, called Owens a "false prophet" for objecting to the "Charismatic Movement." Another called the BFMF "a devisive [*sic*] force" and asserted that its efforts smacked of negativism. That writer asked Owens to discontinue his efforts for the good of the SBC. The BFMF president wrote back, assuring the writer that his organization had no desire to be divisive. Kenneth W. Veazey, a pastor from Norfolk, Virginia, scathingly denounced the BFMF for trying to impose its views on all Southern Baptists. He wrote: "What I hear you very loudly and clearly saying is that you are working to get rid of the so-called 'liberal' element within the SBC. That's wrong! That's un-Christian! And certainly that's not Baptist!" In another letter Veazey called the BFMF's activities a "witch hunt" and said he hoped it would fail "miserably." When it was alleged that the BFMF showed signs of Landmarkism, Owens admitted that "there are some men in our Fellowship who take the Landmark line," but he said he believed the "majority of them" were not of that "persuasion."[36]

It is remarkable that Owens could carry on the work of his church and the work of the BFMF without being overwhelmed. He was doubtless a man of great energy and determination, for answering countless letters was far from all he did for the BFMF in 1973. His most significant initiative was launching the fellowship's newspaper, called *The Southern Baptist Journal*. In doing that he sought the help of Bill Powell, whom Owens persuaded to become the organ's editor.

Powell, like Owens, Pressler, and Patterson, had been a Southern Baptist all his life. He was born in Dothan, Alabama, September 15, 1925. A graduate of the University of Alabama and New Orleans Seminary, he served as pastor of six churches in Alabama between 1948 and 1957 before moving to Chicago, Illinois, to take a pastorate there. For over five years he was superintendent of missions in Chicago, and he helped organize the Chicago Southern Baptist Association. In 1962 he went to work for the Home Mission Board in Atlanta. Powell married Betty Joyce Pate of Tuscaloosa, Alabama, and the couple had one son, William A. Powell, Jr., who was born in 1954.

As a student at New Orleans Seminary in the early 1950s Powell became alarmed over what he regarded as the liberal views of some faculty members, especially those of Professor Frank Stagg. He wanted to do something to turn the SBC from the liberal direction he believed it was taking, and the only way he could see to do it was by firing all SBC employees, particularly seminary professors, who denied that the Bible was inerrant. After he went to work for the Home Mission Board in 1962, Powell studied the structure of the Convention, poring for hours over the SBC's Constitution and Bylaws. Between 1962 and 1973, when he helped found the BFMF, Powell worked out the strategy that Paul Pressler later adopted and successfully implemented with the help of Paige Patterson. That strategy, which called for electing a fundamentalist president who would use his appointive power to secure the election of fundamentalist trustees to all SBC agencies, has been duly noted by virtually all who have written about the SBC controversy of the 1980s. The problem is that the writers have given the credit for devising it to the wrong man. Paul Pressler *implemented* the strategy. It was Bill Powell who first advocated it.[37]

By the end of June 1973 the hard-driving Owens and the BFMF had decided upon Powell to be editor and "Field Worker" of *The Southern Baptist Journal*, and within a few months Powell resigned from the Home Mission Board to assume the position. Owens expected that it would take "about $50,000 a year minimum" to produce and distribute the paper, and he planned to persuade two hundred churches to pledge $250 each per year to raise the money. He feared that they really needed $75,000, but he was optimistic. "God has the money, if we have the faith," he wrote to a well-wisher. He sent out literally hundreds of appeals for money to publish and distribute the *Journal*. Even before Bill Powell resigned from the Evangelism Division of the Home Mission Board to assume the editorship, the BFMF brought out the first issue of the *Journal* not long after the 1973 meeting of the SBC. The first issue was designated the "Special Convention Issue" and was mailed to "more than 30,000 addresses." R. Dean Ramey, pastor of College Park Baptist Church in Rock Hill, South Carolina, wrote Owens, asking him to remove Ramey's name from the mailing list. Owens wrote back, accusing Ramey of being "so narrow and prejudiced" that he could not "read anything with which you might possibly find yourself in disagreement." Informing the South Carolina pastor that he could not remove his name from the mailing list, Owens advised him to drop the paper in "the post office waste basket, or into File 13." The mailout proved to be frightfully expensive. By the end of the year the BFMF had a balance on hand of $242.17, along with $4,752.75 in unpaid bills and bills anticipated of $3,984.47 for January 1974.[38]

Meanwhile, Owens was busy with other pursuits. At the annual meeting of the North Carolina Baptist Convention in November, he introduced a new baptism amendment, one that would have required "Differing" churches who wished to remain in the state convention to change their policies by receiving only those people into membership who had been immersed "according to the New Testament." This version of his amendment, like the one introduced in 1971, went down to defeat. Again, Owens was attacked for stirring up trouble. Randolph L. Gregory, pastor of the First Baptist Church of Wilmington, North Carolina, called Owens and his supporters "a small group of self-appointed censors" and "a sort of spiritual Gestapo whose aim is to make everyone goose-step with them."[39]

Somehow Owens also found time in 1973 to write an essay entitled "The Crisis We Face." Gerald Primm printed it in *The Sword and the Trowel*. The focus, of course, was on the Bible, for which Southern Baptists, Owens argued, must regain proper respect. Claiming that Southern Baptists, during most of their denominational existence, had believed that the Bible was "the inerrant, authoritative Word of God," Owens insisted that this belief was slipping away because of the liberalism being taught in Baptist schools. In so many words, Owens admonished Southern Baptists to go back to the Bible. He said:

> The basic issue before Southern Baptists today is the nature of Scripture, and its reliability as an historical document or as attestation to the real person of Jesus Christ of Nazareth.
>
> Southern Baptists are now face to face with this issue. If we accept the secularized, rationalistic view of the Bible we have no place to go except to existentialize our thinking. Then we shall find ourselves led down the same path other denominations have gone, and ultimately cast on the trashpile of history. The crisis is upon us![40]

The following year, 1974, turned out to be a shaky one for Owens and the BFMF. The money troubles continued. Bill Powell's salary, as editor of the *Journal*, was supposed to be $12,000 per year plus a housing allowance of $3,600. By March the BFMF had $15,030 in past-due bills, and Powell had not received his salary for January, February, and March. Months later, in October, Powell's salary was ten months in arrears, but he kept going by selling one of his cars and some personal stock, which brought $9,600. He even tried to sell the house he had owned since 1962, and he considered selling his airplane, which he had owned since 1965.[41] No one could doubt Powell's dedication to the Fellowship's cause.

Along with the money problems, the organization became more controversial than ever because of the strident voice with which Powell spoke as editor of the *Journal*. Combative as a Spartan warrior, he became embroiled in a quarrel with Duke McCall, president of Southern Seminary, and the school's dean of theology, William E. Hull. Fundamentalists like Powell had chafed for several years over Hull's sermon of 1970 questioning biblical inerrancy, and in December 1973 Powell sought a meeting with McCall and Hull, purportedly to promote mutual understanding. The meeting was held in Louisville on December 14, 1973, and was taped in its entirety. Several people besides Powell, McCall, and Hull were there, including Laverne Butler, an officer in the BFMF.

During the discussion Powell claimed to be speaking for himself only. He asserted that the BFMF had been founded because of liberal inroads being made in the SBC, and he defined as liberals everybody who raised questions of any kind about such doctrines as inerrancy or the virgin birth of Christ. He charged that leaders of various Baptist agencies and institutions did not adhere to the Baptist Faith and Message Statement of 1963. He asserted that the Bible was infallible—case closed. He denied wanting to establish a creed, but stated that he believed everything in the BFM Statement of 1963. He alleged that only two of the SBC's six seminaries showed any regard for that statement at all. Powell asked Hull if he as a dean in a Southern Baptist institution could expect to continue receiving his salary from Southern Baptists who believed the Bible to be infallible, when he had preached and written that he did *not* believe it was infallible.

Hull responded by saying that his views were consistent with the position of the Convention, including the BFM Statement of 1963. He accused Powell of attacking his views without really knowing what they were. McCall accused Powell of a personal attack on Hull and said that both he and Hull believed the BFM Statement of 1963 as it was written, but not as it was quoted by Powell, who, McCall contended, misquoted it.

Instead of promoting mutual understanding, the meeting at Louisville set off a feud that continued through 1974 and ended with McCall calling Powell "a liar who cannot be trusted to deal openly and honestly with the question of who sincerely accepts the Baptist Faith and Message as adopted by the Southern Baptist Convention." Even after the seminary president told Powell what he thought of him, the fundamentalist editor tried to keep the fight going, inviting McCall to engage in dialogue with the members of the BFMF at the organization's meeting in November 1975.[42]

Powell's biting words not only offended two highly respected Baptist academicians, but many other people as well. One of them was R. G. Puckett, editor of the *Maryland Baptist* in 1974 and later editor of the *Biblical Recorder* in North Carolina. Puckett wrote an editorial attacking the BFMF in general and Bill

Powell in particular. M. O. Owens struck back, accusing Puckett of pursuing a "vendetta against the Baptist Faith and Message Fellowship." He asked Puckett why he did not use some of his "vituperation against those who, by their liberal theology and low view of Scripture" sought "to destroy the vitality and vigor of the Convention?" Owens warned Puckett that he could "crucify" Bill Powell if he wanted to, but he predicted "that the spectre of it will haunt you the rest of your days." So offensive were Powell's words to some that before 1974 was over, he was being threatened with libel suits. He appealed to Charles Stanley to put him in touch with a few competent "conservative Baptist" lawyers who were sympathetic to the fellowship's cause.[43]

Not only Powell came under attack in 1974; M. O. Owens did, too. One Owens critic, James F. Cole, editor of the [Louisiana] *Baptist Message*, implied that the Gastonia minister was on a mission of vengeance because he had not been elected to high office in the North Carolina Baptist Convention. Cole wrote: "Actually it's too bad that he [Owens] was not elected executive secretary of the North Carolina Convention or president of that convention[,] for had he been elected to either office, I feel that his attitude today would be far different." Years later Owens denied that his activities on behalf of the fundamentalist cause were ever motivated by political vengeance.[44]

In spite of the criticism aimed at him and the problems confronted by BFMF in 1974, Owens persisted in the tasks he had laid out for himself. The 1974 SBC meeting in Dallas was a source of both elation and disappointment for Owens and his cohorts. Jaroy Weber, pastor of the First Baptist Church of Lubbock, Texas, and a supporter of BFMF, was elected president, but on the negative side a resolution for which Owens tried to rally support went nowhere. In May, before the Convention in June, Owens wrote W. A. Criswell and asked him to speak on behalf of a resolution that appeared to promote local church autonomy but surreptitiously aimed at providing a means by which churches could bypass the Cooperative Program and give directly to those agencies fundamentalists could support. Criswell returned the letter, scribbling at the bottom, "in all this I am deeply sympathetic. Behind the Co-operative program hide all the liberals. I wish we could get at them directly." The Dallas pastor made no commitment to speak on behalf of the resolution, as Owens had urged him to do.[45]

Finally, in 1974 M. O. Owens made one last attempt to help add an immersion amendment to the constitution of the North Carolina Baptist Convention. James Bulman, the convention's parliamentarian, had reworked the old Owens amendment in an attempt to satisfy those who worried about local church autonomy. Although convinced that the talk about autonomy was nothing more than a "smoke screen," Owens, along with Gerald Primm, agreed to support the Bulman amendment. Like the Owens amendments of 1971 and 1973, this one, too, was defeated.[46]

The BFMF would last until 1989, but it began to fall apart in 1979 and 1980 because of internal dissension, too little support from grass-roots Southern Baptists, and scant funding. The money problems, of course, were nothing new. Owens remained active as a board member until 1980, but he was not as much in the forefront after 1974. He focused more on North Carolina, becoming interested during 1975 in the position of general secretary-treasurer of the state convention. His followers wanted to nominate him, and he would have had considerable support, but doubtless not enough. "After struggling with the decision for several weeks," he decided not to allow his name to be placed in nomination, for he sensed that the search committee "had settled on" Dr. Cecil Ray. Owens urged the convention to unite behind Ray and "give him our cooperation in every way possible." Also in 1975, Owens was replaced as president of Baptists United for Spiritual Revival by Ned Mathews, another North Carolina pastor. The old crusader continued to write articles for *Baptists United News* for at least five more years.[47]

In the meantime, Bill Powell continued as in the past, attacking and being attacked. The pugnacious editor never stopped condemning as liberal anyone who "believes the Bible does or may contain errors in the original manuscript." He asserted, "I won't debate it." Arguments by scholars pointing out that councils of men, such as the Council of Jamnia and the Council of Carthage, decided what would and would not be included in the Scriptures left Powell undaunted. Avowing no animosity toward those he regarded as liberals, the fiery fundamentalist said that all people were free to believe what they pleased as long as they were not employees of the SBC. Especially irate over liberal seminary professors, Powell wrote in 1976, "Let's elect trustees who will fire the Bible-doubting teachers and hire teachers who do believe that the Bible is the verbally inspired and infallible Word of God."

After the 1979 SBC meeting Powell launched an attack against Jack Harwell, editor of the Georgia Baptist paper called *The Christian Index.* Harwell admitted privately that he did not believe the Bible was inerrant. Specifically he did not believe Adam and Eve to be one man and one woman, but mankind and womankind. Powell circulated copies of a letter by Harwell containing those admissions. When Harwell threatened to sue, the petulant Alabamian stopped, but he kept urging that something be done about Harwell. Someone tried, but a resolution calling for Harwell's dismissal as editor of the *Index* failed at the Georgia Baptist Convention when it was ruled out of order.[48] Eventually, though, fundamentalist pressure forced Harwell out.

Over and over the BFMF was accused of standing for a creed, and in the minds of many Southern Baptists creedalism was wrong. M. O. Owens denied that creedalism was a problem, and he wrote an address called "Creedalism Is Not a Danger to Baptists." In it he argued that Southern Baptists were not about to become creedal, insisting that "Baptists believe the Bible; it is their guide. They well know the difference between a confession of faith and their source of truth." On the other hand, Bill Powell did not shrink from the label of creedalist. He argued that "Baptists Do Have a Creed," because a creed was "what you believe" and everyone had one. Once more he asserted that there were certain definite doctrines Baptists believed, such as those stated in the BFM Statement of 1963. As always, he insisted that "the most important article of our faith has to do with our views on the Bible."[49]

Men who would later become closely identified with the moderate group in the SBC in the 1980s hurled critical barbs at the BFMF and Powell during the mid-1970s. Among those who did were Russell Dilday, the pastor of the Second Ponce de Leon Baptist Church in Atlanta, Grady Cothen, president of the Baptist Sunday School Board, and Bill Self, another Atlanta area pastor. Dilday called the fundamentalists "Pharisaical creedalists" who were "wasting precious time in a ministry of casting the mote from other people's eyes."[50]

The constant controversy caused by Powell's militant, inflexible stance eventually proved embarrassing to some of the fellowship's leaders, including Owens. Powell was voted out as editor in 1979, but at the 1980 SBC in St. Louis he outmaneuvered his opponents on the fellowship board in a "power play," according to Owens. By a 9–7 vote the board ousted Russell Kaemmerling, who had replaced Powell as editor, and reinstated the latter. Unhappy with this turn of events, Owens and several other board members resigned from the board and started a new organ called *The Southern Baptist Advocate* with Kaemmerling as editor. Kaemmerling, a Texan and Paige Patterson's brother-in-law, moved the *Advocate* to Dallas. Meanwhile, the combative Powell carried on as editor of the *Journal*, putting out sporadic issues, until 1985 when a "terminal illness" forced him to resign in favor of Dave E. Lucus, pastor of the First Baptist Church of Oak Hill in Austin, Texas. Lack of funds eventually caused Lucus to discontinue the paper, and the BFMF became moribund in 1989.[51]

If success be measured by finishing the race, the BFMF was a failure. On the other hand, if running the race and urging swifter runners with the same objectives to press on to victory counts, then M. O. Owens, Bill Powell, and their fellow workers of the BFMF were indeed successful. Owens launched the first significant fundamentalist movement among Southern Baptists in North Carolina at the beginning of 1969. Four years later he expanded that effort by helping found the Baptist Faith and Message Fellowship and by serving as its president.

Powell, a fellow BFMF founder, was the architect of the strategy employed by Paul Pressler and Paige Patterson between 1979 and 1991 to secure control of the SBC for fundamentalists. Pressler and Patterson agreed that their efforts were minimal between 1967 and 1977, and the judge acknowledged that it was Bill Powell who persuaded him to get involved in the struggle to purge the SBC of liberalism. All of the evidence suggests that Pressler was reawakened and prompted to act by Powell around 1977.

In the meantime, sometime during 1975, Bill Powell had informed fundamentalist SBC president Jaroy Weber of his strategy for redeeming the Convention. Both Weber and Pressler came to have a deep appreciation for Powell's strategy, and Pressler carried it out to perfection. What happened at Houston in 1979 could never have happened if M. O. Owens and Bill Powell had not prepared the way, and, of course, there was a large but relatively uninfluential number of pastors and layman who helped them carry on as long as they did. Thus, there was an important and unmistakable link between the failed first crusade led by Owens and Powell and the successful second crusade spearheaded by Pressler and Patterson. Powell prompted Pressler to become involved and then laid out for him the strategy for winning control of the SBC.

There was little if any difference in what Pressler and Patterson did after 1979 and what Owens and Powell intended to do between 1969 and 1979. For the most part Owens and Powell raised the same issues and fought the same battles, but Pressler and Patterson were more focused (they avoided going off on such tangents as immersion amendments), better financed, and better organized. Pressler and Patterson successfully enlisted the support of many of the pastors who ministered in the "super churches," and the small churches that had supported the BFMF were easily persuaded to go along. This was a coalition that Owens and Powell could never form, partly because they emerged from the Southern Baptist gentry. They had sound credentials and were well respected in middle- and lower-class Baptist circles, but they had no clout with urban "super churches" and their affluent members. Patterson was from the gentry, too, but Judge Pressler, in the words of his younger ally, "brought aristocracy to the movement." He had rich and powerful friends in Southern Baptist ranks and outside the denomination as well. In one sense, the crusade for the SBC holy land did begin at the Cafe DuMonde in 1967. That, however, was the second crusade, which was delayed for a dozen years, while the first was launched with little success in 1969. It began in North Carolina and blazed the trail for the second. Where the fundamentalist crusades began, though, will forever be overshadowed by what happened at Houston in 1979.[52]

3

The Second Crusade

In the Trenches, 1979–1984

IN 1979 THE Southern Baptist Convention experienced perhaps its most bizarre and certainly its most surprising annual meeting ever. Moderates soon called it a "takeover" while fundamentalists called it a "take-back." What happened is clear now, and it was clear to perceptive Southern Baptist leaders almost immediately after it happened. The fundamentalists in the Convention had rallied their troops as never before, electing their candidate as SBC president and paving the way for a seizure of power in the Convention. Houston 1979 marked the beginning of the second crusade to reclaim the SBC holy land from people the crusaders called liberals. The first crusade, initiated and led by M. O. Owens, Jr., in 1969 and continued during the 1970s by Owens and Bill Powell, had failed. What they started, Paul Pressler and Paige Patterson finished. The second crusade got off to a quick and successful start. There was sometimes fierce opposition, but the fundamentalists moved relentlessly forward. Fundamentalist apologist James Hefley, who has written about the controversy of the 1980s in more detail than anyone else, described what occurred in Houston as follows:

> Adrian Rogers' election marked the end of an era in which the Convention and its presidents had been managed behind the scenes by a group who were more concerned about keeping the denominational machinery running smoothly and Cooperative Program money coming in than with doctrinal purity. Although most Southern Baptists didn't realize it yet, a new leadership was already inside the gates. They would not have a majority of trustees on denominational boards and committees for several years, but they were headed in that direction. In the forefront was Adrian Rogers. By his side were Paige Patterson, the theologian of the movement, and Paul Pressler, the strategist.[1]

Although Hefley was well aware of the first fundamentalist crusade, being a friend of Bill Powell's and certainly knowing who M. O. Owens was, he scarcely mentioned it. He even knew that Pressler's strategy was developed by Bill Powell. He noted the fact in his work, but he gave it little emphasis. Hefley simply mentioned that the strategy now renowned as Pressler's had been first articulated by Powell and then moved on. He was definitely correct in saying "most Southern Baptists" did not yet realize what had happened. He should have added, however, that most Convention leaders and the Baptist media certainly knew and immediately let it be known that they knew. This is obvious from an article written in 1981 by Louis Moore, religion editor at that time for the *Houston Chronicle:*

> From the day in 1979 that the fundamentalist controversy in the SBC erupted, the Baptist media as a whole have treated the controversy as a Watergate-like scandal to be exposed and stamped out. I felt like a voice crying in the wilderness in the press room during the 1979 SBC session in Houston when I maintained that the knives should be put back in their sheaths and the Baptist media should back off and simply tell the story as it was happening, accurately quoting leaders from both sides. When I said in the press room that the fundamentalist leader from Houston, Appeals Court Judge Paul Pressler, might not be the devil in disguise, as most Baptist media people seemed to think, but a decent, honored and respected citizen and judge in Houston, I was greeted with glares and insinuations that I must somehow be in cahoots with him.[2]

The SBC, like the ancient Egyptian god Osiris, appeared, flourished, and then died each year only to be resurrected the following year. Presumably, unlike Osiris, the annually resurrected Convention body was never exactly the same two years in a row, for each year there were new churches represented by first-time messengers and often new messengers representing old churches. Of course, there were usually messengers present who had attended the last meeting, but the list of messengers was not likely to duplicate the list of the previous year. Conceivably, but improbably, any SBC meeting could repudiate every action taken at a previous meeting of the Convention. Anything could happen at the annual meeting, and in Houston the unexpected occurred—but not by accident. What happened was carefully planned and orchestrated. This was possible because of the Convention's uniqueness. As strange as an annual meeting of the SBC may have seemed to some, no writer has been more acerbic in attacking those gatherings than Ellen Rosenberg, who referred to the messengers as the "ad hoc multitude." She went further in her sarcasm by writing, "There is a commitment to basic democracy, and to Robert's *Rules of Order* as modified by the president's inexperience and the ignorance of everybody else." And, of course, she had to add that the many opportunities for manipulation had been "increasingly exploited."[3] Unfortunately, as harsh as her observation was, it contained some truth, as will shortly be evident.

Although Paul Pressler was actively trying to alert Southern Baptists to the dangers of "liberalism" in their midst during the early 1960s and met Paige Patterson in 1967 to discuss the subject, he claimed that his involvement in Convention affairs was minimal between 1967 and 1977. The two factors that led him from minimal involvement to vital involvement, according to him, were the proddings of Bill Powell and the reports from his "young people" that liberalism was being taught in religion classes at Baylor University. Powell first contacted the judge in 1976 or 1977; the Baylor students reported to him in 1977. The student reports seem to have spurred him on even more than the promptings of Powell, for in 1977 he decided not to sit by any longer and "help finance the destruction of the faith of my young people." He began at that point, he said in an interview eight years later, to study the structure of the Convention. As he put it in 1985, "The liberals had analyzed the Convention structure and manipulated it for their own purposes. . . . We studied the constitution, studied the bylaws, and, not wanting to be dissident, we [presumably Pressler and Paige Patterson] decided that we would work within the system to effectuate the changes that needed to be made. . . . We just communicated with the people."[4]

What the judge failed to note was that Bill Powell had already done that, and he had passed his findings along to those who would listen. Some listened and did little. Judge Pressler listened and successfully implemented the strategy that Powell had mapped out. According to Paige Patterson, he and Pressler met with twenty or more pastors in 1978 and made plans to change the direction of the Convention. At that meeting it was agreed that he and the judge would take the lead and consequently absorb the barbs from the many who were expected to oppose their movement. The others who met were somewhat apprehensive, and so their names were not revealed. They were to stay in the background and play supporting roles as the group set its sights on winning the presidency at the 1979 convention in Houston. On the eve of the Houston convention Pressler and Patterson confirmed reports that meetings had been held in at least fifteen states for the purpose of encouraging messengers to attend the convention and elect a president committed to biblical inerrancy. And Pressler made it clear that the coming meeting was only the beginning. He was in it for the long haul and would work to get his forces out at all future conventions. He argued that "Conservative men should be at the Convention voting on everything from Convention Officers to Resolutions," for such involvement would lead to "Convention actions" that would reflect "the feelings of grassroots Baptists."[5]

Rosenberg sneeringly referred to the SBC annual meeting as a "circus," and the Houston convention did exhibit some of the attributes of that time-honored form of entertainment. Adrian Rogers dramatically held out as a presidential nominee until 2:30 A.M. of election day, praying with Paige Patterson and Jerry

Vines in his hotel room from midnight until that early hour as he looked for a "clear direction" from God. After receiving his sign from above, Rogers became one of six nominees, the others being Abner McCall, Robert E. Naylor, Ed Price, William Self, and Doug Watterson. McCall and Naylor were already considered elder statesman among Southern Baptists, but Rogers won on the first ballot, as he garnered 51.36 percent of the vote. Naylor, a former president of Southwestern Baptist Theological Seminary, was a distant second with 23.39 percent. McCall, who had been dean of the Baylor University Law School and was then the highly respected president of Baylor University, managed a meager 5.39 percent of the vote.[6]

During the election, according to some reports, Pressler and Patterson "occupied a command post in sky boxes" above the convention floor and maintained contact with fundamentalist floor leaders below. Presnall Wood, editor of *The Baptist Standard* (the journal published under the auspices of the Baptist General Convention of Texas), commented three years later on the Pressler-Patterson tactics at Houston, calling them a "new brand of precinct-style, state-by-state, get-out-the-vote politics." Both during and after the Houston convention, charges of voting irregularities filled the air. Lee Porter, the Convention's registration secretary, studied the matter and reported to the SBC Executive Committee three months later.[7]

Porter's report to the Executive Committee is most interesting. It reveals that approximately 14,000 messengers registered, while 1,516 pre-registered, making a total of more than 15,500 messengers. Some churches apparently sent more messengers than they were allowed by the SBC constitution. One hundred and seven messengers registered twice. Perhaps as many as a thousand people registered who had not been elected messengers by their churches. Many of those were pastors and their wives. Some people cast ballots for other people. Husbands cast votes for wives who had left the hall. Pastors and others voted for church members who were not present when the vote was taken. It was alleged that churches within 150 miles of Houston brought in busloads of people and registered them to vote. Porter later asserted that the registration procedures were quite "loose" and provided every opportunity for abuses, and he noted that there were indeed abuses at Houston on both sides. To prevent a recurrence of the Houston spectacle, he recommended that the Executive Committee instruct churches to elect messengers according to constitutional provisions, to publicize the names of their messengers, and to make sure that their messengers took proper credentials with them to the convention. He further urged the committee to seek a change in the convention bylaws that would outlaw proxy votes, to develop plans to prevent overregistering, to redesign registration cards, and to clarify the constitutional provisions regarding registration.

A motion to implement Porter's recommendations was defeated at the meeting of the Executive Committee in February 1980, but the recommendations were approved a year after that.[8]

One of the more curious incidents concerning voting irregularities at Houston was that Judge Pressler himself was registered as a messenger from the First Baptist Church of Bellaire, Texas. At that time he was a member of the First Baptist Church of Houston; he was only an "honorary member" of the church in Bellaire, where he was serving as interim pastor. When this was made an issue on the convention floor, Pressler gave an impassioned and tearful speech, defending his use of "sky boxes" and denying that he was an illegal messenger. Later he denied charges that he and others encouraged local and area churches to bus messengers to the convention to assure the election of Adrian Rogers or that some churches sent more than the maximum ten messengers allowed by the constitution. He also denied doing anything more to elect Rogers than had been done for previous presidential candidates.[9]

Like Pressler, Patterson denied everything. He claimed that he and his friends had no candidate at Houston, contending that any one of a hundred candidates would have been satisfactory but that Rogers was "the most popular." Although he admitted that he and his supporters encouraged "the grassroots constituency" to go to Houston, he denied orchestrating the convention and expressed amusement about the "furor" over the "sky boxes." With regard to busing in messengers, he contended that it never occurred. The charges that Pressler was at Houston as a messenger from a church in which he held honorary membership did not faze Patterson. He claimed that there were numerous precedents for it and that it was "another smoke screen to avoid the real issue of TRUTH!"[10]

Joining Pressler and Patterson in defending the proceedings at the Houston convention was Robert Tenery, one of the leaders of the failed first crusade. Eager to jump on the bandwagon of the second, he argued that there was nothing in the least fraudulent about Rogers's election. Admitting that there were irregularities at the convention, Tenery contended that Lee Porter's report showed that the irregularities were not limited to messengers of "a particular theological or doctrinal persuasion" and that there was "no evidence of mass bussing of voters, and no evidence of stolen ballots." According to Tenery, Porter's investigation revealed that thirty-one denominational workers, including two professors from Southwestern Baptist Theological Seminary, were registered illegally. It is difficult to know how carefully Tenery read Porter's report, but it is clear that he ignored parts of it, and his argument was less than convincing.[11]

In the midst of the unusual goings-on at Houston there were almost some fireworks over the issue of inerrancy, or what Larry Lewis, then pastor of Tower Grove Baptist Church in Ridgeland, Missouri, and later president of the Home

Mission Board, called "doctrinal integrity." An Oklahoma messenger named Eli Sheldon presented a motion that would have required SBC officers to sign a statement saying they believed in and were committed to the Baptist Faith and Message Statement of 1963. Sheldon eventually withdrew his motion after action on it was postponed. To head off possible trouble, Wayne Dehoney, a former SBC president, moved a reaffirmation of the 1963 statement. He and Adrian Rogers, the newly elected president, joined together in publicly stating that the Bible's "original autographs" were without error. Dehoney exhorted the convention to put aside the question of inerrancy and arrive at unity. Larry Lewis supported the motion, saying he thanked God that Southern Baptists continued to be a people of the Book, but when he presented a resolution on "doctrinal integrity as it relates to Convention seminaries," the resolution was ruled out of order "since the issue had been dealt with" by "reaffirming the Baptist Faith and Message Statement." According to James Hefley, Baptist Press failed to report this action, deliberately choosing not to do so. Apparently Hefley believed there was an attempt to cover up the fact that the matter was acted upon, but word of it was spread through the journals of the state conventions, and his contention that it was not mentioned in the *Annual of the Southern Baptist Convention* was simply wrong.[12]

Adrian Rogers was well aware that the entire Houston convention and especially his election were highly controversial, and he attempted to assure his opponents that he was not looking for a fight. After being elected, he said, "I have not come with blood in my eyes but love in my heart. I learned in the pastorate that you can do more by affirming something than by tearing it down. I am not so much a crusader as a leader and a helper."[13] The Memphis pastor would learn soon enough that he was indeed on a crusade whether he wanted to be or not. In no time at all two hostile camps were in evidence—those who approved of developments in Houston and those who strongly disapproved. Just as quickly the two sides were locked in verbal combat, and turmoil engulfed the SBC. There was constant name calling; accusations were hurled continuously. Both of the contending factions sought the support of the basically conservative but nonaligned majority in the middle, many of whom wanted to remain neutral. Some were no doubt baffled as the warring factions strenuously disagreed over what to call each other and over what the fight was all about. As previously indicated, Pressler, Patterson, and most of their supporters eschewed the fundamentalist label and insisted that they ought properly to be called "conservatives." To them, those on the other side were "liberals." Nearly all of those on the other side insisted that they were true conservatives who were devoted to genuine Baptist traditions and that the Pressler-Patterson forces were clearly fundamentalists. A variety of labels were used during the 1980s by writers trying to accommodate one side or the other, or, in some cases, both sides. As already indicated, the author is convinced that valid designations are "fundamentalists" for those who triumphed at Houston in 1979 and "moderates" for those who opposed them.[14]

The fight over the issue that divided the two sides was even more bitter than the one over labels. There was nothing new about the quarrel. The fundamentalists of the second crusade, like those of the first, argued that the central issue was biblical inerrancy. To them the faith of Southern Baptists and all other Christians survived or perished on what they believed about the nature of the Scriptures. The Pressler-Patterson coalition professed to believe that the Bible was fully inspired by God and without error of any kind. In their minds the moderates not only did not believe that but had caused the denomination to drift away from the doctrine of an infallible Bible. As the fundamentalists saw it, the only hope for the SBC to return to that crucial tenet was for them to secure control of the Convention, put people who would insist upon that tenet in charge of all agencies, and relegate the moderates to the shadows of the denomination or drive them out of it altogether. The moderates, on the other hand, argued that the fundamentalists were simply seeking power and that their movement had little or nothing to do with restoring theological truth. In other words, ideology was being used as an excuse to mask a bid for power. What neither side could ever see, or at least could never admit, was that both sides were right. The second crusade was both theological *and* political, but the moderates refused to recognize the former and the fundamentalists, more often than not, denied the latter.[15] The validity of this conclusion will be clearly established by the evidence that follows.

In some ways the debate over inerrancy was remarkable, for the word *inerrancy* itself was relatively new in theological circles. It could not be found in the Bible itself, nor in any Baptist confession of faith from the earliest Anabaptist to contemporary Southern Baptist statements of faith—not even the Baptist Faith and Message Statement of 1963. The origins and exact meaning of the word were obscure, but that did not trouble Pressler, Patterson, and their supporters, all of whom insisted that the word might be new but that the concept of an infallible Bible was as old as the Scriptures themselves and that true Southern Baptists had always believed in that sacred idea.[16]

Judge Pressler insisted that there was but one issue, the nature of the Bible. He never deviated from that contention. He asserted, "Once you have crossed the theological Rubicon of saying that the Bible is sufficiently man's work so that it can be in error and make mistakes, then you have opened the floodgates for the individual to determine the categories which are truth, and that is [an] extremely presumptuous thing for a man to do." Contending that "liberals" did not believe in the "complete accuracy" and "complete truth" of the Bible, he added, "The issue in the Southern Baptist Convention has been, is, and always will be, as far as I am concerned, what Scripture is, not an interpretation of Scripture, not the personalities of individuals on the various sides."[17]

Other fundamentalists also insisted that the central issue was the inerrancy of the Bible. Adrian Rogers, speaking in Rome, Georgia, in May 1982, said the real question among Southern Baptists was not "unity in diversity," as the moderates maintained, but what members of the denomination believed about the "Word of God." To Rogers it was simple: the Bible was either "infallible" or "fallible," "inerrant or . . . errant." Another Memphis fundamentalist, Vaughn W. Denton, pastor of Southmoor Baptist Church, stated, "Anyone who does NOT accept the Bible as infallible AND inerrant is a heretic and disbeliever." And in the *Southern Baptist Journal*, still edited by Bill Powell and still being published occasionally, the following statement appeared in 1983: "The issue in the current battle in the SBC is: DOES THE BIBLE CONTAIN ERROR? THE QUESTION is: How much longer will Southern Baptists support the liberals who *deny* the *Bible* is the *infallible* Word of God. The issue is *NOT* a matter of the INTERPRETATION. It is NOT a matter of politics or some fundamentalist faction taking control of the SBC." Such statements from fundamentalist quarters became almost as numerous as the stars throughout the 1980s and on into the 1990s. One of the strongest such statements came from Morris Chapman, pastor of the First Baptist Church of Wichita Falls, Texas, soon after he was elected SBC president in 1990. He was quoted as saying, "For us not to believe in inerrancy is not to believe in God."[18]

Moderates refused to believe that inerrancy was the issue, insisting that power was the issue. They wanted to debate the matter, and Paige Patterson, who was far from a babe in the woods when it came to theology, was glad to oblige. In 1981 he debated two well-known moderate pastors, Kenneth Chafin of South Main Street Baptist Church in Houston (until he resigned in 1984 to accept a faculty position at Southern Baptist Theological Seminary) and Cecil Sherman of First Baptist Church in Asheville, North Carolina. Chafin called *inerrancy* a "code word introducing a different spirit" of "anger and hatred"—a "code phrase for a ruthless power grab." Patterson denied the charge, noting that there were seven reasons why inerrancy was important and claiming that there was "no seeking for office or grab for power." He called it "simply a deep theological concern."

In the other debate Sherman argued that "the message of the Bible, not the inerrancy" was the crucial point, while Patterson maintained that the Bible was historically true in the "autographs," or original texts, and that the doctrine of "plenary, verbal inspiration" was held by the founders of the SBC. Although Patterson did not say so explicitly, he in effect qualified the term *inerrancy* by saying that only the "autographs" of the Scriptures were error-free. Even Pressler was aware of the inconsistency in the inerrantist view; when questioned closely, however, he glossed over it by saying, "I believe that the original texts that God gave are inerrant. I believe that the King James Version is a very accurate translation." Yet, because Sherman, during his debate with Patterson, declared that all extant manuscripts and versions of the Bible contain errors (something Patterson and Pressler well knew) and refused to endorse inerrancy, Russell Kaemmerling asserted that Sherman's position proved that "the issue is clearly theological."

Besides defending inerrancy, as *he* qualified it, Patterson consistently denied moderate charges that he and the judge were out to take over the SBC. In 1980 he pointedly declared that no "take-over" of the SBC was planned and that "no political party" would emerge among the various groups of concerned Baptists. He claimed that nothing more was happening than an exchange of information and encouragement to participate in Convention life. He professed to believe that 90 percent of Southern Baptists "support historic Baptist convictions [i.e., inerrancy] without hesitancy." He insisted that "no agenda of permanency exists in the plan of anyone." Six years later, with a fundamentalist takeover fast becoming an undeniable reality, Patterson was still denying that he and his friends were trying to take over the Convention and impose their beliefs on it. He said that they did not insist that anyone believe in inerrancy or use the word, only that "those whose salaries we pay not allege the existence of error and mistake in the Bible."[19] At the very least the fundamentalists intended to impose their beliefs on SBC employees as a requirement of continued employment.

A host of prominent Southern Baptist ministers and laymen declared their belief in inerrancy publicly, but some qualified it in private. Patterson was honest enough to do it publicly in his debate with Cecil Sherman. Most avoided declaring openly that they did not hold an absolute view of inerrancy, perhaps fearing that numerous lay people among Southern Baptists would be confused by their subtle qualifications of the doctrine. It was common for learned inerrantists to deny publicly that there were errors of any kind in the Bible and then turn around in private and admit to "minor errors," "statistical errors," and contradictions between one historical fact and another when pressed by knowledgeable interrogators. In his book *These Issues We Face*, W. A. Criswell contended that the Bible had been "exactly preserved through the fire and blood of the centuries." A few lines later he did a 180-degree turn and admitted that the Bible, in its modern form, contained "additions, deletions, changes, and glosses." In *The Criswell Study Bible*, written by "conservative scholars" and edited by Paige

Patterson, there was admission of scribal errors, and yet some fundamentalists praised the work as the "most important book published in more than 300 years."

Not only did Criswell, Patterson, and other "conservative scholars" admit to scribal mistakes (while insisting that the "autographs" were free of any kind of error), but Clark Pinnock, who had once been regarded as a shining light among Southern Baptist inerrantists before leaving New Orleans Seminary, ultimately concluded in the 1980s, following a long struggle with the biblical evidence, that inerrancy was "a logical deduction not well supported exegetically." He warned, "Those who press it hard are elevating reason over Scripture at that point."[20]

Falling back on the notion that the "autographs," or original texts of the Bible, were perfect and without error, was a clever strategy, but it smacked of searching for a loophole to wiggle through. As indicated above, the idea of inerrant autographs is not explicitly stated in the Scriptures or any Baptist confession or statement of faith.[21] It is an interpretation and nothing more, but it did not seem to bother the inerrantists that no autographs existed and that their presumed perfection could not be verified or even investigated. Nor did it seem to trouble them that councils of *men* had decided what ancient writings would and would not be included in the Scriptures. Even so, it is not difficult to believe that the fundamentalists were sincere in their belief regarding an infallible Bible. In their minds it was God's book, and God could not err. If there were errors, and clearly there were, they were made by the uninspired *men* who subsequently mishandled the perfect autographs. The fundamentalists denied that such a belief amounted to bibliolatry, but at times their declarations appeared to approach it. To make a book (a book that would be perfect if the autographs were available) the unquestioned authority governing the actions of the SBC was what the fundamentalist crusades, the first and the second, were mainly about. This does not mean that there were not cultural and sociological influences at work on the fundamentalists also. Those influences were significant, too, but their main contribution lay primarily in spawning a general, conservative climate of opinion in which fundamentalism could gain sufficient acceptance to promote the fundamentalists' theological agenda.

A puzzling question arises. Why did the idea of inerrancy capture the imagination of so many Southern Baptists in 1979 and throughout the 1980s, when it failed to do so in 1969 and during the early 1970s? The answer is that it took time for society to react in an organized fashion to the disturbing, revolutionary decisions of the Supreme Court under Chief Justice Earl Warren and to the excesses of student protesters and others during the Vietnam War. A reactionary climate of opinion accompanied by organized action did emerge during the 1970s, but it evolved slowly. Finally, by the end of the 1970s, the stage was set for, among other developments, a national inerrancy conference and the election in 1980 of Ronald Reagan to the presidency of the United States.

The BFMF contributed to the promotion of the inerrancy idea, as did the publication of two books by Harold Lindsell, former editor of the conservative biweekly journal *Christianity Today*. Lindsell's first book, *The Battle for the Bible*, was published in 1976, while his second, *The Bible in the Balance*, came out in 1979. The burden of the two books was that denominations that abandon strict inerrancy decay and die. Some writers have argued that Lindsell's books inspired the inerrancy movement among Southern Baptist fundamentalists, but James L. Sullivan, a former president of both the SBC and the Baptist Sunday School Board, called attention to the fact that M. O. Owens and the BFMF first raised the issue of inerrancy at least two years before Lindsell's books appeared. Actually, as has already been demonstrated, Owens raised it in North Carolina as early as 1969.

What should not be overlooked is the fact that Southern Baptists had no corner on inerrancy. During 1978 the International Council on Biblical Inerrancy, made up of representatives from several denominations as well as independent churches, met in Chicago and generated the Chicago Statement. The statement contained nineteen articles and three thousand words, which included articles of "Affirmation and Denial" replete with contradictions and loopholes. The articles maintained that "the very words of the original were given by divine inspiration" and denied "that any essential element of the Christian faith is affected by the absence of the autographs." Fundamentalists of various denominations had their spirits boosted enormously a year later when an extensive Gallup Poll on American religious views revealed that over half the respondents believed the Bible to be inerrant. In 1980, citing the Gallup Poll, Larry Lewis claimed that 94 percent of "our Southern Baptist pastors believe in the inerrancy of the scriptures." According to Lewis, this statistic proved that belief in inerrancy represented the SBC mainstream, not "a radical minority."[22]

Thus the doctrine of inerrancy, which a few Southern Baptist fundamentalists and people of like mind from other religious groups had asserted for years, acquired national respectability beginning in 1978 and soon gained popularity in many quarters. It flourished as never before, as America made a sharp economic and political turn to the right with Reagan's election in 1980. As the general conservative spirit gained momentum, the Pressler-Patterson coalition became steadily more dominant in the SBC.

The moderates, however, did not fold their tents and silently retire to the corners of the denomination. Over and over again they contended that the doctrine of inerrancy was a ruse being used by the fundamentalists to camouflage what amounted to nothing more than a naked power play. They also accused the fundamentalists of being creedalists, arguing that creeds were not in harmony with the Southern Baptist tradition. Robison James, a religion professor at the University of Richmond, called the inerrantists of the 1980s heretics because of their "creedal belief in inerrancy." As has been noted, similar charges were made against M. O. Owens in North Carolina during the early years of the first fundamentalist crusade to redeem the SBC. Larry Lewis, who worked hard for a "doctrinal integrity" resolution until he secured the passage of one at St. Louis in 1980 and another "by an enthusiastic standing vote" at the 1981 annual convention in Los Angeles, denied that the demand for "doctrinal integrity" was "the creedalism of which we are accused."

Agreeing with Lewis was Tom Nettles. With fellow Southwestern Seminary professor Russ Bush, Nettles had written in 1980 *Baptists and the Bible*, another book that gladdened the hearts of fundamentalists. Nettles said, "The 'Doctrinal Integrity Resolution' passed at the 1980 Southern Baptist Convention was entirely in keeping with Baptist precedent. . . . The resulting affirmation did not unduly elevate the confession [Baptist Faith and Message Statement of 1963] itself but focused attention on the sole authority of Scripture as an infallible revelation from God. Such action hardly qualifies as creedalism, for it advocated change and sought to tie the convention constituency more closely to the Scripture."[23]

On the moderate side, Grady Cothen, president of the Sunday School Board, predicted in 1981 that the BFM Statement of 1963, an affirmation he called "our creed which we deny having," would be "further 'interpreted' until it becomes rigid enough to satisfy those who feel we must require such a test of fellowship." He warned that this would drive thousands of pastors and churches from the Convention. Nine years later, in May 1990, Cothen struck a similar chord in his commencement address at Southern Seminary, declaring, "A people historically non-creedal rush headlong into a narrow creedalism that claims superior authority to holy Scripture. A bitter and vindictive anger masquerades as righteousness assaulting everyone who does not do obeisance."

Also looking back on the controversy in 1990 and speaking his mind was Dan Griffin, moderate pastor of Snyder Memorial Baptist Church in Fayetteville, North Carolina. He said the SBC had become "pretty much a totalitarian regime of nouveau-Pharisees who are intolerant of divergent opinion," and he did not hesitate to name them: W. A. Criswell, Bill Hancock, Adrian Rogers, O. S. Hawkins, Jim Henry, James Draper, Jack Graham, Charles Stanley, Jerry Vines, Bailey Smith, John Bisagno, Morris Chapman, Ed Young, Mark Corts, Fred Wolfe, Robert Tenery, and the "two ring leaders," Paige Patterson and Paul Pressler. He called their "spurious argument against liberals" a smokescreen "disguising their greedy power grab." To fundamentalists, Griffin asserted, anyone was a liberal who did not "believe exactly as they do."

Two years earlier Henlee Barnette, professor emeritus of Christian ethics at Southern Seminary, contended that the "inerrancy-of-the-Bible issue" had been "blown all out of proportion to the Christian faith" and had proved "destructive to the fellowship." Barnette added that Southern Baptists had been "swept up into the maelstrom of denominational peevishness and power plays."

One moderate pastor declared in frustration that there were not enough liberals in the SBC "to fill a telephone booth." The real problem, he maintained was "a crusading Fundamentalist wing, no longer willing to cooperate with more moderate, but still theologically conservative, fellow Southern Baptists."[24]

The debate over inerrancy and creedalism raged throughout the 1980s, but Paul Pressler remained altogether single-minded and appeared oblivious to charges that power was the issue and that he and those he led were creedalists. When quizzed by reporters at the 1988 SBC meeting in San Antonio about various allegations, the judge answered, "You see, the issue is . . . whether we approach Scripture with the confidence that this is God's Word. The liberals know they cannot win on that issue. So they're trying to make non-issues so that they will have a chance to win." As for the matter of whether he was a creedalist or not, Pressler brushed that allegation aside almost flippantly during a "Dialogue" at Samford University in Birmingham, Alabama, on October 11, 1990, when he declared, after just being accused of creedalism, that he did not even know what a creed was. He did not elaborate, but repeated his same theme—"The issue is what the Bible is." Again he argued that the Bible contained no error, did not contradict itself, and was "true in all things that it says." The judge further said that peace could be restored in the Convention if the moderates would admit the sincerity of those in power, concede that there were doctrinal problems that had to be addressed, and work with the new leaders to solve the problems. He maintained, however, that seminary professors should not be allowed to teach views that were out of line with what the majority of Southern Baptists believed.[25]

Passionate rhetoric of the kind cited above flew from the pens and pulpits of aroused Southern Baptists between 1979 and 1990, and after 1990 it did not cease but only tapered off slightly. Most of the SBC annual meetings during those years were held in a tension-filled atmosphere. After Houston, year by year and little by little, the ten-year plan of Pressler and Patterson (revealed in the spring of 1980) to gain control of the Convention by stuffing SBC agencies with fundamentalist trustees was put in place. The first steps were taken by Adrian Rogers a few months before the 1980 meeting when, according to Pressler, the Memphis pastor appointed an "absolutely superb Committee on Committees." Pressler praised Rogers as the first SBC president to make appointments designed to "effectuate change," and the judge was well pleased.

Rogers, on the other hand, was not comfortable in the role of crusader. Customarily SBC presidents ran unopposed for a second term, but in 1980 Rogers chose not to run at all. Some argued that the retiring fundamentalist president backed away because he had no stomach for confrontation and the kind of fight that Pressler and Patterson demanded. He was basically a nice fellow (so the argument went) who felt he was being used, and he recoiled from the Pressler-Patterson style of hardball. Robert Tenery, not yet an insider with the new crusaders but bidding for that status, gave an entirely different explanation. He claimed that the SBC's "most dynamic and successful leader in a generation" had been "hounded from office by the Baptist Press." Rogers himself gave as his reasons a desire for more time to "spend with personal pursuits" and the "pressing duties" of his pastorate. He denied that the controversy surrounding his election in Houston and his name being linked with the Pressler-Patterson faction had anything to do with his decision.[26]

Since Rogers refused to run, another candidate of the fundamentalist persuasion had to be found to take his place. Stepping forward was Bailey Smith, pastor of the First Southern Baptist Church of Del City, Oklahoma. Apparently Judge Pressler worked behind the scenes on Smith's behalf, but as the 1980 SBC meeting drew near, Southern Seminary president Duke McCall issued a warning to Southern Baptists that a takeover attempt was under way and that it could succeed. He said the issue was "*not* theology but power," adding that theology was "simply the flag they wave."

Other voices opposing the fundamentalists were raised, too. For example, a few weeks before McCall issued his warning, Presnall Wood, editor of the *Baptist Standard*, challenged the fundamentalists to name liberals among Southern Baptists and cite their proof. In answer, Paige Patterson soon came forth with a list of names and excerpts from their works. He named Temp Sparkman, a professor at Midwestern Seminary, C. W. Christian of Baylor University's Religion Department, E. Glenn Hinson and Eric Rust of Southern Seminary, Fisher Humphreys of New Orleans Seminary, and Frank Eakin of the University of Richmond. Calling his list only a representative sample, Patterson later put out a document called "Evidences" and circulated it to show that some Baptist educators propounded unbiblical views. To the above list he added the names of Frank Stagg, John Claypool, David Moore, John Lewis, Robert Crapps, H. Jackson Flanders, Jr., David Smith, William E. Hull, T. B. Maston, and Roy Honeycutt.[27] The purpose of this eleven-page document was obviously that of smoking out the "liberals" and arousing inerrantist Southern Baptists against them. What the fundamentalists hoped to achieve was clear to many, and that was the ouster of Baptist teachers who did not hew to the line of biblical inerrancy. One story, which could well have been apocryphal, made the rounds. Upon visiting his doctor, a seminary professor was asked if he were engaged in a dangerous occupation. He answered, "Yes, I am a theologian."

While there was as yet no organized opposition to what some were already calling the Pressler-Patterson-Rogers political machine, it was apparent to perspicacious observers of the SBC that the 1980 meeting in St. Louis was not going to be altogether peaceful. Judge Pressler showed up in St. Louis claiming that he had no candidate, but that he could enthusiastically support Bailey Smith who, at the time, was president of the Oklahoma Baptist Convention. There is some evidence that suggests that Pressler and Smith were more in cahoots than the judge acknowledged upon his arrival in St. Louis. A week or so after Smith triumphed over five other candidates in an election that was remarkably similar to Rogers's victory in 1979 (when the Memphis pastor won over five candidates with virtually the same percentage of the vote as Smith received in 1980), he and the judge corresponded. On June 18 Pressler wrote to Smith, "I praise the Lord for the tremendous victory in St. Louis. You are God's man for God's hour, and I admire and appreciate you. . . . You have my unquestioned support." Smith's reply was quite revealing—about his own theological stance and about his connection with Pressler. He wrote, "I know you did much work in the background and I shall always be aware of the investment you have made in my life. The papers have been calling me a 'strict conservative' and a 'fundamentalist' and 'an inerrant constructionist.' Well, guess what—I am guilty. All in all, the News Media has been kind. I sometimes think they don't know what to think." Did Judge Pressler really go to St. Louis without a candidate and endorse Smith at the last minute? That is possible, of course, but Smith's letter implies something different.[28]

Smith won the presidency in 1980 on the first ballot over five other candidates with just under 52 percent of the vote. One of his five opponents was Richard Jackson, an inerrantist pastor from Phoenix, Arizona. Rumors spread that Jackson had made a deal with the moderates, and Smith carried the day. The victory encouraged the fundamentalists to introduce and secure passage of a resolution requiring SBC agencies to hire faculty and staff who believed in the "divine inspiration of the whole Bible, the infallibility of the original manuscripts, and that the Bible is truth without any error." An amendment proposed by Herschel Hobbs would have stricken the word "infallible." It was voted down, and the original motion passed. Many other resolutions passed, including one that called for prohibiting abortion except to save the life of the mother and another opposing ratification of the Equal Rights Amendment to the Constitution of the United States. Judge Pressler was quoted as saying, "The tide is now moving our way." The headline of an article written by Dan Martin, Baptist Press editor, summed up what happened in St. Louis quite succinctly: "SBC Takes Sharp Right Turn in St. Louis." Published in the *Baptist Beacon,* the article noted that "the inerrancy of the Scriptures was a constant presence at the convention, seldom mentioned but always apparent."[29]

Bailey Eugene Smith, a forty-one-year-old native of Dallas, quickly made himself a controversial president. He aroused great indignation by stating on August 20, 1980, "God Almighty does not hear the prayer of a Jew." Moderates condemned Smith for his intolerance, and later he tried to make amends by meeting with some rabbis and explaining his personal convictions. He reportedly offered his hand in friendship and cooperation in causes that were of mutual interest to Baptists and Jews, but moderates and many others did not forgive or forget. Although Smith's statement gave the moderates a point of attack against him, their opposition to him began in St. Louis over two months before his verbal misstep. The opposition that emerged against Smith appeared because he was associated with what many were beginning to call a fundamentalist political machine.

One man who sat through the proceedings at St. Louis left that city committed to launching a countercrusade against the triumphant fundamentalist crusaders. He was Cecil Sherman, the Asheville, North Carolina, pastor who then served as president of the North Carolina Baptist Convention. He later described his thoughts and feelings:

It was June 1980. The place was St. Louis. The Southern Baptist Convention was in session. My wife and I were sitting in the hall taking in the first SBC ever presided over by the new regime of Fundamentalists. Adrian Rogers was in the chair. Believe me, it was different. Speakers seemed compelled to identify themselves as inerrantists. Speeches and business sessions were filled with digressions so the house could be evangelized to the new orthodoxy. My wife and I had not heard it this way before in our three decades of attending the SBC. My wife leaned over and whispered in my ear: "Honey, did we come the wrong week? This must be a political convention, not the Southern Baptist Convention. Maybe we made a mistake. . . . "

It was in St. Louis that I saw our predicament clearly. If we did nothing, the SBC would fall to the Fundamentalists. They were organized; we were not. They had one candidate for the presidency of the Convention; we had several. Their votes were directed; ours were scattered. They had a plan; we had none. They had leadership; we were loathe to give leadership or, as later history would demonstrate, to discipline ourselves to "followship."[30]

Sherman left St. Louis determined to mount some organized resistance against the Pressler-Patterson coalition. He carried through by persuading his brother, Bill Sherman, who was pastor of the Woodmont Baptist Church in Nashville, Kenneth Chafin, and fourteen other pastors to join him at a meeting in Gatlinburg, Tennessee, on September 25–26, 1980. The agreement reached by the seventeen pastors at that meeting was summed up neatly by the man who called the men together:

> It was agreed at Gatlinburg that we would return to our home states and begin putting together a network. This network would become a politic to counter Fundamentalism in Southern Baptist life. We would meet again in February 1981. We would find others to join us. We would find a presidential candidate to carry our banner at the next meeting of the SBC in Los Angeles 1981. If asked about our meeting, we would truthfully answer; if not asked, we would remain silent. And so we left Gatlinburg.[31]

People must have asked about the meeting and been answered "truthfully" about what had happened in the Tennessee mountain resort town, for news of it was soon widespread. Among others, Robert Tenery reported the event, noting in the *Baptists United News* just three weeks after the meeting that "a cadre of liberals" had recently met in Gatlinburg. He identified Cecil Sherman as the man who had convened them and reported that their stated purpose was that of ousting Bailey Smith from the presidency of the SBC at the next annual meeting. He called the Sherman group the "Gatlinburg Bunch." Two weeks later Tenery wrote to Bailey Smith in what appears to have been an attempt to curry favor with the new SBC president and to win his confidence. Tenery had long known Judge Pressler but he apparently did not know Smith. He informed the new president about the *Baptists United News*, declaring that it was the "conservative" antidote to the *Biblical Recorder* (the journal sponsored by the North Carolina Baptist Convention), which "always tilts in favor of the liberal view." He wrote, he said, to let Smith know what was happening in North Carolina and to commend him for his remark about the prayers of Jews. He urged Smith not to back down, even though W. A. Criswell and Jerry Falwell had expressed their disagreement with the statement.[32]

Tenery was apparently the first inerrantist editor—he denied being a fundamentalist or even that there were any fundamentalists in the SBC—to give the Sherman group a derisive name. For the sake of alliteration the fundamentalists soon changed "Gatlinburg Bunch" to "Gatlinburg Gang." Sherman and his friends called themselves "Denominational Loyalists." Whatever they were called, the Sherman group made a strong effort to counter the fundamentalists, only to end up frustrated. Sherman worked diligently over the next few years to organize moderate forces, with considerable help from many cohorts but especially James Slatton, pastor of the River Road Baptist Church in Richmond, Virginia. Statements made in 1992 by both Slatton and Sherman pinpointed the reason their efforts were never very successful. Slatton said, "There were no funds to draw upon as the 1981–1982 campaign began, and there would be no systematic effort to raise funds. There would be no paid staff. All of the first group were pastors or spouses of pastors who had full-time jobs with strong churches. Networking was done on a part-time basis and at personal expense, except where local churches afforded funds or office support."

Sherman noted that on more than one occasion his group rounded up a significant number of votes for moderate candidates at the annual conventions—1981, 1982, 1984, and 1985—only to lose by five to ten percentage points. He attributed the failure of the group's counter crusade to too little money and too little support from the people they were trying to save. Agency heads and seminary presidents, even Russell Dilday of Southwestern (who would later become one of the most outspoken critics of the fundamentalists), tried at first to warn Sherman and his cohorts off. Most denominational executives were sure that the trouble would soon blow over or that they could effectively deal with "these people."

Grady Cothen, president of the Baptist Sunday School Board, Duke McCall, president of Southern Seminary, and Foy Valentine, director of the Christian Life Commission, were among the few denominational heads who embraced the moderate effort at the outset. In the words of Sherman, "The people we set out to save would not own us." In spite of a deficiency in financial backing and influential support, the Denominational Loyalists enjoyed some successes. For example, their movement brought into being "The Forum," the moderates' answer to the Pastor's Conference, which for years had been held for pastors on the two days before the annual SBC meeting. By 1983 the Pastor's Conference was totally controlled by fundamentalists and used primarily as an inerrantist pep rally. At Pittsburgh during the 1983 SBC meeting, Cecil Sherman took the first steps toward establishing an alternative meeting at which interested parties could hear the moderate message. The first Forum gathering was held at the convention in Kansas City the next year, and two thousand people attended. Duke McCall called it "the biggest baby ever born at a Southern Baptist Convention."

The Denominational Loyalists also helped establish a new journal called *SBC Today,* edited by Walker L. Knight, a highly acclaimed Southern Baptist journalist. Fundamentalists had their *Southern Baptist Advocate,* and, beginning in April 1983, moderates had *SBC Today* in which to tell their side of the story. The first issue, which was twenty-eight pages in length, was mailed to forty thousand Southern Baptists. Launching both the Forum and *SBC Today* was accomplished in the face of efforts by some denominational heads to pressure Sherman into standing down.[33]

While the moderate countercrusade could claim only a few victories because it failed to secure adequate funding or support, the fundamentalist crusade apparently had an abundance of both. Yet, the question of where the money came from was never answered. Paul Pressler was independently wealthy and no doubt had affluent friends who were willing to contribute to the fundamentalist campaign. Paige Patterson's comment to the author that the judge brought aristocracy to the movement would suggest as much, but Pressler denied ever spending the huge sums that some claimed he spent. Pressler and Patterson could not have accomplished what they did without a large bankroll, and where that money came from may never be known.

As for political support, it seems that the numbers definitely favored the fundamentalists after 1979, although the moderates contended that the votes at the annual conventions did not represent true Southern Baptist sentiment, because the fundamentalists used precinct-style politics to get the vote out and moderates did not. It seems more likely that the fundamentalists did indeed have the numbers, thanks in part to the rising tide of conservatism throughout the nation during the 1980s. On the other hand, the claims of the fundamentalists that their margins of victory at the annual meetings were not representative of Southern Baptist sentiment and that probably 90 percent of Southern Baptists agreed with the new fundamentalist leadership on the inerrancy question was hardly more than wishful thinking. A reasonable assessment is that the votes at the annual meetings were fairly representative of Convention sentiment and that at that particular juncture in the history of the SBC up to 10 percent (some years a *little* more and some years a good deal less) more Southern Baptists favored the fundamentalist agenda over that of the moderate program.

The fact remains that by 1980 the fundamentalists were gaining momentum, and over the next four years the organized effort of the Denominational Loyalists to slow them down failed. Cecil Sherman was already worried about the SBC's future when he left St. Louis in 1980. His worries had just begun. In August 1980, around the same time Bailey Smith made his unfortunate remark about the prayers of Jews, Russell Kaemmerling started *The Southern Baptist Advocate* in Dallas. Powell's "power play" at St. Louis, discussed earlier, caused a split in the Baptist Faith and Message Fellowship, and one result was the formation of the new journal, which had the support of some of those who left the BFMF as well as Paige Patterson. The *Advocate* soon became an organ promoting the second fundamentalist crusade. Kaemmerling made it clear that his paper would not be a "*National Enquirer* type publication," which, he implied, was what some of the people in the BFMF wanted. That kind of journalism, he asserted, did not help "the conservative cause."

Not only did the fundamentalists acquire a new media voice in the summer of 1980, but two weeks before the Sherman group gathered at Gatlinburg, Paul Pressler, speaking at the Old Forest Road Baptist Church in Lynchburg, Virginia, on September 12 and 13, made one of the most inflammatory statements of the entire controversy. He said, "We are going for the jugular. We are going for . . . trustees of all our institutions, [trustees] who are not going to sit there like a bunch of dummies and rubber stamp everything that is presented to them." Pressler later tried to qualify his comment, claiming that his words had been misunderstood, but moderates, and especially those who soon met in Gatlinburg, were convinced that they understood the judge all too well. The Gatlinburg meeting was held amidst Pressler's protests that he had only been speaking metaphorically in Lynchburg and that he was "only trying to show the source of strength and power, where the lifeblood of Southern Baptists lies." The judge's Lynchburg statement, which included an additional admonition that fundamentalist churches should give at least enough money to the Cooperative Program to allow them to send the maximum number of messengers to the annual conventions, convinced moderates that they were right in thinking that Pressler and his friends were out to secure control of the SBC. Also, the statement clearly indicated a fundamentalist political strategy for the long term, the existence of which Paige Patterson denied again and again.[34]

As Cecil Sherman and friends made their plans to derail the fundamentalist express at the Los Angeles convention in 1981 there were confrontations aplenty. Sherman himself was opposed for the presidency of the North Carolina Baptist Convention in November 1980 by none other than M. O. Owens, who went down to defeat, receiving only 40 percent of the vote. After winning the election Sherman came under heavy attack from North Carolina fundamentalists for his refusal to endorse biblical inerrancy. Mark Corts, pastor of Calvary Baptist Church in Winston-Salem, was among the attackers. He announced flatly in a *Baptists United News* article, "I am an inerrantist." He made it clear that he was bothered by the fact that the president of his state convention was not an inerrantist. Then, in February 1981, there was Sherman's debate with Paige Patterson in Morganton. Robert Tenery claimed that Sherman believed the Bible contained errors because he had been taught that at Southwestern Seminary, and the Morganton pastor accused Sherman of becoming angry and upset during a question-and-answer session following the debate.

More trouble began to brew in the spring of 1981 as the Los Angeles convention approached. Sherman, joined by Kenneth Chafin, found fault with Bailey Smith's appointments to the Committee on Committees and called for a

change in the SBC constitution and bylaws. The proposal called for a realloca-
tion of messengers on the basis of contributions to the Cooperative Program.
Thus large churches, which contributed a small percentage of their budget to
the CP (as did some of the large urban churches that had fundamentalist pastors), would have their allotted number of messengers reduced. Fundamentalists let it be known immediately that they would oppose the proposed change,
ostensibly because it would penalize small, poor churches that could not afford
to give as large a percentage of their budgets as big, rich churches could. The
fundamentalists ignored the point made by moderates that some of the largest
and richest churches gave a pittance to the CP and that the pastors of those
churches were winning control of the denomination and dominating the annual conventions. Another moderate proposal called for amending Bylaw 21 so
that appointments to the Committee on Committees would be made by a committee of the president and two vice-presidents and not simply the president in
consultation with the two vice-presidents. At the convention Adrian Rogers attacked the moderate proposals as "reactionary." They went down to defeat.[35]

The fireworks started before the convention, and there were more at Los
Angeles. On April 29 Texas evangelist Freddie Gage wrote to Presnall Wood and
expressed his displeasure at Kenneth Chafin for saying that "Bailey Smith's
committees were a bunch of fundamentalists." Gage said he was proud to be
"a Bible believing fundamentalist." He went so far as to declare that moderates
should leave the SBC. His exact words were, "I do not feel there is any place for
moderates or liberal[s] in the Southern Baptist Convention." Russell Kaemmerling let his thoughts be known, too. He headlined the upcoming convention,
"Gatlinburg Gang Plans Shoot-Out at LA Corral." He referred to Cecil Sherman,
Kenneth Chafin, Earl Davis, Ralph Langley, C. Welton Gaddy, and others as "the
New Left Gatlinburg Gang" and revealed that they were putting up Abner
McCall to oppose Bailey Smith. The *Advocate*'s editor reminded his readers that
at Houston in 1979 McCall had been a candidate and had received only 643
votes out of 11,184 cast. Kaemmerling noted sarcastically that the 4,155 Texas
messengers present in Houston knew McCall well and had "expressed the to-
tality of their confidence in their candidate."

Moderates, by contrast, praised their candidate, the Baylor University president, as a latter-day Lincoln who could unify the SBC and take it back to the
center. Thus was the stage set for the moderate campaign to unseat an incumbent SBC president. The campaign was a total flop as Smith trounced McCall,
receiving slightly over 60 percent of the vote—more than any other fundamentalist candidate received between 1979 and 1991 (except James T. Draper and
Morris Chapman, elected by acclamation in 1983 and 1991, respectively).

While the convention was still in session there was talk that a split in the

SBC was probably not far off. Abner McCall downplayed the talk, saying that he did not think his thrashing by Smith necessarily would result in a split. He believed, though, that the almost 40 percent who had cast their ballots for him were registering their protest against the Convention's march toward creedalism.[36]

Losing the presidential election was not all that upset the moderates at Los Angeles. There was also the defeat of their proposals to amend the constitution and bylaws, plus another setback. Ten trustees who were eligible for a second four-year term at their respective agencies were removed by the Committee on Boards. A substitute motion by Kenneth Chafin to restore four of those who had been removed was upheld by the convention on a close vote—3,571 to 3,089—in spite of former president Adrian Rogers's opposition to it. This tiny victory was of little comfort to the moderates, who left Los Angeles fully aware that their hopes of thwarting the fundamentalists had been dashed for at least another year. In the months that followed, Chafin revealed his frustration while indulging in some name-calling. He called Pressler, Patterson, and Criswell "people with different sets of sick egos with different ego needs—one old one that should retire, one with a secular vocation wanting to be in a religious vocation and one with a second-rate institution wanting to be in a first-rate institution."[37]

Following the Los Angeles convention the two sides promoted their respective agendas and made plans to fight it out again the following year in New Orleans. The moderates found their candidate, Duke McCall, who retired as president of Southern Seminary in February 1982. Meanwhile, Judge Pressler was in search of a candidate, and it is not at all clear that he had any kind of understanding with James T. Draper, Jr., the man who ultimately won. Draper contended that he was his own candidate and that he wanted to bring the Convention back together. Of course, Bailey Smith had made similar statements following his election in 1980. Shortly before the New Orleans meeting Judge Pressler was apparently still shopping for a winning candidate. The *Baptist Messenger* (organ of the Oklahoma Baptist Convention) stated, "Reports indicate that Houston judge Paul Pressler has made a few trips around the country to meet with potential supporters about the convention. . . . He is concerned about who is going to be elected president of the SBC this year when Bailey Smith steps down. His avowed intention of changing the makeup of the convention is at stake."[38]

Whatever arrangements Pressler made or did not make, one thing was definite: he did not want Duke McCall. Nor did Bailey Smith. In fact, Smith planned to train his guns on McCall in his presidential address. Someone leaked that address to Louis Moore of the *Houston Chronicle* just before the convention. In the address Smith came down firmly for "the holy, infallible, inerrant Word of

God." He condemned those Baptists who identified themselves as humanists, prayed at a dedication ceremony for the "opening of a brewery," called the book of Genesis political rhetoric instead of historical fact, taught evolution, or unashamedly took a "social drink." He called such actions inexcusable, and he had in mind particular moderates who were guilty of them. The "social drink" reference was to Duke McCall, who had drunk some Chinese beer, instead of a "dirty-looking glass of tea," while on a trip to China. An angry McCall tried to set the record straight for the press. He said that he had told the story as a joke and that some people had enlarged upon it to the point of asserting that he had a drinking problem. Paige Patterson publicly denied any part in spreading the story about McCall in China and apologized before the convention for those who had done it. McCall graciously accepted the apology and shook hands with Patterson.[39]

In the presidential showdown between McCall and Draper the fundamentalist margin of victory was not as great as it had been the year before in Los Angeles. Besides Draper and McCall there were two "independent" candidates, and Draper was forced into a runoff with the retired seminary president. In the runoff Draper, a graduate of both Baylor University and Southwestern Seminary, won 57 percent of the vote. The count was 8,331 for the pastor from Euless, Texas, and 6,292 for McCall. After winning, Draper emphasized that his goal was to promote denominational unity.

In addition to the struggle over the presidency, the moderates and fundamentalists fought it out over some substitute nominations for trustee posts and over a resolution in support of prayer in the public schools. The moderates succeeded in obtaining three replacements on the trustee slate, but could not defeat the endorsement of a prayer amendment. At that juncture James Dunn, executive director of the Baptist Joint Committee on Public Affairs, called the passage of the prayer resolution an "incredible contradiction of our Baptist heritage." He had already stated a few weeks before the annual meeting that President Ronald Reagan's proposed constitutional amendment on the subject was "despicable demagoguery." Since the SBC provided a lion's share of the financial support for the Baptist Joint Committee on Public Affairs, Dunn was flirting with trouble. Earlier he had crossed swords with Pressler and Patterson in Texas; now he alienated other fundamentalists who would soon seek to deprive his organization of SBC support. There was also some inflamed rhetoric over abortion. The moderates won a momentary victory by getting one resolution on abortion tabled, but a revised resolution condemning abortion, infanticide, and euthanasia subsequently passed.[40]

Among those who left New Orleans disappointed over Convention developments were A. C. Miller, a ninety-one-year old messenger from Hendersonville, North Carolina, who had spent most of his adult life in the Southern Baptist ministry, and two editors of state Baptist papers—Edgar R. Cooper of the *Florida Baptist Witness* and Al Shackleford of the *Baptist and Reflector,* the publication of Tennessee Baptists. Miller noted that what happened in New Orleans seemed "to run contrary to traditional Baptist beliefs" as he understood them. He opposed the prayer amendment and stated that he favored keeping religion "voluntary and uncoerced." Cooper, the Florida editor, was quite upset over the feuding. He observed, "From the welcoming address . . . to the final amen, there was a feeling of tension and a noticeable division of the messengers. The so-called conservatives and moderates were at it again. Just how long God will put up with His people acting like petulant children no one knows. . . . The bickering and infighting must stop before irreparable damage is done to the convention program."

Shackleford made similar observations but expressed them differently. He noted, "It is now evident that our convention has evolved into two political parties, which could be called the 'Conservative Party' and the 'Moderate Party.' " He declared that the votes in New Orleans were "right down the party line." Pointing out the long-range strategy of the Pressler-Patterson coalition to win control of the Convention by electing presidents and using their appointive power to name the Committee on Committees, Shackleford predicted that future SBC meetings would be characterized by an increase in secular-style politics. If both sides remained about equal in strength, the result would be bitter debates and close ballot decisions. If, on the other hand, one side gained dominance, that would likely lead to the minority's breaking away from the SBC.[41] Shackleford's observations and comments about the proceedings at New Orleans, like those of James Dunn, caused fundamentalists to view him with a suspicious eye. Before a decade passed, both men suffered for their failure to appreciate the success of the fundamentalists.

After the 1982 Convention there was a lull in hostility, mainly because the new president pledged to "get Southern Baptists talking to each other again, instead of about each other." Moderate leaders like Cecil and Bill Sherman and Ed Perry, pastor emeritus of Broadway Baptist Church in Louisville, Kentucky, urged Draper to share his appointive powers with leaders of state conventions. The pastor from Euless rejected the plan they proposed, but he promised to confer with some state convention leaders informally. Draper also called a meeting of moderates and fundamentalists in Irving, Texas. Don Harbuck, a moderate pastor from Arkansas, asserted during the meeting that "the judgmental spirit and exclusivistic posture of fundamentalism" was tearing the SBC apart.

Paige Patterson disagreed and put forth a four-point peace plan for ending the controversy. First, he insisted that inerrantists should be given parity with moderates in employment, especially in seminary faculty positions. Secondly, Patterson wanted SBC employees who objected to the term inerrancy to make a straightforward statement publicly as to what they believed about the Bible and other "essential doctrines." Thirdly, he contended that moderates should find a way to prevent the ridiculing in Baptist college and seminary classrooms of those students who avowed biblical inerrancy. Fourthly, he called for restructuring the Cooperative Program in a way which would permit churches to give only to agencies whose programs they could support in "good conscience." Nothing came of the meeting. Agency heads, apparently hoping to remain neutral, kept silent, taking no steps either to help the moderates or to placate the fundamentalists. Kenneth Chafin said he was giving up because agency heads would not speak up. The moderate cause was going nowhere fast, and the two men most instrumental in launching it were fully cognizant of that fact.[42]

Even before the Pittsburgh convention in June 1983, Cecil Sherman had all but given up, too. On May 18, 1983, he wrote a letter to the heads of the SBC agencies and the thirty-four state convention presidents and said, "In the last three years Mr. Pressler has been more successful than I have ever dreamed he would be. Though some of us have done our best to offer options to Southern Baptists and though we have done some organizing, most of our options have been turned down by the convention in session and our organization has little to show for its effort. Small victories are our best prizes. The structure of the SBC has moved in the direction of Mr. Pressler's agenda." Sherman expressed sympathy for the agency heads who, he acknowledged, were under the pressure of having to serve "two different kinds of people." Even though he and his friends had been "pushed to the edge of our denomination" and "eased out of policy-making posts," they retained a deep and abiding love for the SBC and were not sure what they would do in the future.[43]

While the Denominational Loyalists were contemplating whether to continue their active opposition or not, a new moderate group was forming in North Carolina under the leadership of W. Henry Crouch, pastor of Providence Baptist Church in Charlotte. Robert Tenery labeled those involved as an organization of "liberal North Carolina Baptists." The announced purpose of the new group was that of giving support to the newly established moderate organ, *SBC Today*, and "to preserve the Southern Baptist Convention as it was before the fundamentalists started to take over."[44] Those who followed Crouch would emerge four years later as the Southern Baptist Alliance, a moderate group that tried to take up where the embattled Denominational Loyalists left off.

Meanwhile, just prior to the SBC meeting in Pittsburgh, Cecil Sherman acknowledged that the Pressler-Patterson strategy was working to perfection. He said, "This committee on boards has surgically excised the kind of Southern

Baptists who will not conform (to their kind of fundamentalism). The exclusion is not an accident; it is a very meticulous thing." At the convention Sherman told the fundamentalist chronicler James Hefley why he thought the fundamentalists had won. He said that they "tagged into our greatest fears and dreams." The dreams were about large sanctuaries and many baptisms, while the fears were about those dreams being prevented by liberalism. Sherman claimed that Rogers, Smith, and Draper had won the presidency "because they embody the dreams of so many pastors." The dejected moderate asserted that it was wrong to contend that growth was the result of correct doctrine, since the Moonies, the Muslims, and the Mormons were growing at a phenomenal rate and no Baptist would allow that those groups taught correct doctrine. He argued that many pastors preached correct doctrine, but, for various reasons, had no growth in their churches.[45]

The point Sherman did not make was that fundamentalist pastors offered their congregation's members essentially the same thing that Moonies, Muslims, and Mormons offered theirs—a dogmatically presented package of pat answers to their questions. If Erich Fromm was right, countless people wish to "escape from freedom" with its attendant obligations and responsibilities, and so they seek out and find (if they are not found first) leaders who will *confidently* tell them what to believe. There can be little doubt that the fundamentalists were convinced that they had *the* truth to impart and that disaster awaited those who refused to receive it.

The Pittsburgh convention was amazingly quiet in view of the bitter battles which had been waged the two previous years at New Orleans and Los Angeles. Moderates were momentarily too discouraged to throw down the gauntlet again, and the fundamentalists were well pleased with developments to that point. Just before the convention, Paige Patterson said, "We really don't have much [of an] agenda for Pittsburgh." He noted that he and his friends had a president generally sympathetic to their views, a very conservative slate of nominees to serve on SBC boards, and previously passed, strong, conservative statements on abortion, doctrinal integrity, and Reagan's prayer amendment. He declared that the "inerrancy faction" planned no new battles; they would simply react to any challenges to the gains they had already made. In short, neither the moderates nor the fundamentalists arrived in a fighting mood at Pittsburgh. James Draper, because of his low-key approach and his church's solid record of giving to the Cooperative Program, was expected to win reelection handily, and he did. In fact, he was reelected by acclamation. His presidential address, entitled "Southern Baptists: People of Deep Beliefs," played down the controversy. He did not use the word "inerrancy" and even denied that the SBC had made a sharp right turn. He called the changes that had taken place "a midcourse correction with our leadership being responsive to the constituency. A turning back to where we were."[46]

The "Peace of Pittsburgh" was not destined to last. In the months following the convention the moderates found the will to mount another campaign to elect their kind of president at Kansas City in 1984. They held rallies, wrote letters, and made telephone calls. North Carolina pastor Warren Carr wrote Draper and gently implied that those of the fundamentalist persuasion were heretics. He said, "As for the most immediate matter of inerrancy, I am not one of those who primarily opposes the doctrine of inerrancy on intellectual grounds. It seems to me that there is a latent heresy of a very destructive kind in this particular dogma. Those strongest advocates of the dogma impress me as substituting an inerrant Bible for a life of prayer and communion with God. In fact, God may be rendered unnecessary by the inerrancy tenet."

The fundamentalists did not sit idly by while the moderates took their shots at Draper and made plans to win the presidency in Kansas City. They were far better financed and organized than their opponents, and they looked to Charles Stanley, pastor of Atlanta's First Baptist Church, to carry them to victory again. Stanley was well known for dwelling in the shadows of the denomination, never before playing a significant part in the Convention's affairs. His very wealthy church gave only sparingly to the Cooperative Program.

Two candidates stepped up to oppose Stanley. One was denominational elder statesman Grady Cothen, who had just retired as president of the Baptist Sunday School Board and who was identified as a thoroughgoing moderate. The other was John Sullivan, a pastor from Shreveport, Louisiana, who was avowedly conservative but who believed in the moderate concept of "unity amidst diversity." Although he held some of the flexible views of the moderates, Sullivan was considered an independent candidate.[47]

Some Southern Baptists who tried desperately to walk the tightrope of neutrality grew anxious as the 1984 Convention approached. One who did was Bobby S. Terry, editor of *Word & Way*. He had counted on Draper to be thoroughly neutral, and he felt disappointed. To Draper, he wrote:

> I recall that at your first meeting with the editors, as president, you took pains to put distance between yourself and the Pressler-Patterson movement. You told us you had not talked to Paige for months before your election and reiterated that you wouldn't appoint Paige Patterson or Cecil Sherman. But, as your term of office ended, you gave public support to Paul Pressler being a member of the Executive Committee, and told me that you not only consulted with Paige about the Missouri nominees to the Committee on Committees but on several other nominations. Obviously I was surprised.

Terry reported to Draper that someone had warned him that "Jimmy is going to do the same thing to us that Bailey did in New Orleans." The Missouri
editor admonished Draper not to throw away in Kansas City the efforts he had
made toward reconciliation. He reminded the lame-duck president that Southern Baptists had already "experienced 'stacked' conventions" in Houston, St.
Louis, and New Orleans and had no desire "to go through another." He warned,
"you know how damaging it would be if moderates leave Kansas City saying,
'I told you so.' " Terry dreaded the thought, he said, of seeing the Convention
again "forced into warring political camps," for it would not survive long.[48]
Thus the moderates and fundamentalists headed for Kansas City to do battle,
while some among the nonaligned looked to the outgoing president, but none
too confidently, to prevent a bloodletting.

The 1984 SBC meeting in Kansas City turned out to be a full-fledged donny-
brook. Over seventeen thousand messengers registered for the free-for-all. Once
again, however, the moderates could not dent the armor of the fundamentalists.
Charles Stanley, only recently recruited by the latter to help promote the inerrantist cause, won the presidency on the first ballot, receiving 52 percent of the
votes to Cothen's 26 percent and Sullivan's nearly 22 percent. The fundamentalists won numerous other victories at Kansas City. Zig Ziglar, a motivational
speaker and an outspoken fundamentalist from W. A. Criswell's church, was
Stanley's "first choice" for first vice-president, in spite of the fact that Ziglar had
never before served as a messenger to any Baptist body at the associational,
state, or national level. Even so, Ziglar was elected, prompting David Simpson,
editor of the *Indiana Baptist*, to write, "The election of Charles Stanley and Zig
Ziglar reflect[s] the desire for conservative leadership. Both men espouse the
view that the Bible is inerrant, without error of any kind. Both have, likewise,
taken very conservative lines on such issues as abortion." Simpson merely stated
the obvious when he pronounced the fundamentalists "well entrenched." That
conclusion was placed beyond doubt by the election of Judge Pressler to membership on the Executive Committee as the replacement for moderate Welton
Gaddy, who had moved from Texas and forfeited his right to serve as a member
from that state.

The moderates made a strong effort to prevent Pressler's election when
Winfred Moore, pastor of Amarillo's First Baptist Church and president of the
Baptist General Convention of Texas, nominated Dallas pastor Bruce McIver for
the post. Robert Tenery reported that Pressler was "handily sustained by the
Convention," but the victory was not sweeping. The judge received about 54
percent of the vote. Until then Pressler had purposely remained in the background, planning and manipulating. When asked in 1985 why he agreed "to
run," he answered, "I felt that I had been so slandered and so misrepresented

in the Baptist Press, that it would give me an opportunity to be known for what I believed and what I thought, rather than for what people were saying that I believed and thought. And my sole objective in serving on the Executive Committee is opening up the processes so we can communicate, so that we can understand each other, and so that we are available to one another."[49]

Moderates were certain that they already understood the judge completely, and they quickly made much of the fact that both the church of which Stanley was pastor and the one of which Pressler was a member gave piddling amounts to the Cooperative Program. The average church in the Convention gave 9 percent of its budget to the CP, but in 1984 Stanley's gave 3.15 percent and Pressler's 3.34 percent. One moderate claim held that churches with pastors waving the inerrancy banner gave only 29 percent of the funds received by the CP, while churches with moderate pastors gave the other 71 percent.[50]

The elections of Stanley, Pressler, and Ziglar were only the beginning of moderate discomfiture at Kansas City. Fundamentalist-sponsored resolutions against abortion (except to save the life of the mother), the teaching of secular humanism in the public schools, and ordination of women were all adopted. One reason cited for opposing the ordination of women was that woman was "first in the Edenic fall." The moderates could take some comfort in the fact that an attempt to defund the Baptist Joint Committee on Public Affairs was barely defeated, but such a close call boded ill for the future of James Dunn's organization. Fundamentalists had not forgotten his remarks in New Orleans two years earlier. Even they, however, appeared a little tired of doctrinal integrity resolutions. When Texas pastor Dave Lucus, who would succeed Bill Powell as editor of the *Southern Baptist Journal* the next year, moved that the convention "affirm our abiding and unchanging objection to the dissemination of theological views in any of our Southern Baptist agencies which would undermine faith in the historical accuracy and doctrinal integrity of the Bible," his motion failed.[51]

Perhaps the moderates had some reason for optimism during and after the Kansas City convention, because they convened their first Forum, which was well attended, and because some agency heads, three seminary presidents in particular, came storming off the sidelines to join the battle. Preaching the convention sermon was Russell Dilday, the Southwestern Seminary president who, several years earlier, had attempted to dissuade Cecil Sherman and his Denominational Loyalists from pursuing their campaign against the fundamentalists. By 1984 Dilday had finally awakened to the dangers of a fundamentalist takeover, and he told the convention, "I shudder when I see a coterie of the orthodox watching to catch a brother in a statement that sounds heretical, carelessly categorizing churches as liberal or fundamentalist, unconcerned about the adverse effect that criticism may have on God's work." He warned that there was "an incipient Orwellian mentality" in the air. As could be expected, editor Robert Tenery blasted the sermon as "the poorest excuse we have heard for a sermon in a long time." He called it "a vicious, vitriolic tirade against conservative men" and condemned Dilday for using the opportunity to make "political hay."[52]

Before long Roy Honeycutt, Southern Seminary's president, and Randall Lolley, president of Southeastern, would join Dilday in an all-out attack on the fundamentalists. No one knew, however, upon leaving Kansas City that Honeycutt would soon call for a "Holy War" against the inerrantists. Some moderates went home very discouraged. For example, Dillard Mynatt, a Tennessee pastor, was convinced that it was "the darkest day in the history of our denomination."

In contrast, the fundamentalists, having won numerous victories, were elated. A few weeks after the convention Paul Pressler wrote to Charles Stanley, glorying in the "tremendous victory" at Kansas City. "Thank you for your availability," the judge told Stanley, and he promised, "You know that I am always available. I will not be calling you frequently because I do not want you ever to feel that I am being pushy." Pressler offered to assist Stanley in any way that he could. He made the offer during a time of personal duress, for the judge's son had been diagnosed as having multiple sclerosis and was in intensive care.[53]

Moderate gloom and fundamentalist glee in the summer of 1984 soon turned into hostile words from the moderates and bitter replies by the fundamentalists. At the fall convocation of Southern Seminary, Roy Honeycutt called for a "Holy War" against the "unholy forces" that were "seeking to hijack" the denomination. He recounted what had happened between 1979 and 1984, as he understood it. He contended that an "Independent Fundamentalist" conspiracy, led by Paige Patterson and Paul Pressler, had been under way for five years to seize control of the SBC by electing fundamentalist presidents who would then appoint the Committee on Committees, which in turn appointed the Committee on Boards. The latter, of course, nominated trustees for all the agencies. Also, by dominating the Convention's Committee on Order of Business, they had scheduled voting at times when they were able to "bus in and otherwise generate the largest number of messengers to elect their nominees and to approve party legislation." Honeycutt charged that in Kansas City they had used floor managers, caucuses (to receive instructions on how to vote), and floor lieutenants. In his words, "Neither the Republican nor Democratic party orchestrated a more efficient political machine than did the Independent Fundamentalists in Kansas City." Moreover, said the angry president, they elected as president of the SBC a man who by his own admission had never before taken time to participate in the life of the denomination. Not content to stop there, they elected a first vice-president who had never before served as a messenger to a Baptist associational meeting, state meeting, or the SBC. The new president, Charles Stanley, was, Honeycutt charged, a "non-participant" in Baptist affairs until he was enlisted in 1983 to help "the inerrancy cause." The fired-up, moderate seminary president called upon Baptists to go to Dallas in 1985 and "deliver the convention from the bondage of its political exile."

Some of Honeycutt's charges were aimed directly at Paul Pressler, whom the seminary president accused of recruiting seminary students as spies for the fundamentalist cause. One Southern student, J. Stafford Durham, had been questioned by the judge as the latter poked around trying to uncover liberal utterances by the Southern faculty. It happened that Durham had once served as President Honeycutt's chauffeur. At first Pressler denied knowing anything about the charge, saying, "I do not know anyone who drives for him." Then, on September 14, 1984, Durham filed a formal complaint with the Federal Communications Commission, alleging that the judge had taped a telephone conversation between them without Durham's knowledge. Pressler was compelled to admit that he had indeed been in touch with the student, and in response to the formal complaint lodged against him, he replied, "No honest person should object to a record being kept of what he says." The holy war declared by Roy Honeycutt was heating up rapidly, and it promised to become very ugly.[54]

Behind the scenes there were private exchanges of bitter words, and most of those went unpublicized. For instance, in the fall of 1984 inerrantist Dave Lucus, trying to win support for purging the seminaries of liberalism, mailed out material to some Baptist ministers whose help he hoped to enlist in the enterprise. Among those he contacted was John T. Bunn, who at that time was pastor of First Baptist Church in Sylva, North Carolina. Bunn was a former member of the Executive Committee, but, to say the least, he had no interest whatsoever in helping Lucus. After receiving the material from Lucus, he responded with harsh words: "You, sir, are the epitome of an educational incorrigible with every entrance of your mind closed and every exit open. About you is the stench of the inquisition and the insidiousness of a witchhunter. When you use the term religion you mean the Christian faith and when you use the expression 'Christian faith' you mean right-wing fundamentalism. You 'come across' as one who has a sense of manifest destiny, chosen of God to be *the* champion of the faith . . . not unlike Saul, before he became Paul."[55]

Clearly the controversy was intensifying both publicly and privately. The fundamentalists in general and Paige Patterson in particular were incensed over the charges leveled at them by Roy Honeycutt. Never one to be attacked without responding, Patterson challenged Honeycutt to a debate in a large neutral auditorium open to anyone who wanted to attend. The fiery Texan said he would present evidence to substantiate his charges that liberalism had invaded South-

ern Baptist seminaries. Although he declared that Southern Seminary had nothing to hide, Honeycutt declined to debate, saying he was open to dialogue but
not debate. He added, "The crisis facing Southern Baptists is neither biblical nor
theological. It is political. However much [Patterson] and his political party may
use biblical and theological smokescreens, this is the issue: our convention is
being wrenched apart by an unprecedented political crisis engineered by Dr.
Patterson and Judge Pressler."[56]

In the closing months of 1984 and the early months of 1985 moderates
vowed an all-out effort at Dallas in 1985 to reclaim the Southern Baptist Convention. Rumors spread that if the moderate effort succeeded, the SBC would
split. Patterson indicated that his group might well leave, form its own mission
board, and run its own schools. There were already two schools that he and his
friends supported—Mid-America Seminary in Memphis and the school of
which Patterson was president, Criswell College. Evangelist Freddie Gage of
Houston predicted that more than eight thousand churches would pull out of
the SBC if Charles Stanley were not reelected president in Dallas. Paul Pressler,
Paige Patterson, and Russell Kaemmerling traveled around the country, sometimes together and sometimes separately, enlisting support for their cause at
Dallas. The judge hammered away monotonously and relentlessly, arguing as
he had from the outset that the issue was the historical accuracy of the Bible and
that all other issues hinged on the belief that the Bible was inerrant. When it
was suggested that the moderates might abandon the Convention, he replied
that the "liberals" would not leave because they were afraid to do so. He put it
thus: "Liberals don't build churches, just institutions. Liberalism is parasitic.
That's why they won't split—they'll show their inadequacies."

When Pressler attacked the "liberals," they returned the fire. Just before the
convention in Dallas, Norman Cavender, a deacon and Sunday school teacher at
the First Baptist Church of Claxton, Georgia, alleged that Pressler organized and
maintained the inerrancy faction through a mailing list on his personal computer and that the judge lied about it when the editor of the *Indiana Baptist* asked
him if it were so.[57] Obviously the controversy had turned bitter and ugly again.
In the spring of 1985 tension filled the air as moderates and fundamentalists
prepared to meet in Dallas for the most acrimonious showdown yet. What the
outcome would be, no one was quite sure. Some wondered if the Convention
would survive the confrontation intact.

The first phase of the second crusade for the SBC holy land ended with the
fundamentalists in command of the field and the moderates vowing to continue
the struggle. Between 1979 and the convention in Dallas the inerrantists successfully rallied enough grass-roots Southern Baptist support around them to win
the presidency six straight times, to place more and more fundamentalist trus-

tees on agencies and boards, and to pass most of their conservative resolutions. And they did it all amidst constant denials by the two spearheads of the movement that they had an organization or even an agenda. Paige Patterson continuously denied that there was any fundamentalist party or that he and his friends sought to control the Convention. Pressler said he had no agenda for the SBC and had never had one. He, too, declared that there was no organization, only "communication" between likeminded people.[58] Yet the two men, along with the thousands they had won to their cause, were well on their way to implementing their ten-year plan to win control of the denomination and to purge it of what they called liberalism. Would the gathering at Dallas disrupt the fundamentalist timetable or give it further impetus? That was the question many concerned Southern Baptists—those on both sides of the controversy and especially those who tried to remain neutral—waited anxiously to see answered. The Dallas convention promised to be a watershed event in the life of Southern Baptists, and it was.

4

The Second Crusade

Showdown at Dallas and the Futile Search for Peace, 1985–1987

A s the Dallas convention approached, several highly respected SBC officials made it quite clear that Charles Stanley, the incumbent president, was
not acceptable to them, and they urged that he be defeated in his quest for a second term. Among those who took this stand were seminary presidents Russell
Dilday, Roy Honeycutt, and Randall Lolley. Joining them in their effort to unseat
Stanley was Keith Parks, president of the Foreign Mission Board. Parks criticized the incumbent president for the minimal support he had given to Convention causes, and he urged Southern Baptist missionaries to go to Dallas and vote
for officers who would support the Bible *and* "our convention approach to missions." Honeycutt was considerably more forthright in his criticism, accusing
the fundamentalist leaders of "unscrupulous use of power and manipulation."
He called for the election of new leaders "who will embrace our diversity as a
blessing." Furthermore, he attacked Paige Patterson and Paul Pressler for
"charging hundreds of Southern Baptists with heresy and deceit" and for con-
spiring to "control the selection of trustees of the agencies through the appointive powers of their handpicked presidential candidates." In the process the fundamentalists were destroying the SBC, Honeycutt asserted.[1]

The hard-hitting rhetoric continued from both sides right up to meeting
time. Moderates kept saying that a group of "independents" were using power
politics to "take over" SBC institutions and creedalize the denomination. Fundamentalists replied that no one could creedalize autonomous churches and
their members. Paige Patterson, finally admitting that fundamentalists had
gained control of the Convention, noted that moderates could now understand
how people on his side had "felt for 25 years." Some moderates admitted that
there was some truth to what Patterson said.[2]

Five years earlier, in St. Louis, Pressler had observed that the tide was moving "our way." He was most certainly correct in that observation, and the Dallas
convention clearly demonstrated that five years had brought little hope of the

moderates' reversing the tide. The 1985 convention saw over 45,000 messengers register, a total more than twice that of any previous convention. At least 20,000 attended the pre-convention Pastor's Conference, while over 4,000 were present for the Forum. Those attending the Forum wore "TEN PLUS" buttons, indicating that each Southern Baptist church should give a minimum of 10 percent of its budget to SBC agencies through the Cooperative Program. Dallas, like Houston six years before, quickly took on circus-like characteristics. It was alleged that at least a hundred children aged six years or younger showed up as messengers. Because they had proper credentials and because the SBC bylaws mentioned no minimum age requirements, the children were registered and given ballots. Lee Porter, the registration secretary, said that nine persons told him they saw computerized ballots being passed out prior to the Wednesday night business session. Someone, it was reported, had been seen distributing ballots to people getting off a bus. Paul Pressler denied all of the allegations and challenged Porter to produce proof of voting irregularities. The judge was sure, he said, that no supporters of Charles Stanley were guilty, and he added, "I am sure no one who is a friend of mine would stoop to such tactics as that." Besides the charges of voting fraud, over 625 writers and broadcasters were there to report on the convention. It became an enormous media event.[3]

The effort to oust Stanley fell flat. Moderates nominated Winfred Moore, the congenial and folksy pastor of the First Baptist Church in Amarillo. Just before the vote was taken word circulated that evangelist Billy Graham had endorsed Stanley, who had already been endorsed by W. A. Criswell. The Texas challenger received a good vote, but not good enough, as Stanley won with 24,453 votes to Moore's 19,795. In spite of the outcome of the presidential vote, for a moment it seemed that harmony might overcome acrimony among the messengers, when someone expressed a desire to nominate Moore for first vice-president. Stanley called Moore to the podium and asked if he would permit his name to be placed in nomination. The Amarillo pastor asked the reelected president if *he* were asking Moore to do it. Stanley responded that he would welcome such a nomination, since he intended to do all he could to reunite the Convention around missions and evangelism during the coming year. The nomination was made, and Moore won easily over Zig Ziglar, the incumbent first vice-president. Stanley, indicating his willingness to work with Moore, predicted "you're going to see everybody in this convention coming closer together than you've ever seen them before." At the time, all of this was viewed as a goodwill gesture and a sign of restored harmony. Rosenberg has observed that the entire episode was a "comedy of errors" that "created a fog of good feeling that lasted a whole day." This caustic critic of Southern Baptists was not far wrong, for not all fundamentalists were comfortable with the outcome of the election. Not only was

Moore elected first vice-president, but Henry Huff, a moderate layman from Louisville, Kentucky, was elected second vice-president. Russell Kaemmerling expressed concern.[4]

Whatever harmony there was vanished the next day when moderate leader James Slatton challenged the report of the Committee on Committees with regard to its nominees for the Committee on Boards. Slatton proposed a substitute slate of nominees to the Committee on Boards, calling for it to consist of state convention presidents and the state presidents of the Woman's Missionary Union. In offering his motion, Slatton said, "The one chance this body has for peace is to adopt a committee that this whole body can trust." Stanley ruled Slatton's motion out of order. His ruling provoked shouts of "point of order," but Stanley ignored them and put the official slate to a hand vote. A formal vote was eventually taken, and the official slate was approved 13,123 to 9,581. At a press conference later, Slatton, Cecil Sherman, and Bill Sherman asserted that the vote on Slatton's motion did not represent the messengers' true views. The three moderate leaders were especially critical of Stanley for ignoring messengers who tried to raise procedural points. Years later Slatton wrote of the incident, "I was designated by Cecil Sherman to bring the motion, and appealed the decision of the chair when Stanley ruled that I could not offer the entire slate as a substitute slate. He ruled that I must nominate each person individually. When the house sustained my right to offer the entire slate, Stanley's overruling of the house and his manner of presiding afterwards impressed many in and out of the hall as extremely undemocratic and high-handed."[5]

The fight over Slatton's motion was both heated and dramatic. His successful appeal to the body had resulted in a vote of 12,576 to 11,801 to overrule the president. It was obvious that Stanley had ignored the convention body's wishes by not allowing a vote on the motion and that he had been extremely arbitrary in refusing to allow anyone to speak who attempted to present an opposing point of view. When asked later why he had not recognized calls for point of order during the debate, Stanley answered, "The chair recognized no points of order so there are none." William J. Cumbie of Virginia, who had served as parliamentarian at three conventions, called Stanley's ruling "bizarre," noting that Bylaw 32 allowed the convention body to amend "all committee reports." In addition to Stanley's questionable ruling there were, once again, charges of voting irregularities during the vote on this issue. One observer was convinced that about four thousand more votes were counted than there were people in the auditorium.[6]

Stanley's high-handedness in handling the Slatton motion led to a lawsuit against the Southern Baptist Convention. One messenger who took umbrage at Stanley's actions was Robert Crowder, a layman from Birmingham, Alabama.

Since 1982 Crowder had been highly dissatisfied with nominations to various offices, because many of the nominees were members of churches that contributed little to Southern Baptist missions through the Cooperative Program. At the Pittsburgh Convention in 1983 he challenged the nominations of Fred Wolfe as chairman of the Committee on Order of Business and that of Dick Thomasian of Whitesburg Baptist Church in Huntsville, Alabama, as a trustee of the Foreign Mission Board. Crowder contended that both men came from churches that gave too little money to the CP. At the SBC meeting in Kansas City the following year, he offered a motion requiring all Convention leaders to come from churches "which support the Cooperative Program with a minimum of 6 percent of the church's total receipts." The motion was referred to the Executive Committee. What happened in Dallas regarding Slatton's motion was the proverbial last straw to Crowder, his wife, and a host of other messengers.[7]

Soon after the SBC meeting in Dallas, Crowder called Harold Bennett, president of the Executive Committee, to discuss the business sessions at the annual meeting. He questioned the election of the nominees to the Committee on Boards and argued that Stanley's action violated Convention bylaws and *Robert's Rules of Order*. He asked Bennett to initiate some action that would make the election of the Committee on Boards null and void. The EC president agreed to consult the EC officers about the request. On August 2, 1985, Bennett notified Crowder that the EC officers refused to do anything to reverse the action of the Convention. In a letter dated August 27 Crowder responded, saying he "had hoped that these questions might be resolved peaceably within the machinery of the Convention." Before the end of the month James Guenther, the Convention's attorney, was notified by attorneys for Robert and Julia Crowder that the Birmingham couple, along with other registered messengers, were bringing suit against the SBC, the president of the SBC, and the EC. Over the next three months attempts were made to negotiate a settlement of the dispute. Attorney Emmet J. Bondourant of Atlanta spoke to the EC on behalf of the Crowders on September 16. He presented the Crowders' grievances, but the EC upheld the action the Convention had taken in Dallas.[8]

Finally, on December 5, 1985, the Crowders, joined by Henry C. Cooper, a layman from Windsor, Missouri, filed suit against the SBC in federal district court in Atlanta. The Crowder-Cooper suit was followed by a suit filed in an Atlanta superior court by messengers from Georgia, Louisiana, North Carolina, and Kentucky. The plaintiffs in the state suit asked for an injunction that would force Southern Baptist leaders to adhere to Convention bylaws. They also asked the court to require Convention officials to reconsider the positive vote taken on the report of the Committee on Committees at the Dallas meeting.

Perhaps because it was heard in a federal court, the Crowder suit, as it came to be called, received more attention. The Crowders and Cooper were soon joined in their suit by H. Allen McCartney of Vero Beach, Florida. They asked the court to void the election of the fifty-two persons chosen at the Dallas convention to the Committee on Boards and to bar them from serving. President Charles Stanley was accused of violating Convention bylaws 16, 32, and 35. On May 5, 1986, Judge Robert Hall ruled that "civil tribunals have no power to resolve disputes that are ecclesiastical in nature." Stanley praised Hall's ruling as a "significant decision for the constitutional principle of separation of church and state." An appeal by the plaintiffs to the Eleventh Circuit Court resulted in that court's sustaining Judge Hall's ruling. The Crowders and their fellow litigants unsuccessfully attempted to have the case reinstated in 1987. After Judge Hall's decision and before the Eleventh Circuit Court in effect dismissed the Crowder suit, the case pending in the state superior court was "voluntarily dismissed."[9]

When, on February 22, 1988, the United States Supreme Court refused to hear the case and thus left Judge Hall's ruling intact, Robert Crowder was convinced that his suit was dead and buried. In March 1988 he sent a check for $223.79 to Harold Bennett, explaining that forty or fifty people had contributed $51,505.65 for the purpose of pursuing the suit and that he was contributing all that remained of that amount to the Cooperative Program. He then issued a news release in which he asserted that the "price of religious freedom had gone up in the SBC." Legal fees paid by the SBC amounted to $243,006.73. Defending an SBC president who maintained that he did in Dallas what he "thought was right," obviously carried a high price tag, too.[10]

The suit brought against the SBC for Charles Stanley's arbitrary ruling at Dallas was not the only sign that the denominational ship was heading straight into a dangerous storm. Some fundamentalist leaders, including former president Bailey Smith, had come to doubt that the Convention's factions could be reconciled. Even before Dallas one proposal circulated that called for reelecting Stanley as president and then establishing a committee to divide SBC assets among the contending parties and adopt "a plan whereby we could depart from each other in peace." Such talk spurred into action men who thought that a schism would be an awful catastrophe. Charles Pickering, a Laurel, Mississippi, attorney and president of the Mississippi Baptist Convention, called a meeting of twenty-three Baptist state convention presidents in April 1985. The state presidents made a plea for the fundamentalists and moderates to "bury the hatchet" and to reconcile. They also appointed a seven-man secret task force to devise a plan for easing tensions in the SBC. Wallace Henley, president of the Alabama Baptist Convention and pastor of the McElwain Baptist Church in Birmingham, played a key role on that task force, which soon discovered that Franklin Paschall of Tennessee, a former SBC president, planned to propose a peace committee similar to one which task force members envisioned. Paschall, upon hearing about the plans of the task force, became offended, believing that the state presidents were "stealing his thunder." Behind the scenes Henley contacted Paige Patterson, only to learn that Patterson had agreed to support Paschall's effort. The task force held meetings with SBC President Charles Stanley and kept them "top secret," trying to refine their ideas for a peace committee. Before the meeting in Dallas they attempted to reconcile with Paschall.[11]

After the secret meetings, the state convention presidents planned to meet in Dallas on June 9. That meeting lasted until 1:30 A.M. and closed with the presidents leaving it up to the task force to proceed with a proposal to the convention. Since the task force wanted all views—fundamentalist, moderate, and nonaligned—represented, they were prepared to recommend nineteen specific persons for service on the peace committee. Task force members decided to ask Paschall to present the motion to establish the nineteen-member "Peace Committee." The state convention presidents would sit on the platform to signify their support of the proposal. Thus it would come out as the motion of Paschall and the state convention presidents. The former SBC president agreed to do it. Then, at a press conference held at the Dallas Hilton, the task force, with Paschall seated right in the middle, "announced to the world" what they planned to do. Plans soon went awry. When time came to present the proposal to the convention, Paschall, because he forgot to take his ballot with him, was not permitted to enter the convention hall. Task force member Bill Hickem, who was president of the Florida Baptist Convention and pastor of Riverside Baptist Church in Jacksonville, had to offer the motion in Paschall's place. Meanwhile, trying to win Judge Pressler's support for the proposal, Henley visited with the fundamentalist leader in his hotel room. The judge did not mince words. He flatly refused to support the effort, saying, "Whitewash [Herschel] Hobbs is on the committee and will see that nothing substantive comes out of this committee, and it's going to be like any other, and I'm not going to support it."[12]

As it turned out, the Peace Committee was established in spite of Pressler's opposition, and Paschall ended up in the limelight after all. Action on the motion that created the Peace Committee was postponed until the next morning. Although Hickem again offered the motion, he deferred to Paschall to handle the discussion. The personnel of the committee was called into question because it had no women on it. Elaine Rasco, a messenger from the First Baptist Church of Chalkville, Alabama, commented, "Women in the ministry is an issue. How can you address it without a woman on the committee?" Paschall soon requested the addition of two members to the committee—Jodi Chapman of the First Baptist Church of Wichita Falls, Texas, and Christine Gregory of Danville, Virginia, a former first vice-president of the SBC and former WMU president.

Although Judge Pressler refused to support the motion, Paige Patterson accepted it and mounted the platform when Hickem introduced it. When the motion was amended to include two women, Patterson was asked if he would accept the committee with women. On the spot before forty-five thousand people, he replied, "Uh, yes, I will." Also added to the committee was the newly elected first vice-president, Winfred Moore. Wallace Henley nominated Charles Fuller, the pastor of the First Baptist Church of Roanoke, Virginia, for chairman of the committee. Fuller was regarded as nonaligned in the controversy. With these amendments the SBC created the twenty-two-member Peace Committee in hopes that it could find a formula for reestablishing peace in the Convention. Henley was optimistic about the committee's ability to bring reconciliation, and J. Everett Sneed, editor of the *Arkansas Baptist Newsmagazine*, also viewed the committee's creation as a sign of hope.[13]

While many Southern Baptists were hopeful about the future because of the creation of the Peace Committee, there were others on both sides who feared that the committee was stacked in favor of the other side. Five distinct groups were identified among the members. Those considered staunch supporters of the fundamentalist movement were Charles Stanley, Adrian Rogers, Jerry Vines, co-pastor of Jacksonville, Florida's First Baptist Church, Jodi Chapman, wife of fundamentalist pastor Morris Chapman, and Edwin Young, pastor of Houston's Second Baptist Church. Avowed moderates on the committee consisted of Cecil Sherman, who had moved from North Carolina to become pastor of Broadway Baptist Church in Fort Worth, Texas, Winfred Moore, and William Hull, then pastor of the First Baptist Church of Shreveport, Louisiana. Members who were considered sympathetic to the fundamentalist cause but not visibly active in it were Jim Henry, pastor of Orlando's First Baptist Church, Bill Crews of Magnolia Baptist Church in Riverside, California, and Ray Roberts, retired executive director of the Ohio Baptist Convention. Those thought to be in sympathy with the moderates but not overtly active in their cause were Albert McClellan, retired associate executive secretary-treasurer of the Executive Committee, Christine Gregory, and Harmon Born of Rex, Georgia. All other members were viewed as neutrals without attachment to either side. They were Charles Fuller, Herschel Hobbs, Dan Vestal, then pastor of the First Baptist Church in Midland, Texas, John Sullivan of Broadmoor Baptist Church in Shreveport, Charles Pickering, Doyle E. Carlton, Jr., of Wauchula, Florida, and Robert Cuttino of Lancaster, South Carolina.[14]

The Peace Committee met less than two months after the Convention on

August 5 and 6 in Nashville. Seventeen of the twenty-two members were present. Other meetings were held in October and December and then another in January 1986. The meetings were well attended, but on February 19, 1986, Charles Fuller reported that it was "difficult to translate into words all that has transpired within the committee" and that the committee had "by no means reached a breakthrough." Five subcommittees were formed and assigned the task of visiting the seminaries and some denominational agencies to make inquiries. It was reported that the leadership at each place had been cooperative. Very defensive about its work, the committee reported: "Regardless of how those committee visits have been perceived, they have *not* been designed to be *miniature inquisitions*. They were honest attempts to dialogue with Southern Baptist leaders about issues which the committee has been assigned to analize [sic]."[15]

As the Peace Committee subcommittees visited the seminaries, allegations were made that some seminary presidents were trying to keep students who supported the fundamentalist side from talking to subcommittee members. These reports prompted Paul Pressler to introduce a resolution at the Executive Committee meeting in February 1986 "reaffirming the right of all to have free access to the peace committee." After fierce debate the judge's resolution was tabled by a thirty-six to eight vote.[16]

Although the Peace Committee was actively pursuing information that many hoped would result in a plan for ending the controversy, the fundamentalist crusaders went forward with their plans to cleanse the SBC of liberalism. It soon became clear that Dallas had chased away no suspicions, settled no issues, and created little or no goodwill by establishing the Peace Committee. At a midwinter conference in Jacksonville, Florida, over 350 of those in favor of a fundamentalist-controlled Convention attended a luncheon hosted by Homer Lindsay, Jr. Among those present was Bobby Welch, pastor of First Baptist Church in Daytona. He announced his intentions of rallying the troops to attend the 1986 meeting in Atlanta and to vote for a man "that will put an end to liberalism within our Convention." Lindsay then announced that Adrian Rogers was the group's choice for president at Atlanta. The fundamentalists proceeded to have an enjoyable time bashing "liberals." Welch accused them of using such "smoke screens" as local church autonomy and the priesthood of the believer to hide behind. Jerry Vines, though a member of the Peace Committee, attacked some Southern Baptist seminary and college professors who "rape" the faith of their students through liberal teaching. He provided no names.[17]

Peace Committee or no Peace Committee, there was no sign of a moratorium on hostility between the fundamentalists and the moderates. Convention president Charles Stanley insisted that there had always been and still was only one real issue—inerrancy—and he praised Paige Patterson "as one of God's choice servants" for his leadership in raising that issue. Nor were the moderates silent or inactive. In April, with the Atlanta convention two months away, Winfred Moore proposed his own four-point "fairness" or peace plan for ending the controversy: (1) establish the principle that no more than two persons from the same church could serve on SBC boards and agencies; (2) ask for nominations to SBC offices from each state convention president, the WMU presidents, state executive directors, and chairmen of the state conventions' executive boards; (3) appoint people to serve on boards and agencies from churches with a history of supporting the Cooperative Program; and (4) hire a professional parliamentarian for each national convention to maintain proper procedures. Moore's plan prompted Lee Roberts, chairman of the Committee on Boards, to remark sarcastically, "If you can't win the game, change the rules." Paul Pressler was also critical of Moore's proposal, calling it tantamount to "endorsing a hierarchical form of church government for Southern Baptists." On the other hand, Keith Parks, president of the Foreign Mission Board, enthusiastically endorsed Moore's plan as a means of getting Southern Baptists back to their "basic biblical purpose."[18] Peace seemed beyond reach.

While the debate raged over the "fairness plan," Stanley released his list of appointees to the Committee on Committees, and the chairman of the Committee on Boards, Lee Roberts, announced the nominees of that committee for service as agency trustees. Stanley had been urged to confer with vice-presidents Winfred Moore and Henry Huff before making his appointments. According to Moore and Huff, they gave Stanley a list of nearly two hundred names, and from it he chose two. Fundamentalists were happy with the Stanley appointments to the Committee on Committees, and the president defended them as fair. Roberts, of course, defended the nominations from the Committee on Boards, but one member of that committee, Fred Morgan of West Virginia, claimed that nominees from his state were rejected by Roberts because they were pro-abortion or did not believe in inerrancy. In Morgan's view the West Virginia nominees did not receive fair treatment.[19]

A few weeks before the Atlanta convention, Stanley announced that he would allow one-by-one challenges to nominations submitted by the Committee on Committees for the Committee on Boards, but he would not allow entire slates to be placed in nomination. The SBC's Executive Committee had already recommended that this be made Convention policy by amending Bylaw 16, and that bylaw would be so amended in Atlanta. Until it was, however, Stanley's position on the matter was rooted in his own arbitrary interpretation of the bylaws. As a consequence, he was regarded by many as the most controversial president the SBC had ever had. Apparently this did not bother the Atlanta pastor in the least, for a week prior to the 1986 Convention he compared himself to Jesus

Christ and the Apostle Paul, noting that both of them had been highly controversial, as was just about everyone who accomplished much in life. He contended that his election had forced Southern Baptists to deal with issues that the Convention had avoided for years.[20]

The stage was thus set for another demonstration of fundamentalist power at the annual SBC gathering. W. A. Criswell announced just before the convention that the pastor was the "ruler of the church," and a Florida pastor named Harold Hunter said that he wanted no messengers going from his church to the convention who were not going to vote the way he voted. He was certain, he argued, that "the Spirit of God" was leading him to the right candidate for president. He intended to vote for that candidate, Adrian Rogers, and he expected messengers from his church to do the same.[21]

Emerging as the moderate candidate to oppose Rogers was none other than the incumbent first vice-president, Winfred Moore, who had announced on May 11, 1986, that he was willing to be nominated again. Thus, two members of the Peace Committee squared off in the presidential election, and both claimed to be peace candidates. Moore said he would bring the Convention back together by implementing his fairness plan. When Georgia pastor Nelson Price nominated Rogers, he called the former president a "peace candidate" who was "owned by no man" and whose "clearly stated stance" would bring "stability." Moore was nominated by Phoenix, Arizona, pastor Richard Jackson, who arose from his sickbed to fly to Atlanta for the convention. In nominating Moore, Jackson said, "Winfred Moore knows the truth, believes the truth, preaches the truth, lives the truth—and above all tells the truth. That's the Baptist way, and I like it." Jackson's heroics were not enough to stem the relentless fundamentalist tide. Rogers defeated Moore by a vote of 21,201 to 17,898, or 54.22 percent to 45.78 percent.[22]

As in other recent SBC presidential elections, charges of voting irregularities were made. When the balloting was in progress, Kelly Brown, a pastor from Meigs, Georgia, appealed to President Stanley, saying:

> I saw with my own eyes a woman who voted two ballots. She covered up her name [on her messenger tag] when I approached her.
> Mr. President, I call upon you to correct this action. I want you to tell this woman she can't vote two ballots, even if her husband has gone to relieve himself.

Stanley's response to the appeal was that he would ask for a new vote if the margin of difference was one vote.[23] Once again the Atlanta pastor revealed himself as an arbitrary and arrogant man.

Not only did Rogers win in Atlanta, but two fundamentalists won the offices of first and second vice-president, demonstrating beyond question that fundamentalists had secured control of the annual meetings. They were also well on their way to gaining control over the denomination's agencies and institutions. After the convention, Larry Coleman, a New York pastor, made an effort to categorize all the trustees who presided over the Convention's boards and seminaries. He went through the entire list of trustees and identified them as fundamentalists, moderates, swing voters, or unclassified. He concluded that the fundamentalists had the highest percentage of votes, but in every case they were short of an outright majority. Over the next three years that would change, and they would gain their majority. Still, the Convention picture was far different from that painted by either the fundamentalists or the moderates. Soon after his election in Atlanta, Adrian Rogers asserted that his margin of victory was not a true reflection of Southern Baptist sentiment. He made the farfetched claim that the split in the Convention was closer to 90 percent to 10 percent in favor of the fundamentalists. Cecil Sherman was on target when he called this comment by Rogers "silly talk," but Winfred Moore was just as silly when he claimed that his defeat was the will of the messengers and not "the people" in the thousands of Southern Baptist churches. He said, "When the rank-and-file understand you'll see a rising up of Baptists who have been denied their liberty."[24] Who were the messengers in Atlanta but Southern Baptists from the Convention's thousands of churches?

The obvious fact was that the fundamentalists had greater grass-roots support than did the moderates, but the latter kept insisting that it was not so. On the other hand, the fundamentalists did not have the support of 90 percent of Southern Baptists, even though a survey taken by Nancy Ammerman in 1985 indicated that 80 percent of those who responded "agreed" or "strongly agreed" that "the scriptures are the inerrant Word of God, accurate in every detail."[25] Even if her survey was truly reflective of Southern Baptist opinion regarding inerrancy, it did not follow that all Southern Baptists who believed in inerrancy supported the movement initiated by Paul Pressler and Paige Patterson. Richard Jackson was an excellent example. Though an inerrantist, Jackson never supported the fundamentalist bid for power; in fact he actively opposed it. As previously noted, it seems entirely possible that the convention votes of 1979 to 1991 accurately indicated the sentiments of Southern Baptists during those years. The votes resulted regularly in fundamentalist victories by margins ranging from one or two to ten percentage points.

That the fundamentalists controlled the Convention by the mid-1980s was not in doubt. The likelihood that peace could be restored was in grave doubt. Peace was nowhere apparent in Atlanta, whether in the presidential election or in the business sessions. Four times moderates offered substitute candidates for trustees, and four times they were voted down. The slate offered by Committee on Boards chairman Lee Roberts passed. Bylaw 16 was changed to suit the fundamentalists, as was Bylaw 31, but tense debate broke out during two sessions held by the Executive Committee. A subcommittee proposed "that the Executive Committee express its concern concerning the unfounded charges made in both Baptist Press releases and secular news reports concerning widespread voting irregularities at the 1985 SBC and that the Peace Committee take appropriate action to correct such statements and eliminate such unfounded accusations in the future." Committee member Paul Pressler led in trying to secure the proposal's adoption. After acrimonious debate, however, the proposal was defeated 38 to 16. On the convention floor Pressler and his cohorts had the votes, but not yet did they have a majority on the Executive Committee. Even so, one observer was correct in concluding that "there was absolutely no question that in Atlanta, the fundamentalist-conservatives were firmly in control from the opening gavel to the closing prayer."[26]

Moderates left Atlanta deeply disappointed, despairing of any relief from fundamentalist control. Robert W. Bailey, pastor of Southside Baptist Church in Birmingham, Alabama, said, "A lot of us feel like we've been to a funeral. We're waiting and watching to see what they will do. This marks eight of the ten years they said it would take to gain control." North Carolina pastor Marion D. Lark, who was chairman of the Southern Baptist Historical Commission, said that Baptists had to stand firm against those who would take them into the "foreign land" of theological uniformity, creedal statements, and Convention hierarchy. He added, "Cooperative missions, not theological uniformity, is our heritage. Biblical authority, not biblical inerrancy, is the waymark that stands tall in Baptist history. Confessions of faith, not creedal statements, give voice to our affirmations."[27]

As the moderates criticized and moaned, the Peace Committee searched in vain for a formula to effect reconciliation. Although it would deliver its final report to the Convention at its annual meeting in St. Louis in 1987, the committee made a preliminary report in Atlanta. It indicated that "significant theological diversity" had been found in the seminaries and admitted that "political activity within the Convention since the late 1970s has reached a new level." The preliminary report immediately became another source of controversy because of a sentence that stated that "the limits of legitimate diversity are at the heart of our ongoing process to bring about reconciliation." Moderates objected to the word "legitimate," while fundamentalists heartily approved its use.

For the time being there was no peace. Instead, tension continued to mount. On October 25, 1986 Cecil Sherman abruptly resigned from the Peace Committee because he believed the seminary presidents were knuckling under to fundamentalist demands that they take a more conservative theological stance. Also in October the Home Mission Board voted to cut off funds to any church which called a woman to be its pastor. There were numerous objections from those who believed that the decision infringed on local church autonomy. Defenders of the new policy, however, argued that it was not fair for Southern Baptists who did not believe in ordaining women pastors to have to fund churches that did. Meanwhile, fundamentalist leaders encouraged new fundamentalist trustees who had been elected to agencies and boards to be active and to contribute to decision making. James Guenther, attorney for the Executive Committee, remarked, "The laid-back good old boy trustee was never very helpful and today he is absolutely unacceptable." Moreover, the fundamentalists began promoting the idea of the "authority of the pastor."[28]

Two significant developments in the fall of 1986 further indicated that there was little hope for peace in the SBC. The Georgia Baptist Convention had already become politicized by the presidential election in 1984, which had pitted a fundamentalist candidate against a moderate. The moderate candidate, Floyd Roebuck, won over fundamentalist Clark Hutchinson, and the victors apparently gloated over their triumph. In 1986 the fundamentalists turned the tables by electing Hutchinson. They also attacked Mercer University, a school supported by Georgia Baptists, for being a "party school." President Kirby Godsey was condemned for allowing drinking and R-rated movies on campus. Godsey defended Mercer as one of the greatest Baptist institutions in America, but the pressures on the school continued to build, as friction intensified between moderates and fundamentalists all over the state. The other development that boded ill for peace was the rejection of a new eight-point moderate peace plan that James Slatton proposed to fundamentalist leaders. Adrian Rogers, Paul Pressler, and Paige Patterson all responded negatively when the Richmond pastor offered his proposal. Slatton reported dejectedly, "There was no give and no offer to meet us halfway."[29]

After Dallas, and especially after Atlanta, a complete fundamentalist victory in the quest to take the holy land of the SBC was a foregone conclusion. Moderates went all out at both conventions only to find that their legions were fewer in number than those of the fundamentalists. Over 45,000 messengers— the largest number ever—attended the SBC meeting in Dallas, and more than 40,000 registered in Atlanta. No matter how many moderates appeared, they were regularly outnumbered by supporters of the fundamentalists. Fewer moderates bothered to go to annual conventions after Atlanta. Attendance at St. Louis in 1987 to hear and vote on the report of the Peace Committee hardly exceeded 25,000 messengers.

Months before the St. Louis meeting some moderates made plans to form a smaller body of like-minded Baptists within the Convention with the idea of meeting from time to time for fellowship, while other moderates announced their intention of conducting what amounted to guerrilla warfare against the fundamentalists for as long as it took to recapture the SBC and restore it to what it had been before 1979. Thus, the moderates themselves became divided over a proper course to pursue and formed two different groups to fight the battle in their respective ways. In less than two years there emerged the Southern Baptist Alliance and Baptists Committed to the Southern Baptist Convention.

Following a preliminary meeting at Mercer University in August 1986 the Southern Baptist Alliance was organized on February 12, 1987. One of the early officers of the organization was Dan Ivins, pastor of Baptist Church of the Covenant in Birmingham, Alabama. Ivins asserted that fundamentalists could "not accept any views but their own" and declared that after eight years "we've had enough." He further noted that the SBA wanted to "give a voice to the people who have been disenfranchised by the Southern Baptist Convention." The SBA incorporated as a nonprofit corporation with a Charlotte, North Carolina, post office box, elected officers, and named a board of directors. Henry Crouch, pastor of Charlotte's Providence Baptist Church, was elected first president of the SBA and indicated that the new organization might help the Baptist Joint Committee on Public Affairs financially, if that agency's funding was slashed by the Convention. He also hinted that the SBA would provide supplemental salary support to ordained women pastors who might be denied funds by the Home Mission Board.[30]

Besides Crouch and Ivins, other early leaders of the SBA included Alan Neely, then a professor at Southeastern Baptist Theological Seminary, who became interim executive director, John Thomason, a Mississippi pastor who succeeded Crouch as president, and Anne Neil, a former Southern Baptist missionary of Wake Forest, North Carolina, who served as third president of the SBA. Over the next five years the SBA held several "convocations" and "listening sessions," devised a strategy for diverting the money of its member churches from SBC agencies that had fallen under the control of fundamentalists, and founded a seminary at Richmond, Virginia, in collaboration with American Baptists and Presbyterians. In November 1988 the SBA board of directors hired Stan Hastey as its first executive director to replace Alan Neely, who had served until a bona-fide director could be found. Hastey had once been a member of the SBC Executive Committee, and at the time of his appointment by the SBA was associate executive director of the Baptist Joint Committee on Public Affairs, an agency already under heavy fire from some Southern Baptists. He accepted the SBA appointment, Hastey said, because the position gave him an opportunity to fight for freedom and "soul liberty."[31]

Two months before Stan Hastey was appointed executive director, the SBA sponsored a three-day listening session in Nashville, Tennessee. At that meeting Alan Neely declared that the future of the SBA was uncertain, but it would "remain active in its support of Baptist principles and Baptist heritage and freedom until . . . oppression is relieved or until a new promised land is reached." Both Neely and Henry Crouch denied that the SBA sought to divide the SBC, but the latter emphasized that its members would "find it very uncomfortable to support indefinitely the present trend of leadership." Some prominent moderates, including Cecil Sherman, joined the ranks of the SBA, and Hastey offered dynamic and energetic leadership. Yet, in spite of all its efforts and a long list of supporters—seventy-three member churches in thirteen states with an overall enrollment of 44,000 and 3,000 individual members from forty-one states by 1989—the organization could do little to slow the pace of the fundamentalist crusaders. (In 1992 the SBA changed its name to the Alliance of Baptists and appeared headed for absorption by the Cooperative Baptist Fellowship, still another moderate organization established over a period of months during 1990 and 1991.)[32]

As the time approached in 1987 for Southern Baptists to meet in St. Louis and consider the report of the Peace Committee, it became painfully obvious that many put little faith in that committee's ability to offer a formula for peace. A little over a month before the convention the six seminaries of the SBC sponsored the Conference on Biblical Inerrancy at Ridgecrest Baptist Conference Center in Rigecrest, North Carolina, held May 4–7. Thirty-six scholars, most but not all of them Baptists, presented papers explaining their particular views on the question. The papers revealed that there was a wide variety of opinions, even among those who affirmed inerrancy. Some were perhaps surprised to discover that there were different kinds of inerrantists. There were inerrantists who insisted that the autographs of Scripture were perfect and true in every detail (of course no autographs have survived!); inerrantists who insisted that some current translations were inerrant; inerrantists who admitted to scribal errors in translation; and inerrantists who qualified the term with a list of disclaimers. Former inerrantist Clark Pinnock publicly repudiated the doctrine, while Adrian Rogers and Paige Patterson repudiated Pinnock and forthrightly reasserted their belief in inerrancy, as they understood the term. There was no indication that anyone was swayed by the opinion of anyone else or that those who had turned the Convention upside down using inerrancy as their rallying cry would make any concessions to noninerrantists.[33] The conference was apparently meant to promote understanding between those of different views, but in all likelihood it merely confirmed the opinion of some that denial of inerrancy (which they regarded as a sure sign of liberalism) abounded both inside and outside the SBC.

To most moderates it appeared there was little to be hoped for in conferences to promote understanding or in the impending report of the Peace Committee. Layman Norman Cavender from Claxton, Georgia, spoke to a crowd of moderates a few weeks before the St. Louis convention. He accused President Adrian Rogers of playing politics with committee appointments, charging that forty-three of the sixty-six people Rogers appointed to the Committee on Committees were aligned with the fundamentalist leaders. Even so, Cavender expressed hope of defeating the fundamentalists at some point in the future. He said, "In the end the fundamentalists will lose. I hope it comes within my lifetime." He called fundamentalism "bankrupt." Echoing Cavender's sentiments were James Slatton and retired Auburn, Alabama, pastor John Jeffers. The three men vowed to fight the fundamentalists and asserted, "We do not expect to drop out, give up or go away."[34]

Moderates went to St. Louis with little expectation of peace breaking out in the Convention, but with the hope of salvaging something of the old Convention. Dan Ivins indicated that many moderates would stay away, because they did not want to have "to put up with that [fundamentalist] junk." He intended to go, however, to help defend Southern Seminary against fundamentalist attacks and to thwart attempts to undercut Convention support for the Baptist Joint Committee on Public Affairs.[35]

Fundamentalists headed for St. Louis in a different frame of mind. They went confidently expecting to reelect Adrian Rogers as president and to approve a Peace Committee report which they believed would vindicate their longtime contention that the controversy was primarily rooted in theology and that there were indeed "theological problems" regarding what was being taught at the SBC's six seminaries.

The convention produced no surprises. Rogers was handily reelected over Richard Jackson, receiving 59.97 percent of the vote. Rogers said some days before the election that the number one issue at that moment was the adoption or rejection of the Peace Committee report. He called the report a compromise with which no member of the committee was *entirely* satisfied, because "no one's point of view has been completely adopted." Jackson asserted that he had long been an inerrantist and preached the doctrine "long before anyone began screaming about it in our Convention." What Southern Baptists needed, Jackson claimed, was to stop emphasizing inerrancy and to emphasize instead the need for "believer-priests who are charged with the responsibility of studying the Word of God for themselves."[36] The margin by which Rogers won the election clearly demonstrated that the inerrantists remained in the ascendancy.

Developments following the election could scarcely have been more satisfying to the fundamentalists. Bylaw 16 was amended once again, this time to change the name of the Committee on Boards to the Committee on Nominations. President Rogers claimed that his appointments in the coming year would represent the "broad spectrum" of Southern Baptists but that he would continue to appoint only inerrantists to the key Committee on Committees. Jerry Vines delivered the convention sermon, and he, too, thrilled the fundamentalists by reaffirming inerrancy. He declared, "If one cannot believe what the Bible says about history, one cannot believe what it says about eternity. And if one does not believe what it says about creation, one cannot be sure of what it says about salvation."[37]

The most publicized development at St. Louis, of course, was the presentation and approval of the Peace Committee's report. In commenting on that matter Ellen Rosenberg did not spare the vitriol. She condemned the report as "the outrage of the year." Promised a month in advance of the Convention, the report was not delivered until 7:00 A.M. of the first day, and it was voted on at 9:00 that night with only thirty minutes allowed for discussion. Chairman Charles Fuller presented the report. Efforts were made to delay discussion and amend the report, but all such efforts were voted down. Paul Kennedy, pastor of the First Baptist Church of Swannsboro, North Carolina, moved to table the report until the 1988 convention. On the advice of Parliamentarian Barry McCarty, Rogers ruled the motion out of order. The report concluded that the primary source of the controversy was "theological" but recognized that there were "political causes as well." No attempt was made to deny that a bitter political struggle was plaguing the Convention. The report described how the struggle had developed: "When people of good intention [i.e., Southern Baptist fundamentalists] became frustrated because they felt their convictions on Scripture were not seriously dealt with, they organized politically to make themselves heard. Soon, another group formed to counter the first, and the political process intensified." In the report the committee admonished the Convention to "move beyond this kind of politics." Specifically the committee urged "all organized political factions" to stop their activity and all Baptist news journals and private persons to tone down their rhetoric and refrain from labeling people as fundamentalists, moderates, and so forth. Fuller moved the adoption of the report "as printed in the *Convention Bulletin.*" The report was adopted overwhelmingly.[38]

Some points of the report were highly controversial, as was obvious during the brief discussion of the document. The report denied that the Baptist Faith and Message Statement of 1963 was a creed to be imposed on others. Instead it was a "commonly held interpretation which sets out parameters for cooperation." There was no convincing many moderates that such a description meant anything except "creed." Moreover, it was not clear whether the report insisted that all employees of Convention agencies subscribe to the BFM Statement, but that expectation was surely implied. Still, Chairman Fuller maintained that the 1963 statement was not a creed. Another controversial provision extended the Peace Committee's work for another three years to "encourage compliance." Winfred Moore resigned from the committee minutes after the report was adopted, asserting that he did not think the Peace Committee should continue as an "oversight" committee, sitting in judgment on denominational institutions and agencies. Charles Fuller insisted that there would be no policing tactics and that the methods for monitoring compliance were yet to be worked out.[39]

Reactions to the report and its adoption were varied. Two committee members, Herschel Hobbs and William Hull, were optimistic, believing that the report would at least start to move Southern Baptists down the road to peace. Hull, who had left his pastorate in Louisiana to become vice-president for academic affairs at Samford University, called the report a "trade-off on both sides." Paul Pressler was "elated." Larry Lewis, newly appointed president of the Home Mission Board, called it a "mandate" to hire as employees only those who subscribed to the BFM Statement. Adrian Rogers said he hoped those "out of step" would "willingly step aside," since the Convention had spoken. Some moderates were far from pleased. Russell Dilday rejected the idea that the controversy was caused by theological differences. He insisted that the cause was the "political activities of conservatives." Carolyn Weatherford, executive director of the WMU, had a "negative" reaction to the report, and James Slatton said its approval made him feel like being "aboard the *Titanic* after hitting the iceberg." He observed that "the denominational ship is still afloat and a lot of wonderful people are aboard. But the damage is grave." Henry Crouch contended that the Peace Committee report struck a blow at the "heart" of what being Baptist was all about—"religious freedom." Extending the committee's work, he argued, turned the committee into an "investigatory enforcement committee for doctrinal uniformity."[40]

The Peace Committee, it had been hoped, would find a way of easing tensions and bringing the warring factions in the SBC back together. Instead of easing tensions, the committee's report heightened them. In the eyes of the moderates the adoption of the report was a clear sign that the fundamentalists were moving ever closer to total victory. Desperately trying to prevent that dark day of an ultimate fundamentalist triumph, the moderates vigorously renewed their opposition over the next three years. What they attempted bears strong resemblance to General Robert E. Lee's defeat in the Battle of the Wilderness and his retreat toward Richmond during the closing months of the Civil War. Lee fought magnificently and inflicted heavy casualties on the Union army, but after his last, bloody hurrah at Petersburg he was forced to retreat and finally to surrender. For those moderates who would continue to hold out for another three years, the 1990 SBC meeting in New Orleans would in effect be their battle of Petersburg, their final defeat.

5

The Second Crusade

The Moderates' Last Stand, 1988–1990

ST. LOUIS OFFERED convincing evidence that the Pressler-Patterson plan was on track, moving relentlessly toward total realization and precisely according to the fundamentalist timetable. More and more trustees sympathetic to the fundamentalist crusade served on the boards of SBC agencies and institutions. Two more presidential victories would be followed by 1989 with fundamentalist majorities on all boards except the board of Southwestern Seminary, and it was expected to "tilt" over in 1990. Already more than half the trustees of the huge Sunday School Board were in sympathy with the fundamentalists, and earlier in 1987 longtime fundamentalist spokesman Larry Lewis had been chosen as the Home Mission Board's new president. Lewis lost no time in announcing a policy of doctrinal integrity in the hiring of Home Mission Board employees, which meant that only those who professed inerrancy need apply. He argued that such a policy was mandated by the Peace Committee report. If the fundamentalists could continue to focus on biblical inerrancy as they had done for eight years and as Pressler insisted they must do, there seemed to be little hope of keeping them from achieving their ultimate goal of acquiring control of the denominational machinery by 1989.

While fundamentalists agreed on inerrancy, they were not of one mind on some other matters. One such matter had to do with how the SBC ought to relate to the Catholic Church. President Adrian Rogers announced in the summer of 1987 that, for reasons he chose not to reveal in "the public media," he would not meet with Pope John Paul II when the pontiff arrived in America in September. Professor Glenn Hinson of Southern Seminary claimed that most of the fundamentalists who supported Rogers were anti-Catholic and that the SBC president could not afford to offend them. When Executive Committee president Harold Bennett did meet with the pope in Columbia, South Carolina, on September 11, 1987, he was criticized. Colorado pastor Kenneth R. Barnett, angered by Bennett's audience with the pope, introduced at the Executive Committee meeting later that month a resolution precluding EC members and EC staff from attending ecumenical meetings without prior consent of the committee. Barnett argued that Bennett had been trapped "by the Pope's PR extravaganza." That the fundamentalists were badly divided on this issue was indicated by the fact that W. A. Criswell had met with the pope once and said he would be glad for the opportunity to have another audience with him. Also, Paige Patterson had twice met with the pope at the Vatican.[1]

Still, there were not enough chinks in the armor of the fundamentalist crusaders to offer the moderates much hope of stopping them. Even so, some of the most determined opposition mounted so far by the moderates got under way in the fall of 1987 at several state conventions. In Georgia, Louisiana, North Carolina, and Texas, moderates were elected over fundamentalists in the presidential elections. For the first time in 166 years Georgia Baptists failed to reelect an eligible incumbent president, but the next year they turned around and did the same thing by ousting the moderate in favor of a fundamentalist. There could be little doubt that Georgia Baptists were about as evenly divided as possible on the controversy. In Texas, Fort Worth pastor Joel Gregory presented himself as a nonaligned peacemaker and was unanimously elected president of the Baptist General Convention of Texas, but three years later he would declare himself firmly in the fundamentalist camp, shortly before being chosen to succeed W. A. Criswell as pastor of Dallas's First Baptist Church. Fundamentalist political activities were condemned at the annual conventions of Virginia and Missouri Baptists, but in Florida, fundamentalist pastor Bobby Welch was elected state convention president.[2]

Between 1987 and 1990 the struggle between moderates and fundamentalists in the state conventions produced mixed results. In 1988 the South Carolina Baptist Convention elected as its president moderate pastor Douglas Baker from Greenville over fundamentalist Michael Hamlet, but the fundamentalist element still had enough strength to deprive Furman University of funding by the convention. Only in Virginia was the fundamentalist cause dealt a severe blow in the late 1980s. Of all the state conventions, the Baptist General Association of Virginia took the strongest stand against the SBC's fundamentalist leadership and followed words with action. In the fall of 1988 Virginia Baptists adopted and sent to the SBC a "Memorial" that threatened to divert funds from the Cooperative Program if the SBC continued to ignore "consultation and consensus leadership." Similar plans were promoted in North Carolina and South Carolina, but they failed to win enough support. The North Carolina Baptist Convention did take action that allowed individual churches to participate in an "alternative funding" plan, if they chose, but their local church autonomy afforded them that option anyway. One North Carolina church that did indeed opt to change its giving habits was Snyder Memorial Baptist Church of Fayetteville, North Carolina. In times past Snyder Memorial had sent 23 percent of its budget to the North Carolina Baptist Convention, which kept 64.5 percent and sent 35.5 percent to Nashville for the CP. Beginning in 1989 the church voted to allow members "to specify that they want none of their gifts to go to the Southern Baptist Convention causes beyond the state level." Thereafter Snyder Memorial sent two separate checks—one to be divided by the usual formula and the other to be retained in toto by the North Carolina Baptist Convention.[3]

Although SBC fundamentalists had come under heavy attack in the state conventions, by 1990 they were still in control at the national level and had suffered only minor damage at the state level. Most states still approved budgets that included increased contributions to the CP. Some states in 1990—Alabama, California, Indiana, and Oklahoma—passed strongly worded statements supporting the CP. Florida Baptists refused to allow a supporter of alternative funding to serve as a trustee of one of its agencies. The 1990 SBC annual meeting angered moderates throughout the Convention by reducing the SBC's appropriation to the Baptist Joint Committee on Public Affairs to a fraction of previous amounts, but only Virginia Baptists provided a line-item appropriation for the BJC. Efforts to provide such funding in the Hawaii, Kentucky, Missouri, New England, and Tennessee state conventions all failed. The fight over alternative funding was most bitter in a number of state conventions, but in the end the messengers chose to stick with traditional giving through the Cooperative Program, even though fundamentalists controlled most of the agencies it supported.[4]

While the fundamentalists lost little ground to the moderates in the state conventions, they gave up no ground at all on the national level as they consolidated their control in 1988, 1989, and 1990. At SBC headquarters in Nashville on February 24, 1988, Adrian Rogers, along with former presidents Bailey Smith, James Draper, and Charles Stanley, issued "An Inerrantist Manifesto" at a press conference. That document strongly reaffirmed the Baptist Faith and Message Statement of 1963 and went even further by affirming the so-called "Glorieta Statement," which the seminary presidents had approved at a meeting in New Mexico during 1986. The BFM Statement asserted that the Bible was "truth without any mixture of error for its matter," but the statement approved at Glorieta said that the Bible "is not errant in any area of reality." Russell Dilday accurately captured the meaning of the action of the fundamentalist presidents in Nashville: "I hoped for a statesmanly proposal from the four SBC presidents, but instead we were given another defense of the take-over strategies of the past ten years. Instead of offering Southern Baptists a way forward toward reconciliation, we were given a statement which merely solidifies the hard line position of those who have gained control of the SBC."[5]

Not to be outdone, the moderates responded to the Nashville press conference with their own "press statement." It was released on March 3, 1988, by seven prominent moderate leaders—Winfred Moore, James Slatton, Henry Crouch, Walker Knight, Missouri pastor and Forum officer George Steincross, Houston layman and millionaire John F. Baugh, and Libby Bellinger, a former WMU president from Waco, Texas. Their two-page statement was sent to Baptist state papers and "other news media." It asked if the SBC—ten years after the takeover—were better off with the denomination's boards "stacked with people who march to one tune." Calling for a "new direction," these Baptist moderates argued that it was not the "Baptist way" to "focus on control instead of ministry; to minimize the priesthood of the believer; to hold up a high-priestly authoritarian concept of ministry instead of a servant model; to depreciate the service of women; to tamper with the authority of the local church; to try to manipulate local church pulpit committees; to flirt with creedalism; to let the denomination be used for secular political purposes; or for people to present themselves as speaking for all Baptists." Finally, the statement asserted, "This denomination is on the verge of neutralizing its great witness to a lost world."[6]

Thus, in total disregard of the Peace Committee report's admonitions to end all political activity, the moderates and fundamentalists stepped up their political campaigns after the St. Louis convention. In addition to answering fundamentalist media announcements tit for tat, some moderates formed the opposition group called Baptists Committed to the Southern Baptist Convention in December 1988, partly out of the frustration caused by their failure to elect Richard Jackson president at the SBC meeting in San Antonio six months earlier. No presidential election after 1979 was harder fought or won by a narrower margin than the San Antonio contest. The soon-to-be-elected fundamentalist candidate was Jerry Vines, who was as unswerving in his commitment to inerrancy as the other SBC presidents of the 1980s. Vines, a native of Carrollton County, Georgia, had been educated at Mercer University, New Orleans Seminary, and Luther Rice Seminary. His involvement in fundamentalist causes went back to the Baptist Faith and Message Fellowship during the 1970s (although he denied being a fundamentalist), and he had gradually eased into the inner circle of the SBC's new fundamentalist leadership. In promoting Vines's candidacy prior to the convention, Judge Pressler said, in a mailout to his friends, "The issue is thus very clear. Do we wish to correct the problems we have, and which the Peace Committee has recognized, or do we wish to turn the direction back to the days when theological liberalism was leading us down the path of doctrinal weakness?" Pressler also wondered aloud why the moderates were so eager to elect inerrantist Richard Jackson. He implied that some kind of deal regarding appointments had been struck between Jackson and the moderates.[7]

The judge might well have been worried about the outcome in San Antonio, for Vines, despite his having held important pastorates, was not as prominent or popular as Rogers, Stanley, Draper, or Smith. Richard Jackson, on the other hand, was pastor of the large and wealthy North Phoenix Baptist Church in Phoenix, Arizona, and he had many followers from the ranks of both the moderates and the fundamentalists. Though personally an inerrantist, Jackson was flexible, and he seemed fully committed to the idea of unity amidst diversity. San Antonio promised to be a close contest. Besides Vines and Jackson, two minor candidates were nominated at the Convention. Together the latter received but 358 votes, while Vines won with 50.53 percent of the total vote. Jackson had 48.23 percent, just 692 votes less than Vines out of a total vote of 31,000. After being elected, Vines promised to "stay the course of his predecessors." He would appoint only inerrantists and continue the "theological renewal already underway." Even so, he spoke of periodically issuing "proposals for reconciliation" and urged all Southern Baptists to renew their commitment to the Cooperative Program and to reach out to one another.

Rumors soon circulated that moderates would finally say that enough was enough and leave the Convention. However, Southern Baptist Alliance spokesman Alan Neely said, "I do not want to bury my mother until I'm sure she is dead." Some of his comments suggested that Neely thought she was gravely ill and all but dead. He declared that the SBC was "now a fundamentalist-dominated convention." When asked if he took consolation in the very close vote between Vines and Jackson, he answered that he did not. He said that if the moderates could not win in San Antonio with Richard Jackson, they could not win with "the Apostle Paul."[8]

Neely would not be ready to bury "his mother" for two more years, but he was certainly determined to chastise her by withholding support as long as she remained under the sway of men he regarded as extremists. Along with others in the SBA he advocated designating funds to SBC agencies "not yet implementing a conservative agenda." His strategy was to bring peace by threatening the fundamentalists and letting them know that "moderate churches are not going to pay the bills for them." The Southeastern Seminary professor claimed that immediately after the San Antonio election the SBA office was "swamped" with about twelve hundred telephone calls asking what moderates should do next. Paige Patterson ridiculed the report of countless calls, saying, "One man's swamp is another man's bathtub." The fundamentalist leader criticized the SBA for "siphoning off funds from the convention."[9]

Besides the bitterly contested presidential election at San Antonio, there was serious conflict over a resolution that in effect repudiated the doctrine of the priesthood of the believer. As far as fundamentalists were concerned, that doctrine was used by "liberals" to believe whatever they wanted to believe and still be loyal Southern Baptists. To correct this problem, they introduced Resolution No. 5 at San Antonio, a resolution that emphasized "the role, responsibility, and authority of the pastor." They cited Acts 20:28 and Hebrews 13:17 to prove that the resolution was scripturally based, and the resolution itself claimed that the priesthood of the believer doctrine was of "recent historical development." W. A. Criswell had already laid the groundwork for the resolution's passage by proclaiming in a sermon to the Pastor's Conference, "we have taken the doctrine of the priesthood of the believer and made it cover every damnable heresy you can imagine." That the priesthood doctrine was under such heavy attack in June was ironic, since at their press conference in Nashville five months earlier the four fundamentalist presidents had affirmed the priesthood of every true believer.[10] In their minds, of course, *true* believers would likely affirm biblical inerrancy.

Resolution No. 5 was adopted by a vote of 10,950 to 9,050. Its passage stirred up considerable adverse reaction, especially among the editors of Baptist state journals. *Biblical Recorder* editor R. G. Puckett called it "nothing short of heresy to a genuine Baptist." Even Herschel Hobbs, who was seldom given to forthright public declarations, criticized the resolution, insisting that pastors should lead and inspire, not rule. Dictatorship might be more efficient, Hobbs observed, but Baptists had rejected it in favor of democracy in church government. Randall Lolley, formerly president of Southeastern Seminary and now a pastor in Raleigh, North Carolina, led several hundred protestors to the front of the Alamo, where they tore up copies of the resolution. Lolley called it "the most non-Baptist document" he had ever seen.[11]

Defending the divisive resolution was none other than new SBC president Jerry Vines, who said that the priesthood doctrine had been used as "an excuse to step outside the parameters we have set in the Baptist Faith and Message." Another defender was Calvin Kelly, pastor of Valleydale Baptist Church near Birmingham, Alabama. He contended that criticism of the resolution was "unwarranted and unfounded."[12] The comment by Vines must have convinced moderates that the fundamentalists were indeed creedalists, for what else could setting "parameters" of belief mean? Other fundamentalist victories were won at San Antonio, including the adoption of Resolution No. 8, which called on all Southern Baptists "to take an active stand in support of the sanctity of human life"—in other words, to fight abortion.

Moderates, having come so close to capturing the presidency with Richard Jackson, left San Antonio utterly frustrated. Joseph M. Jones, a messenger from Huntsville, Alabama, went home "unsettled and greatly bothered." A statement he made indicated that he was on the verge of leaving the Convention: "I cannot live with an omniscient dictatorial view which tells me what I must believe if I am to be acceptable. It is a narrowness . . . that brings complete revulsion and argues that it's time to find a place to go." Lynn Clayton, editor of the *Baptist Message,* summed up the situation almost perfectly: "The outsiders are in, and the insiders are out. . . . Fifteen years ago, some more conservative constituents of the convention belonged to the Baptist Faith and Message Fellowship and published the *Southern Baptist Journal* because they felt disenfranchised and unheard. Now, some moderates belong to the Southern Baptist Alliance and publish *SBC Today* because they feel disenfranchised and unheard."[13]

The Peace Committee, which had brought no peace, declared its work ended at San Antonio and went out of business. In view of the fact that the next two years were the most avowedly and intensely political two years that the fundamentalist crusades had yet produced, the disbanding of the committee was most appropriate. Few on either side showed any inclination to end the conflict. The moderates, obviously all but defeated now, still made plans to do battle again by establishing the opposition group called Baptists Committed to the Southern Baptist Convention. Members of this group called themselves centrists. Their principal leader was Winfred Moore, who, at the meeting of the Forum in San Antonio, had urged all Southern Baptists to join one side or the other because in the middle of the road there was nothing but "a yellow line and dead possums." The new opposition group was born in Dallas in December 1988. About two dozen Southern Baptists from around the country answered Moore's call to create a "centrist coalition." Claiming that contributions and baptisms were down and unity shattered in the SBC, they announced their intention to reunite the Convention around its "historic principles" of (1) the priesthood of the believer, (2) the autonomy of the local church, (3) the separation of church and state, and (4) cooperative missions. They denied having any intentions of leaving the Convention or starting a new denomination.[14]

From the beginning the "centrists" had impressive support. Their leaders included convener and chairman Winfred Moore, whose church ranked third in the SBC in contributions to the Cooperative Program, Richard Jackson, whose church ranked first in that category, and Dan Vestal, who had recently resigned from a church in Midland, Texas, that ranked second in giving to the CP. Vestal's new church in Dunwoody, Georgia, also supported the CP generously. Other leaders of the centrists included longtime moderate warrior James Slatton, Steve Tondera, a Huntsville, Alabama, layman who had recently served two years as president of the Alabama Baptist Convention, and John F. Baugh, whose money largely bankrolled the Baptists Committed group. The centrists hired a full-time field director, David Currie of Paint Rock, Texas, and announced a long-range plan to recapture the SBC presidency and restore the Convention to what it had been before 1979. Currie, who had once been employed by the SBC's Christian Life Commission, was quoted as saying, "It may take us 10 years to accomplish our goals. It took 10 years for others to do what they have done in the takeover crusade. But I am committed to the task for that long, if necessary."[15]

The creation of Baptists Committed set off two years of unprecedented political fireworks, and when it was over the fundamentalists were more firmly entrenched in power than ever. In fact, they had won their crusade; they had seized the SBC holy land. There were still pockets of resistance in various state conventions, but at the national level they had total control. The centrists fought a good fight, twice putting up Dan Vestal as their candidate for president, but they suffered the same devastating disappointment that the other moderate groups had previously suffered. Like Winfred Moore and Richard Jackson, Vestal was a theological conservative by most people's definition. Also like them, he was flexible and accommodative and was committed to the principle of unity amidst diversity. He made a strong candidate, but in 1989 at Las Vegas he ran against incumbent Jerry Vines at a sparsely attended convention, and at New Orleans in 1990 he was flattened by the same fundamentalist steamroller that had rolled to impressive victories earlier at Houston and Dallas.

Tension filled the denominational air early in 1989. At its February meeting the Executive Committee provoked a quarrel with Bill Moyers. Trained in theology at Southwestern Baptist Theological Seminary, Moyers was a popular television journalist who had been an assistant to President Lyndon Johnson during the 1960s. He had produced a three-part documentary called "God and Politics" for national television. Judge Paul Pressler was convinced that the program disparaged him, and he persuaded the EC to adopt a resolution critical of the production. Moyers asked for an audience with the EC in Las Vegas, with Pressler in attendance, to discuss the matter. When he found out that the EC would vote in Las Vegas on whether to give him an audience in September, the television journalist withdrew his request, stating in a fax message of June 11:

Forget it.

When you and Pressler would not allow me to present my case this week at your meeting in Las Vegas and when Pressler refused my offer of free time on PBS (Public Broadcasting Service) to discuss the issue following the repeat in May of the documentary, I realized that I am up against a situation most un-Baptist: closed minds and in the parlance of your host city, a stacked deck.

There is no way to get a fair hearing from an Executive Committee that has become a rubber stamp for a secular politician who has infected this Christian fellowship with the partisan tactics of malice, manipulation, and untruth. Under his thumb you do only his will. I want no part of it.[16]

A few weeks after the EC censured the work of Moyers about a hundred fundamentalist leaders held a closed meeting at the First Baptist Church in Atlanta. The four fundamentalist SBC presidents who had preceded Jerry Vines called the meeting, although Bailey Smith was prevented from attending by a previous engagement at Jerry Falwell's Liberty University. The only reporters who were allowed entry were James Hefley and Robert Tenery, who had replaced Russell Kaemmerling a couple of years earlier as editor of the *Southern Baptist Advocate*. Baptist Press was denied permission to attend. SBC president Jerry Vines stopped in on his way to another meeting in Alabama. Adrian Rogers took the lead and indicated it was a strategy meeting brought on by the "shenanigans of the Alliance compounded by the intentions of the erstwhile group now calling themselves 'centrists'." Those in attendance listened to a tape recording of a confrontation between Judge Pressler and Richard Jackson that had occurred recently in Nashville. Next they held a panel discussion, with Rogers, Stanley, and Draper serving as panelists and Paige Patterson as moderator. Several participants claimed that the purpose of the meeting was simply that of promoting the Christian causes of the SBC![17]

Much attention was given at the Atlanta meeting to the Jackson-Pressler dispute in Nashville. That confrontation had taken place during the EC's February meeting, and it was clear that Jackson became both angry and animated. Since 1983 the fundamentalists had tried to reduce the SBC's contribution to the Baptist Joint Committee on Public Affairs. Unable to secure the votes to bring that about, Pressler and others began to advocate the creation of a new Religious Liberty Commission, which presumably would take over the work of the BJC in handling SBC concerns about religious liberty. When Pressler spoke in favor of this idea at the EC meeting, Jackson, who was in attendance as a concerned Southern Baptist, accused the judge of "blowing smoke" and of trying to run everything in which Southern Baptists were involved. The thrice-defeated contender for the SBC presidency also claimed that he had two witnesses who had heard Pressler say in the early 1960s that he would change the Convention or split it. There was a sharp exchange, but Pressler apparently kept his composure. It was reported that the judge's last words to the Phoenix pastor were, "God bless you, Richard, my brother."[18]

Again inflamed rhetoric from both sides filled the air as Southern Baptists moved toward another annual brawl in Las Vegas. Robert Tenery accused John Baugh of promising to speak the truth in love, only to speak "untruths in hatred." The fundamentalist editor contended that there was no way to work with the centrists. Larry Holly, a fundamentalist physician from Beaumont, Texas, who was a trustee on the Sunday School Board, also had harsh words for Baugh. A few weeks before the convention, Holly wrote to Jerry Vines and said, "The conservative monolith which he sees and fears is a myth of his own imagination. The oligarchy of Pressler and Patterson is equally fanciful." Furthermore, Holly denied Baugh's charges of voting fraud at SBC elections, contending that the Peace Committee found such claims to be false. Baugh had asserted that voting frauds were indelibly etched in the history of recent conventions, but Holly claimed that "the only place this idea is 'indelibly etched' is in the mind of the men who have lost their toy [i.e., the SBC] with which they had exclusive privilege for so many years."

Younger fundamentalists were no less vocal than Holly and Tenery. On May 25, 1989, seventy "Young Conservatives" held a meeting in Euless, Texas, at James Draper's church. The purpose was to promote the fundamentalist crusade among younger Baptists. One of the speakers was Dwight ("Ike") Reighard, fundamentalist Georgia pastor and president of the Georgia Baptist Convention. He likened the battle against "liberalism" to the slaying of Goliath by David, asserting that the giant was only knocked down and his head had yet to be cut off. Another speaker, Kerry Peacock, called the "liberals" in the SBC "rats" and "skunks."[19]

With such attacks coming from both sides and with the pre-convention announcement by Jerry Vines that he had not knowingly appointed anyone to any post who did not believe the Bible, Las Vegas promised to be a veritable free-for-all. Again, however, the moderates went to the convention short on votes, and they lost the presidency the same way they had during the ten elections preceding Las Vegas. Vines defeated Vestal, receiving 56 percent of the vote. That was only the beginning of the moderates' losses at the gambling mecca in Nevada. During the convention the EC held its annual organizational meeting and elected Paul Pressler vice-chairman, thus further upsetting the moderates. An attempt by moderates to pass a new resolution on the priesthood of the believer was defeated, as was a motion to rescind Resolution No. 5, which had been adopted in San Antonio the year before. Another motion to censure the Executive Committee for letting itself be used in the personal quarrel between Bill Moyers and Judge Pressler was ruled out of order. About the only vote taken at Las Vegas in which the moderates could find consolation was the one that elected Richard Jackson as a trustee of the Home Mission Board.[20] The process that began in 1979 continued unabated. Little by little the moderates were being pushed into the corners of the denomination, and more and more they sounded like voices crying out in the wilderness to no avail.

During the months following the Las Vegas convention political activity and rhetoric were as intense as they had been at any time since 1979, for many moderates realized at last that their position was similar to General Lee's at Petersburg. Like the outmanned Confederate commander they prepared for one last battle to save the SBC. Centrist laymen John Baugh and Steve Tondera frantically tried to rally support, calling upon pastors and laymen to "wake up to this takeover threat." They warned that the fundamentalists were expanding their efforts with a view to seizing the state conventions, the fifty-four Baptist colleges and universities, and "even local associations and churches." Baugh even argued that the takeover was "part of a larger scheme of Reconstructionism, an attempt by zealots who are passionately committed to dismantling democracy and replacing it with a theological oligarchy in the United States." In other words, Baugh tried to link the fundamentalists to an extremist, right-wing political movement in America that was diametrically opposed to democracy and the cherished Baptist belief in the separation of church and state.[21]

In January 1990 President Jerry Vines issued an open letter to all Southern Baptists calling for nominations for the 1990 Committee on Committees, the Resolutions Committee, the Credentials Committee, and the Tellers Committee. He said he wanted "Bible-believing, cooperating Southern Baptists." He promised to appoint "as many new people" as he possibly could. Vines noted that he had used the same procedure in 1989 and did not have "as much participation as he anticipated." By this time nothing that Vines could have done would have placated the moderates, for to them his deeds spoke louder than his words, and they were not about to support his efforts. At the February Executive Committee meeting there was a bitter confrontation between Vines and Russell Dilday, apparently initiated by the latter. The seminary president told Vines he would publicly endorse Dan Vestal for SBC president in 1990 and work for him every way he could. Vines was taken aback because Dilday had made an agreement with his trustees to keep out of denominational politics. Dilday accused the fundamentalists of lying and named Paul Pressler as an example. He called the fundamentalist crusade "the most devastating in the history of the SBC"—even more devastating than the "Norris movement."[22]

Meanwhile, in North Carolina John Hewett had seen the proverbial handwriting on the wall and had come to fear that the 1990 convention in New Orleans would mark the final, futile stand by the moderates. He served notice on the fundamentalists that, even though they had all but won the war, they had not defeated him personally. He lashed out fiercely at the fundamentalist crusaders, calling Judge Pressler a "swaggering little Napoleon" and warning that if the judge planned to go for the jugular in North Carolina, "he'd better be eating his Wheaties, for he's got a fight on his hands!" He filled the air with epithets as he called the fundamentalists "servants of Dagon," "misbegotten fools who defend truth, but fear knowledge," "the new pharaohs of the Foreign Mission Board," and "the hanging judge and his courthouse stooges." Hewett warned that "if the final eviction notice" should be served in New Orleans, he would stay away from "Southern Baptist officialdom" but would remain a North Carolina Baptist "free and unfettered in kingdom service."[23]

As the heated verbiage filled the air and many a printed page, Dan Vestal was already running for the SBC presidency in 1990. On February 4 he told the congregation of Mountain Brook Baptist Church outside Birmingham, Alabama, that he thought he had a good chance to win. Vestal said that he was an inerrantist, but that the "issue now is not really whether you believe in the Bible. It's will you pledge allegiance to this continued control." He said he wanted to include *all* Southern Baptists in the decision making, not just those "who will subscribe to continued control of the denomination." For a while it appeared that Vestal's fundamentalist opponent in New Orleans would be Fred Wolfe, pastor of Cottage Hills Baptist Church in Mobile, Alabama, but Wolfe had some misgivings about running, perhaps because the fundamentalist leaders doubted he could match the visibility of Vestal. In any case, on February 12, 1990, fundamentalist spokesmen endorsed as their presidential candidate Morris Chapman, pastor of the First Baptist Church of Wichita Falls, Texas, and urged all Southern Baptists to join them in a coalition around "the perfect, infallible Bible."[24]

Leading the charge for Chapman's candidacy was John Bisagno, pastor of the First Baptist Church of Houston. Until 1990 Bisagno had claimed to be nonaligned in the controversy and had asserted that one side had gone too far to the left and the other too far to the right. In 1986 he had advocated the election of a "non-political" man to the SBC presidency, and he had even suggested Dan Vestal for consideration. By 1990 Bisagno had changed his mind, apparently because he had finally determined which way the winds of triumph were blowing and had set his sails accordingly. He claimed he was trying to prevent a split in the Convention. The main issue, Bisagno said, remained the same after eleven years—"Does the Book mean what it says or not?" He called politics, control, women in the ministry, priesthood of the believer, and other such issues "secondary." He offered what he called a simple solution for ending the controversy. All it required was for all Southern Baptists to acknowledge that theology *was* a denominational problem, just as the Peace Committee report said it was. His solution, when examined carefully, in effect called upon moderates to surrender.

The Houston pastor's statement that Morris Chapman could complete the "correction begun eleven years ago," could only mean that he desired a fundamentalist victory.[25]

Shortly after Bisagno called for a new Southern Baptist coalition "of those committed to a perfect, infallible Bible," Charles Stanley invited fundamentalist pastors and lay people to Atlanta to map out their strategy for electing Chapman SBC president in 1990. All five of the fundamentalist SBC presidents of the 1980s came out strongly for the Texas pastor. Dan Vestal called Bisagno's announcement a "very clear political strategy" and condemned the five presidents who endorsed Chapman as "a college of cardinals." To meet the political challenge, the moderate pastor from Dunwoody, Georgia, put together a team that included Carolyn Weatherford Crumpler, former executive director of the WMU, for first vice-president and Steve Tondera for second vice-president.[26] From this time on claims by either side that its candidates and supporters were not playing politics could hardly be taken seriously.

Prominent pastors who had previously claimed to be nonaligned enthusiastically endorsed Bisagno's proposed coalition and emerged from the fundamentalist closet. Some of them included Charles Fuller, the man who had led the Peace Committee, Joel Gregory, Fort Worth pastor and former president of the Baptist General Convention of Texas (and soon to be named W. A. Criswell's successor at First Baptist in Dallas), Norfolk, Virginia pastor Kenneth Hemphill, and Jim Henry, the Orlando pastor who had served on the Peace Committee. Baptist Press came under heavy attack from the fundamentalists for not publishing a big story on these men's shift in position to the fundamentalist side. More than ever, fundamentalists were convinced that developments favoring them received only slight mention by the Baptist media, both in Nashville and at the state level.

Insistence by the fundamentalists on adequate coverage in the Baptist media attracted the attention of the secular media, which proceeded to give the Pressler-Patterson coalition some negative publicity. Less than two months before the annual meeting of the SBC Gustav Niebuhr, in a *Wall Street Journal* article entitled "House Divided," accused Pressler and Patterson of setting off "a purge of an unprecedented number of teachers and staffers who don't agree with their fundamentalist views." The reporter maintained that the SBC was losing more members than it was adding and that fewer and fewer missionaries and seminary students were signing up to spread its word. Moreover, the money was not coming in as fast as it had in the past. Niebuhr noted that Pressler and Patterson played down the problems and argued that others would come to take the place of departing members. The two men were convinced that "conservative, grassroots Southern Baptists" would open their pocketbooks when they had complete confidence in their institutions.[27]

Although Pressler and Patterson seemed undaunted by the negative publicity, they were probably feeling somewhat less secure on the eve of the New Orleans convention than they were willing to reveal. A huge fight was shaping up, as usual, over the report of the Committee on Nominations. Within hours after the committee had finished its work in Nashville on March 24, David Montoya, pastor of the First Baptist Church of Gravette, Arkansas, had announced that he would present a minority report containing alternative nominations for about half of the 260-plus nominations listed in the report.

A graduate of Criswell College, Montoya had already caused the fundamentalists considerable embarrassment earlier in the year by defecting from their ranks and condemning their "Machiavellian machine." Because many doubted the existence of a fundamentalist political machine, Montoya, who was one of that machine's eight district leaders in Arkansas from 1982 to 1989, had taped a strategy session and leaked it to Arkansas Baptists. This created an uproar, causing one of the "founding fathers" of the movement to call the young minister a traitor in the inerrantists' "war with the liberals." The fundamentalists also revealed that Montoya had been arrested in the 1970s for a variety of serious crimes and that he had hidden this information from Criswell College and his church in Arkansas. While Montoya owned up to his police record, he explained to those who would listen that it had all happened before he "came back to God." After working for the fundamentalists for seven years, he had become an active moderate late in 1989. He argued that the initial movement to preserve the doctrine of inerrancy had been "perverted, polluted, and prostituted by a select group that has seized the moment for its own advantage." Montoya further asserted that the fundamentalists had turned "to pursuing political power politics, focusing not on inerrancy but on personal advancement, prestige, vendettas, power, and, of course, money."[28] How much trouble the Arkansas pastor could stir up in New Orleans was a matter of speculation, but he was clearly a fly in the fundamentalist ointment.

Just before the convention Judge Pressler predicted that a moderate victory at New Orleans would result in a return to turmoil, while there would be peace if the "conservatives" won. At the same time moderates were beginning to view New Orleans as the place where they would make their last stand. Stan Hastey of the Southern Baptist Alliance already expected another fundamentalist victory, and he announced that Alliance people would go to no more conventions after New Orleans. As had been the case for eleven years, wild rumors circulated. One of them was that John Baugh had reserved twenty-seven thousand rooms in New Orleans, when in fact he had reserved only one—the one to be occupied by him and his wife. Besides the wild rumors, there was a variety of predictions. No one doubted that the Convention's future for some time to come would be decided in the city of the Superdome.[29]

With more than thirty-eight thousand registered messengers in attendance the New Orleans convention turned out to be the third largest in SBC history. As planned, John Bisagno nominated Morris Chapman for president, calling him the man who would "put this issue [of the Bible] to rest once and for all." Phil Lineberger, president of the Baptist General Convention of Texas, nominated Dan Vestal and hailed him as the man who would take Southern Baptists through the open door of evangelism "together." Again the results favored the fundamentalists, as Chapman won with almost 58 percent of the vote. Asked afterward if his election settled the inerrancy issue once and for all as Bisagno had claimed it would, Chapman replied that the answer depended on the 42 percent who had voted against him. Then he repeated the extravagant assertion by Adrian Rogers several years earlier that at least 90 percent of Southern Baptists adhered to inerrancy. The new president claimed that he wanted to "enhance the cooperative spirit" while "standing steadfastly for biblical truth."[30]

A native of Mississippi and, like his defeated opponent Dan Vestal, a graduate of Southwestern Seminary, Chapman was as adamant on the inerrancy question as any of the five fundamentalist presidents he succeeded. He exhibited more presence than Jerry Vines, but he was not as flashy and personable as Adrian Rogers, Bailey Smith, and James Draper. Though by no means as supercilious as Charles Stanley, Chapman was stubborn and unyielding in his stance, and moderates put little stock in his promise to "enlarge the tent" of Southern Baptist participation. To most moderates Chapman's election meant that a fatal blow had been dealt to their cause of returning the SBC to what it had been prior to 1979.

Nor was Chapman's election the only defeat the moderates suffered at New Orleans. Carolyn Weatherford Crumpler and Steve Tondera, the moderate candidates for first and second vice-president respectively, also lost. The moderates lost the fight over the report of the Committee on Nominations, too. They first challenged the right of Roland Lopez of McAllen, Texas, to be chairman of the committee, since his church was not a cooperating Southern Baptist church. Vines overcame that objection by ruling that at the time Lopez was elected as chairman of the committee he had been a member of a cooperating church. David Montoya's attempt to present a minority report had been ruled out of order by Vines before the convention, but the president had explained the ground rules to Montoya for presenting substitute nominations. In trying to amend the report at the convention, however, Montoya was voted down, and he alleged that Robert's Rules of Order were violated and that he had been "steamrollered." The committee report, as presented by Lopez, was adopted.[31]

Two other blows fell on the fatally wounded moderate cause. The fundamentalists' seven-year struggle to defund the Baptist Joint Committee on Public Affairs was finally brought to a successful conclusion when the convention voted to appropriate a mere $50,000 for that auxiliary agency. The appropriation the year before had been $391,796, meaning that the 1990 appropriation represented an 87.24 percent budget cut. Since the SBC provided a huge share of the BJC's budget each year, the agency, whose cause had long been championed by the moderates, was placed in financial jeopardy. Another turn of events that was shocking from the perspective of the moderates was the passage of a resolution offered by Cactus Jack Cagle, an attorney from Houston, Texas. Cagle moved that "all agencies, institutions, commissions, boards, and other entities who have trustees elected by the Southern Baptist Convention or receive money from the Cooperative Program" not "support one element of our Convention in opposition to any other members." In other words, there was to be no partisan political activity by denominational employees. The motion further required all SBC agencies to investigate and confirm in a written report at the next convention in Atlanta that there had been no such political action. The agencies did affirm the following year that none of their funds had been used for political purposes. Even the Sunday School Board, which was self-sustaining, reported that its trustees had instructed their president "to make every effort to avoid any activity which could reasonably be perceived as political."[32]

Developments at the New Orleans convention made it clear to most Southern Baptists that the fundamentalist crusade to capture the SBC was over and that the crusaders had established their Latin Kingdom of Jerusalem. Soon after Chapman's election three hundred fundamentalists went down to the Cafe Du-Monde to celebrate their victory at the place where Pressler and Patterson had first discussed liberalism in the SBC over twenty-three years earlier. They sang "Victory in Jesus" and presented certificates of appreciation to their political strategist, Pressler, and their theological guru, Patterson. Some moderates who happened to be in the cafe at the time cried out "Shame, shame, shame." One moderate, Jay Robison from Kentucky, attempted to report the event to the convention the next day on a point of personal privilege. Twice he was not recognized, and twice his microphone went dead.[33]

People left the convention knowing that the SBC would never be the same again. Moderates, fundamentalists, and the nonaligned reflected on the final outcome in the months that followed. One North Carolina pastor, Frank Turner of Clinton, had mixed feelings. He told the author that the moderates had lost the power struggle and no longer enjoyed the control over the Convention that they had had for so long. Turner, a graduate of Southwestern Seminary, admitted that he preferred the theology of the fundamentalists, but noted that he did not appreciate their political tactics. If there was a formal schism, which he believed was a real possibility, he jokingly said that he would probably follow the Annuity Board. That board, of course, provided the bulk of retirement pensions for Southern Baptist pastors. Marse Grant, a moderate and retired editor of the Biblical Recorder, predicted "a restructuring of budgets in mainstream North Carolina Baptist churches," since such churches had been "invited out" of the SBC by Adrian Rogers. Moderate pastor Dan Griffin predicted that his church would be "dually aligned by this time next year," meaning that Snyder Memorial would retain membership in the SBC but would also join the new denomination he assumed would soon be established. Alabama moderate Randall Simmons of Blountsville wondered if the fundamentalists could hold the Convention together in view of the fact that they were trying to "maintain a power structure" and were "attempting a neo-inquisition."[34]

Before the summer was over the specter of a formal schism arose in the SBC. Defeated presidential candidate Dan Vestal issued a call in July for moderates to meet in Atlanta the following month to explore a plan of "alternative funding," meaning a plan to divert money from the SBC's Cooperative Program. The idea was not new, of course, since the Southern Baptist Alliance was already doing it. Now that the centrists, too, had given up hope of defeating the fundamentalists politically, more and more moderates wanted to find a way to withdraw financial support from agencies committed to the fundamentalist agenda. Initially it was expected that about five hundred participants would attend this so-called "national consultation," but when the meeting was held on August 24 and 25, over three thousand registered for it! Participants representing Baptists Committed, the Southern Baptist Alliance, the Forum, *SBC Today*, and Southern Baptist Women in Ministry established an elaborate "alternative funding mechanism" called the Baptist Cooperative Mission Program. Whether or not such action was a prelude to the creation of a new denomination was not clear. Stan Hastey predicted that there would be a new denomination, and so did Dan Griffin, who even proposed a name for it—the Continental Baptist Convention.[35]

The end result of "alternative funding" could not be discerned with certainty, but the fundamentalists were most critical of it. Paige Patterson and James Draper called the moderates hypocrites, pointing out that they had once condemned fundamentalists for advocating similar tactics. Now that the moderates were out of power, they suddenly saw nothing wrong with diverting funds. Draper was disturbed and called for a meeting between fundamentalist and moderate leaders to try once more to settle the controversy. Nothing came from that meeting, but at a second meeting in October, called by Morris Chapman, the new Convention president flatly refused to include in Convention leadership roles those who were not committed to the "perpetuation of allegiance to God's perfect word." In a word, Chapman hated to lose moderate money but not enough to compromise on the inerrancy issue.[36]

Out of the movement to organize an alternative funding mechanism there would emerge during the next two years an incorporated group called the Cooperative Baptist Fellowship which, for all practical purposes, became a denomination within a denomination, and the struggle continued on a different level. Supporters of the fundamentalists lashed out at those who had withdrawn their financial support from the denomination simply because they no longer had the votes to control it. Some moderates, including eighty-seven-year-old Nan Knight of Birmingham, Alabama, were convinced it was time to get out of the Convention and let the fundamentalists have it. Reacting to the firing of Baptist Press's director and news editor in the summer of 1990, Ms. Knight vented her anger to Morris Chapman by letter and announced her intention to leave the SBC.

That fall the struggle in the state conventions was as bitter as ever, as Texas Baptists fought over Baylor University, Florida Baptists over Stetson University, and South Carolina Baptists over Furman University. Some still spoke of reconciliation, and Judge Pressler even participated in a "dialogue" at Samford University in Birmingham, Alabama on October 11, a dialogue built around the theme of "Hope for Reconciliation." Standing with Pressler to represent the fundamentalists was Wayne Dorsett, pastor of Central Baptist Church in Birmingham. Representing the moderates were David Montoya and San Antonio attorney Randall Fields. Although Pressler promised to do everything he could to avoid a split in the Convention, no one present could have thought there was much hope for that when Montoya compared the fundamentalists to Nazis and Fields accused them of becoming a "police force enforcing specific doctrines on our schools."[37]

At the national level the struggle for the SBC holy land was over by the closing days of 1990, for the fundamentalists achieved a definitive victory at New Orleans. That became increasingly obvious in the aftermath of the convention. The road to final victory started at Dallas in 1985 when the fundamentalist crusaders demonstrated that they could "get out the vote" better than the moderates, even when the moderates made a supreme effort to rally their forces. Between Dallas and New Orleans the fundamentalists had only one genuine scare, and that was at San Antonio in 1988 when Jerry Vines defeated Richard Jackson for president by a razor-thin margin. The fundamentalists not only won the presidency at each of the six conventions from 1985 to 1990, they also secured approval of most of the major items on their agenda, including the adoption of the Peace Committee report at St. Louis, Resolution No. 5 at San Antonio, and the virtual defunding of the BJC at New Orleans. The Peace Committee's report, instead of bringing peace, intensified the fighting and led to a definitive fundamentalist victory at New Orleans. Within weeks of the New Orleans convention the victors purged director Alvin Shackleford and news editor Dan Martin at Baptist Press. While the firing of those two journalists was the most dramatic episode associated with fundamentalist domination up to that time, there had been other purges, and more were to follow. As 1990 slipped into 1991 there was no doubt that the fundamentalist crusade to take the SBC holy land had succeeded. The question was: What would the triumphant crusaders ultimately do with the holy land they had conquered? Moderates were convinced, because of what they had already witnessed, that the victors would turn the SBC into a wasteland of uniformity by purging all who did not march in lock step with them.

6

The Fundamentalist Purges

RECLAIMING THE Southern Baptist Convention from its "liberal" captors and cleansing the denomination of "liberalism" was what the fundamentalist crusades were mainly about, at least in the minds of the fundamentalists. Given such a mindset, no one should have been surprised at the denominational purges that began as soon as the fundamentalists gained control. The fundamentalists' first priority was to stamp out liberalism in Southern Baptist educational institutions, and their efforts to do that will be treated in the next chapter. In addition to being troubled over what they regarded as the heresies being taught in the seminaries, colleges, and universities, the fundamentalists were disturbed by the presumed liberal attitudes and views of SBC agency heads and their employees. During the mid-1970s Bill Powell of the failed first crusade had shown Pressler and other fundamentalists that new trustees with the right views could fire the "liberals" and thereby cleanse the denomination. By the mid-1980s the fundamentalists of the second crusade were gaining their trustee majorities and were poised to purge those agencies they considered liberal. Among those given special attention by the fundamentalists were the Christian Life Commission, the Home Mission Board, the Foreign Mission Board, the Sunday School Board, Baptist Press, and especially the auxiliary agency known as the Baptist Joint Committee on Public Affairs.

The SBC and the Baptist Joint Committee had a peculiar relationship, one that did not allow for the denomination to control that independent agency except indirectly by cutting off funds to it. That, of course, was what the fundamentalists did when they realized there was no way to dominate it. Besides the seminaries, the BJC was the first agency to come under fire from the fundamentalists. As early as the fall of 1982 Morris Chapman's church in Wichita Falls, Texas, passed a resolution "that all monies be withdrawn from support of the Baptist Joint Committee and the contractual relationships be duly terminated." All of this began because earlier that year the agency's executive director, James Dunn, responded to President Ronald Reagan's proposal of a prayer amendment to the Constitution by calling it "despicable demagoguery" and accusing Reagan of "playing petty politics with prayer." Subsequently, when the New Orleans convention adopted a prayer amendment resolution in support of Reagan's proposal, Dunn called it an "incredible contradiction of our Baptist heritage" and vowed to fight it. Dunn hoped that the Convention might rescind the prayer amendment resolution in 1983, and he planned to work toward that end. Unfortunately for him, he underestimated the ability of the fundamentalists to sustain their political advantage at the annual conventions, and his agency would ultimately pay dearly for his miscalculation.[1]

Defunding the BJC, which fundamentalists set out to do late in 1982, was destined to take nearly a decade of hard fighting, for the agency had worked successfully with the SBC for over forty years and had endeared itself to countless Southern Baptists. The Baptist Joint Committee was actually "inaugurated" in 1939 by the SBC and three other Baptist bodies. Ultimately nine Baptist bodies came to comprise it, and it began operating as a full-time agency in 1946 under the name of the Joint Conference Committee on Public Relations. Not until 1950 did the committee change its name to the Baptist Joint Committee on Public Affairs.[2] There appears to have been little friction between the Convention and the BJC until James Dunn, a former director of the Texas Baptist Christian Life Commission, assumed the directorship and antagonized the SBC's new fundamentalist leaders and their followers in 1982.

The first big push by the fundamentalists to vanquish the BJC was launched at the Kansas City annual meeting in 1984. Ed Drake, a Dallas attorney and a messenger from W. A. Criswell's church, moved that the $411,436 recommended for the BJC in the 1984–1985 budget "be set aside and reallocated as the convention may hereafter determine." The Dallas attorney argued that the SBC needed its own separate agency in Washington. His motion was barely defeated by a vote of 5,854 to 5,480. At Dallas the following year the fundamentalists focused on problems that were more pressing than the BJC, but in 1986 at Atlanta an Alabama messenger, M. G. "Dan" Daniels, moved that the convention "vote to remove the Southern Baptist Convention from participation in the Baptist Joint Committee on Public Affairs and establish an exclusive Southern Baptist presence in Washington, D.C. for the purpose of more truly reflecting our views." Another motion was made to refer Daniels's motion to the Executive Committee, and it passed by a vote of 12,001 to 9,556. The chair declared the motion referred. A year later in St. Louis Daniels went after the BJC again, calling for changes in the "personnel of the operational staff" of BJC "for the purpose of more truly reflecting our views." This motion was referred to the Public Affairs Committee, which consisted of the fifteen Southern Baptist members on the BJC.[3]

Meanwhile, the Executive Committee had appointed a nine-member subcommittee to investigate the SBC's relationship with the BJC. At the same time fundamentalist PAC members began pushing for a merger of PAC and the SBC's

Christian Life Commission for handling "legislative and governmental issues" in Washington. They also began independently to take partisan actions, such as urging President Reagan to veto a piece of civil rights legislation and endorsing Robert Bork, whom Reagan had nominated for the Supreme Court. Among the members of the EC subcommittee appointed to investigate the SBC-BJC relationship was Judge Pressler, who doubtlessly relished the actions of the vocal, right-wing PAC members. Pressler himself attacked James Dunn for his remarks against President Reagan and condemned Dunn's associate director, Stan Hastey, for "absolutely terrible journalism." Hastey had admitted to "an honest mistake" in a story he wrote about the judge. In February 1987 the subcommittee and the full EC recommended a change in the Convention bylaws that would increase "grassroots" participation on the BJC by having the annual meeting elect twelve PAC members at large and make them eligible to serve two four-year terms instead of one. The other Southern Baptist members would be agency heads and the SBC president. Additional fundamentalist representation on the BJC was the obvious objective of the recommendation.[4]

In "going for the jugular" of the BJC, Pressler demonstrated political acumen and patience. He moved gradually, winning any ground that he could and waiting for his next opportunity to move ahead. With regard to funding, the best Pressler could do in 1988 was persuade the EC to recommend a $48,400 reduction of the amount appropriated for the BJC the year before in St. Louis. At San Antonio Henry Green, pastor of the First Baptist Church in Cocoa, Florida, introduced a motion to restore the $48,400 plus $19,060, which represented the average increase the EC recommended for other SBC agencies. Green's motion was defeated, but under questionable circumstances. Adrian Rogers asked for a show of hands and declared the motion defeated. There was a call for a ballot. After the ballot vote Rogers ruled that the motion had been defeated, but when no count was given, Robert Crowder, the man who had sued the SBC, asked for the numbers. Rogers refused to give the results of the ballot tally![5]

The numerous fundamentalist victories at the San Antonio convention must have emboldened Judge Pressler to attempt a final settlement of accounts with the BJC. When the Executive Committee held its September meeting, he moved for defunding the besieged agency by taking $400,000 from it—money allotted to the BJC in the 1988 Convention budget. SBC attorney James Guenther advised the EC that it lacked the authority to override the Convention, so the motion was ruled out of order. Then another study committee was appointed to devise an "alternative plan to accomplish the program and distribution of funds traditionally assigned to BJCPA." Frank Ingraham, a Nashville attorney, called the maneuver another attempt to "defund the Baptist Joint Committee."[6]

Early in 1989 the study committee proposed the creation of a new Religious

Liberty Commission to work with the BJC. The proposal called for giving SBC money to the new commission, which would then allot money to the BJC. Moderates immediately charged that such a step would mean the end of the SBC's participation on the BJC. There was considerable opposition to the proposal from many quarters. Kentucky editor Jack Sanford declared that the SBC needed a new agency "as much as we need the pox." While the controversy raged over the proposed Religious Liberty Commission, Pressler continued his efforts to take funds away from the BJC. At the EC meeting in February 1989 the judge clashed with Lloyd Elder, president of the Sunday School Board. Because of a budget shortfall at the EC the trustees of the SSB had offered to give the EC $400,000. When Pressler tried to amend the budget that was to be recommended to the convention in Las Vegas by taking away more than $300,000 from the BJC and diverting most of that sum to the Public Affairs Committee, Elder objected. The SSB president explained that the offer of $400,000 by his trustees was based on the SBC budget's remaining unchanged. If the EC was going to have over $300,000 at its disposal as a result of cutting off funding to the BJC, then perhaps it did not need the SSB's $400,000. He said he would inform his trustees of the change, not knowing if they would withdraw the offer or not. Pressler, of course, charged that Elder was playing politics with the $400,000 offer. No doubt both men were playing politics with SBC money, and on this occasion, at least, Elder prevailed. The EC voted down Pressler's motion by the barest of margins—one vote.[7]

Even so, the EC came within two votes of slashing the BJC's budget allocation by $150,000 and voted forty-two to twenty-seven to recommend the creation of the Religious Liberty Commission to the convention. There was so much opposition to the proposal that Jerry Vines wanted to delay it, and it was not brought up in Las Vegas. Especially outspoken on the issue of the Religious Liberty Commission was Keith Parks, who argued that the new commission would take funds away from the Foreign Mission Board. Home Mission Board president Larry Lewis opposed it, too, arguing that it would deprive his agency of needed funds at a bad time. Several moderate leaders—Winfred Moore, Richard Jackson, Dan Vestal, James Slatton, John Baugh, and Steve Tondera—also spoke in opposition. In the midst of the deliberations at the EC meeting in February 1989 Richard Jackson and Paul Pressler had their big quarrel over the judge's ubiquitous involvement in SBC affairs. Because the two men appeared to be headed for a spirited argument, it was suggested that they might discuss their differences outside the room. Thus, it was outside the meeting room that the two men had their sharpest exchanges. Pressler kept saying that he was willing to sit down and talk with Jackson, but the latter showed no interest. At one point Jackson reportedly commented that the judge's idea of cooperation was "I'll operate and you cope." The Phoenix pastor told reporters later that he would not sit down with Pressler because he had no confidence in him.[8]

As word spread among Southern Baptists that the EC had voted to recommend the establishment of the Religious Liberty Commission to the convention at Las Vegas, opposition mounted during the early months of 1989. Keith Parks and Larry Lewis remained steadfast in their opposition, and a number of editors of denominational state papers condemned the whole idea. R. G. Puckett of the *Biblical Recorder* said that the SBC did not need such a commission "now or ever." Jerry Vines, claiming that he wanted the Las Vegas convention to focus on evangelism and missions, asked EC chairman Charles Sullivan to defer recommendation of the commission. At its June meeting the EC agreed to defer the matter until the 1990 convention in New Orleans.[9]

The EC soon scrapped plans for the RLC and took a different tack. At its September meeting, three months after Las Vegas, the committee voted to consider "assigning the convention's religious liberty program to the SBC's Christian Life Commission." Right after the EC took this action, Jerry Vines told the committee that he wanted the Baptist Joint Committee issue settled. He asked the EC to ascertain "the facts concerning the funding of the Baptist Joint Committee and provide the same for publication in our Baptist papers, thus enabling our people to clearly understand them." Then, at New Orleans, the issue could be settled in "a clear-cut, uncomplicated way." The SBC president added, "Whatever the outcome, let the majority not gloat, the minority not gripe, and let us move on." When asked if he would encourage the fundamentalists to "move on" if the moderates won, he said he "would take no position on the matter."[10]

Instead of ascertaining the facts regarding the SBC's funding of the BJC and disseminating them, the EC attempted to discredit the BJC and took steps to terminate the relationship between the Convention and that agency. At the EC meeting in February 1990 a motion was made to cut the BJC's budget appropriation from the previous year by $341,796, leaving only $50,000 for that agency. EC member Ann Smith strenuously opposed the motion, saying that the BJC had earned its money, because it had stopped a "tax on missionaries that saved the Foreign Mission Board $10,000,000 in the last eight years." She accused some EC members of being "so set on political goals" that they were willing "to sell their Baptist heritage for a mess of pottage." In spite of Smith's impassioned opposition, the motion passed. The EC's recommendation to slash the BJC's funding listed seven reasons for doing so. In essence the reasons amounted to the BJC's failure to support ultraconservative political and social legislation in Congress.[11]

The fundamentalists' assault on the BJC made one thing perfectly obvious to any serious observer—namely that the fundamentalist crusaders required far more of those who received their approval than a mere belief in biblical inerrancy. Those who would win approval must also interpret the inerrant Bible on moral and social questions in the same way the fundamentalist leaders did. And those leaders clearly advocated a right-wing political and social agenda that, they insisted, was reflected in the Bible so plainly that there could be no compromise on it. The monotonous claim of Judge Pressler that the only issue in the SBC was biblical inerrancy began to have a hollow ring to it by early 1990. In its call for drastically reducing the BJC's budget, the EC made no mention of James Dunn's theological beliefs or those of his staff members. They were unacceptable because of their political and social "liberalism" and thus not entitled to SBC money.

Efforts by Southern Baptist fundamentalists to replace the BJC with the SBC's Christian Life Commission as its voice on matters of religious liberty brought on verbal exchanges between James Dunn and CLC director Richard Land. In April 1990 Dunn questioned the CLC's ability to function effectively as both a church-state watchdog agency and as a prophetic voice for social justice. Land responded that he was puzzled by Dunn's concern, since Dunn had previously served as the executive director of the Texas Baptist Christian Life Commission, which, according to Land, performed "both roles for many years."[12]

The controversy surrounding the BJC grew and intensified as news spread that the agency's budget would be drastically cut at the convention in New Orleans. Fifteen church historians from Baptist seminaries and universities circulated an open letter of protest among Southern Baptists. The Administrative Committee of the Baptist General Convention of Texas urged the EC to recommend the existing level of funding to the convention. If the messengers still wanted to reduce the funding, then let the EC recommend that it be done gradually over five years "in the interest of harmony." The fundamentalists were in no mood for compromise and appeared little concerned about harmony. William D. Powell III, a Birmingham, Alabama, dentist and EC member, said the BJC did not reflect Southern Baptist views on such issues as school prayer and abortion, and that he would prefer to defund the agency totally if the fundamentalists had the votes.[13]

When the vote was taken at New Orleans on June 13, 1990, to reduce the BJC's appropriation from $391,596 to $50,000, attorney Frank Ingraham, who was a former EC member, offered an amendment to restore the funding. He argued that the EC's recommendation was "fatally flawed." He said that it would "unsaddle a joint voice in Washington and double-saddle the CLC." He warned that the "issues of morality and the separation of church and state do not mix.

It's like crossing an antelope with a jack-rabbit. You don't know what you'll get, but you know you won't like it, and its bound to have horns." Ingraham's opposition was to no avail; his amendment was defeated by a vote of 17,915 to 13,608. At a news conference afterward, James Dunn said that he expected concerned Southern Baptist individuals, churches, and state conventions to cover the huge loss with direct gifts.[14]

The vote at New Orleans left matters of religious liberty and separation of church and state to the CLC, and the convention increased its budget by $300,000. Richard Land announced plans to expand the CLC's office in Washington and to carry out the SBC's wishes as expressed in resolutions on abortion and prayer in the public schools. He participated in the 1990 Rally for Life and put pressure on President George Bush to come out more forthrightly on the abortion issue. The CLC director threatened to call for the abolition of the National Endowment for the Arts if the government did not eliminate obscenity in tax-funded art. He also protested the invitation of homosexuals to the White House for bill-signing ceremonies. The BJC had chosen to ignore such issues. The SBC, through its Christian Life Commission, now spoke with a fundamentalist voice in the nation's capital.[15]

In the following year the relationship between the SBC and the BJC was dealt the finishing blow. The BJC changed its bylaws to reduce SBC representation on the committee and to give additional seats to a new "national member body" called the "Religious Liberty Council, an umbrella organization representing state conventions, churches, and the Southern Baptist Alliance." The bylaw changes were made in the fall of 1990 and were to take effect on March 4, 1991. The EC voted in opposition to the proposed changes when it met in September. At its spring meeting a few months later the EC paved the way for the SBC's Public Affairs Committee to be merged with the CLC and again included a recommendation in the budget of $50,000 for the BJC. As recommended, the 1991 convention in Atlanta merged the PAC with the CLC, but it did not approve the $50,000 appropriation for the BJC. Instead it eliminated *all* funding to that agency. Among those who argued for this course of action was Fred Minix, a Virginia pastor who said that the BJC better represented "Norman Lear's organization, People for the American Way." In vain James Dunn appealed to the convention to maintain its relationship with his organization.[16]

The fight waged by fundamentalist leaders to defund the BJC was long and bitter, and while it was in progress other battles were fought to gain control over agencies within the Convention. As longtime agency directors approached retirement, the fundamentalists took steps to make sure their successors would be men sympathetic to their agenda. The first board to fall under the control of fundamentalist trustees was the Home Mission Board. As a result one employee,

George Sheridan, lost his job because he claimed that Jews retained a "covenantal" relationship with God. Next the board adopted a policy refusing to give financial aid to churches hiring women pastors. After the Dallas convention in 1985 a rift developed over the appointment of Janet Fuller to do student work at Yale University. She was an ordained woman, and fundamentalists believed ordaining women was unscriptural. By late 1986 the board not only had a majority of fundamentalist trustees, it had a new fundamentalist president, Larry Lewis, formerly president of Hannibal-LaGrange College in Missouri and one of the earliest advocates of the fundamentalist cause. Under his leadership the HMB policy allowed for the appointment of ordained women as missionaries and chaplains but refused funds to support a woman pastor of a local church.

Lewis, who had been a strong advocate of "doctrinal integrity" for years, persuaded the trustees in 1987 to adopt a policy of hiring only biblical inerrantists as employees of the HMB. Robert Tenery praised the policy, claiming that the HMB was taking Southern Baptists back to where they wanted to be, but Alan Neely called it "an ominous sign." And, of course, Larry Lewis claimed that he was only doing what the Peace Committee recommended.[17] It is clear that the fundamentalists were having their way at the HMB relatively early— three years before their final triumph at New Orleans.

Another SBC agency which was of special interest to the fundamentalists was the Christian Life Commission. For years that agency had been directed by a Texan named Foy Valentine who was accused by fundamentalists of using CLC money to support liberal positions "on everything from economics to nuclear disarmament, while remaining virtually silent on abortion." He had come out in support of the *Roe v. Wade* decision and had been peripherally involved with People for the American Way. By 1984 he was drawing heavy fire from the fundamentalists. He was accused of sponsoring liberal writers in *Light*, the agency's publication, and liberal speakers at its conferences. Valentine responded that the CLC had invited to its conferences such people as Republican stalwarts Howard Baker and Robert Dole and even fundamentalist Baptist preacher Jerry Falwell, founder and leader of the Moral Majority. In 1986, two years before his expected retirement, the controversial director of the CLC retired. Fundamentalists charged that he did it so that his successor could be chosen before new fundamentalist trustees took their places on his board. The Texan denied the charge, saying that his decision was prompted by poor health.[18]

The search for and selection of Valentine's successor was acrimonious. Larry Baker, forty-nine-year-old professor of ethics at Midwestern Seminary, was elected by the trustees by a secret ballot vote of sixteen to thirteen. Not a prolife activist, Baker was in trouble with the fundamentalist members on his board from the day of his installation in March 1987. They wanted a strong prolife advocate who would lead the charge for a human life amendment to the U.S. Constitution, and, because Baker would not, they soon called for his ouster. Judge Pressler predicted that the new CLC director would be looking for another job "as soon as the trustees meet after St. Louis."[19]

Besides his moderate views on abortion, Baker opposed capital punishment and accepted the idea of women being pastors. None of this was acceptable to the fundamentalist trustees, and they moved to replace the new director. Their first attempt to fire him ended in a tie vote of fifteen to fifteen. Unable to function under such circumstances, Baker resigned soon after the San Antonio convention in 1988 and received $41,835 in severance pay and an automobile. An interim director replaced him until a search by the trustees resulted in the appointment of Richard Land, holder of an Oxford University doctorate and vice-president of Criswell College. The new director took office on October 24, 1988.[20]

In searching for Baker's replacement the trustees announced that they were seeking a director who opposed abortion, favored the death penalty, was "doctrinally sound," and had "political acumen." It was made clear that no woman would be considered. Land turned out to be the ideal candidate on all counts as far as most of the fundamentalist majority on the CLC board was concerned. He opposed legalized abortion and the ordination of women, and he favored capital punishment. He obviously met the fundamentalists' standard with regard to "political acumen," and no one could quarrel with Land's academic training. Besides his Oxford Ph.D., Land held an A.B. magna cum laude from Princeton University and a Th.M. with honors from New Orleans Seminary.

Even Land, however, did not go far enough for some of the extreme fundamentalists on the board. One of them was Curtis W. Caine from Jackson, Mississippi, who lamented the coming of integration, condemned Martin Luther King, Jr., as a fraud, and denied that apartheid existed any longer in the Republic of South Africa—but said it had been beneficial when it did exist. In November 1988 the Mississippi Baptist Convention adopted a resolution repudiating some remarks Caine had made to the press two months earlier. Yet, when the CLC adopted a resolution condemning racism "whenever and wherever it occurs" at its meeting in January 1989, Caine abstained.

Apparently there were other CLC trustees who also held extreme views, for at their spring meeting in March 1990 they voted twelve to eleven to "respectfully request our executive director to refrain in the future from inviting speakers who support the so-called 'pro-choice' position on abortion." Actually Land did not favor such a restrictive stand, for it precluded a prochoice speaker from speaking at a conference having nothing to do with abortion. While Land's actions did not totally satisfy all of his trustees, the new director definitely led the agency down a far more conservative path than had the two men who immediately preceded him in that office.[21]

The CLC was a small agency with a relatively tiny budget, but because of its mission to promote SBC social causes, it was considered a prize worth winning by the fundamentalists. Once in control they set out to use it for the promotion of their own social agenda. An even more valuable prize to seize was the huge and quite wealthy Sunday School Board, which the fundamentalists set their sights on about 1986. The SSB had hundreds of employees (close to two thousand), assets of more than $150 million, and sales of over seventy million pieces of literature annually. No Cooperative Program money went to the SSB; it was self-sustaining. In fact, the SSB contributed money to the Convention. Grady C. Cothen, who had had a long and distinguished career as an administrator of various Southern Baptist institutions, retired as president of the SSB in 1984. Lloyd Elder, a Texan who held the position of executive vice-president at Southwestern Seminary, was elected as Cothen's successor. At the time, Elder was fifty years old.[22]

In mid-1986, after less than two years on the job, Elder ran afoul of the fundamentalists, especially Larry Holly and Robert Tenery, two of his trustees. James Sullivan, a former president of the SSB and the SBC, made a speech at Nashville in May in which he called the new SBC leaders "inexperienced" and noted that their movement included "Pharisaical legalists, extreme literalists, and snake handlers." He further asserted that they wanted as SBC trustees only those who were from their "extreme rightist group." The speech was printed in *Facts and Trends*, the SSB newsletter. At a meeting of the SSB trustees Larry Holly asked Elder to apologize for publishing the speech. The president refused, saying, "I don't feel in a position to apologize for a great Southern Baptist who has expressed his position." When another trustee, Roy Gilleland from Tennessee, came to Elder's support, asserting that the SSB president had the ability to fill the leadership void among Southern Baptists, Robert Tenery called his remarks "an insult to the denomination's current conservative leadership."[23]

From that day until he was forced to resign in January 1991, Lloyd Elder was a marked man. He was often accused of playing favorites in SBC politics. His reported criticism of the Public Affairs Committee for endorsing Robert Bork for the Supreme Court further alienated the fundamentalist element. Elder was plainly impatient with the champions of inerrancy, causing Larry Holly to claim, "Those of us who are inerrantists have been held up to ridicule—a caricature that is offensive, objectionable, uncalled-for and must stop."[24]

Elder was able to hold his fundamentalist critics at bay until early 1989, when the matter of the SSB's proposed gift of $400,000 to the EC became an issue. Elder's threat to retract the offer stirred up several fundamentalist members of the EC as well as some of the members of his own board. EC member Jerry D. Brown wrote other members of the committee and said he was "shocked and totally outraged by the actions of Lloyd Elder!" He added that some SSB trustees were "plenty upset" because they had cautioned him "about his politicking in the convention's business." Another EC member, Doyle J. Collins, called Elder's action an "attempt to bribe the Executive Committee." And, of course, Larry Holly was disturbed. He accused Elder of playing politics with the four hundred thousand dollars and of manipulating "the restoration of funds to the [B.] J. C. P. A." Although conceding that Elder was a "conservative, Bible-believing Baptist," Holly alleged that the SSB president had "obstructed dynamic growth and many creative initiatives of the Sunday School Board" because he was "resistant to trustee initiatives" and prone to "oppose anything which did not originate from his office." By this time Holly had had enough of Elder and launched a campaign to remove him. Paige Patterson encouraged Holly in his opposition to Elder's policies.[25]

By midsummer 1989 Holly had drawn up a bill of particulars against Lloyd Elder. He called it the "History of the Presidency." Elder, according to Holly, opposed the "conservative resurgence" and clearly revealed his sympathies for the moderates. He had gone out of his way to promote moderate presidential candidates Winfred Moore, Richard Jackson, and Dan Vestal. The SSB president had been asked to stay out of SBC politics but had refused to comply. He had offered $400,000 to the EC and then threatened not to give it if the BJC's funding was cut. Elder had permitted publication of Southeastern Seminary professor John I. Durham's Sunday school lesson on the book of Job, a lesson espousing liberal views, and an article by Robert L. Cate, the academic dean of Golden Gate Seminary. Cate's article suggested that King David might have believed in other gods along with the God of Israel. The case against Elder was cut and dried as far as Holly was concerned. He forthrightly called for Elder's ouster, saying he wanted a man in his place "who will walk in concert with the great presidents being elected by our convention."[26]

A few weeks after writing his "History of the Presidency," Holly, several other trustees, and Elder met with the SSB's General Administration Committee on August 7, 1989, at Glorieta, New Mexico, ahead of the general board meeting. There was a four-hour closed session. At issue was Holly's letter-writing campaign against the president. Elder asserted that the "crisis of leadership" at the SSB was a figment of Holly's imagination. Later, at the general board meeting, Elder spoke for forty-five minutes in his own defense. The trouble at the SSB, Elder maintained, was the fault of one man—Holly, but another trustee objected, saying there were others who had been concerned. There was heated discussion, which led to a motion to fire Elder. It was made by Joseph T. Knott III, an attorney from Raleigh, North Carolina. Holly spoke in support of the motion, but during an hour of discussion Trustee Tommy French from Louisiana urged Knott to withdraw the motion, since it would not pass. Elder objected, arguing that the motion belonged to the body. French reportedly told Knott, "We've been set up. This is why Elder attacked Holly; he wanted to precipitate this [motion to fire.] With twenty new trustees and the first order of business of their tenure, they would certainly not vote to fire you. It was a power play to destroy the influence of the conservative faction." Knott finally asked the committee's permission to withdraw the motion, and the request passed by a substantial voice vote. Later, Elder called Knott's withdrawal the "depth of cowardice."[27]

The targeted SSB president took a hard pounding at Glorieta. He said afterward that he had not felt so abandoned since his daughter was killed in a car wreck. He was not abandoned, of course, because there were many Southern Baptists who were appalled at the way he was treated at Glorieta. One of them was Don Wainwright, pastor of Woodmont Baptist Church in Mobile, Alabama. He wrote that he was "greatly disturbed" by what had happened in New Mexico. Wainwright described himself as "a Bible believing Southern Baptist preacher for almost forty years, never once having any doubts . . . about the inspiration and authority of the Word of God." Even so, he forthrightly condemned the fundamentalists for their "mean and unchristian spirit." "Who is going to be next?" he asked. What leader would be attacked by "diatribes and charges?" He said he was "offended and appalled" at the attempt to remove Elder and lamented the "bitter and contentious spirit that is so prevalent in the convention today."[28] Unfortunately for Elder, people like Wainwright were out in the churches. The fundamentalists were in the majority on his board, and they held the fate of Elder and the SSB in their hands.

If Elder intended to keep his highly prestigious position, he needed to mend some fences, and he tried. At their meeting in February 1990, some SSB trustees claimed that healing and reconciliation had taken place between them and their president. A motion of support for Elder passed without opposition. In a matter of months, however, there was more trouble. This time it was over a centennial history of the SSB. H. Leon McBeth, a professor of church history at Southwestern Seminary, had agreed in May 1988 to undertake the work with the clear understanding that it was to be an "interpretative history." He signed a contract for $18,000 with Broadman Press on September 16, 1988. He was to receive his money in three $6000 installments, the last when the work was published. In August 1990 SSB trustees contended that the manuscript should be scrapped because, according to Larry Holly, it was "totally skewed to the liberal side." Holly specifically charged that McBeth's work was not history, for it made no mention of Lloyd Elder's failures and did not demonstrate how he had "polarized the convention by pressing the moderate-liberal agenda in a number of ways." Another trustee called the work "unbalanced." In the final analysis the project was suppressed. One copy of the manuscript was to be preserved and kept on file in the board archives, while all others were to be destroyed.[29]

McBeth defended his work, denying that he did a "puff job" on Elder. He argued that he had produced "a fair and honest, interpretive history," and he warned that the attempt by the fundamentalists to manage history would backfire. James Hefley contended that quite a few editors and administrators, along with a couple of attorneys, examined the manuscript and judged it to be of a "liberal mindset" and unfair to fundamentalists, but he quoted without documenting the quotations. He claimed that such "inter-office communications" turned out to be the "smoking gun" that caused the trustees to call for Elder's resignation.[30]

The controversy over McBeth's manuscript in the late summer of 1990 led directly to Lloyd Elder's announcement in January 1991 that he would retire January 31, 1992, or thirty days after the appointment of his successor, whichever came first. The trustees claimed that the agreement was made because of "honest differences of opinion . . . with regard to management style, philosophy, and performance" and was not "based upon political or theological differences." One trustee, Al Jackson of Auburn, Alabama, said, "The mismanagement of the centennial history is merely the latest of a series of incidents in which the president needlessly involved the Sunday School Board in controversy." Still the trustees entered into an agreement that included payment of Elder's salary of over $135,000 per year until April 1, 1993, along with all benefits, since he would remain on as a consultant until that time. He would then receive half-salary for life. If he died before his wife, she would receive the half-salary for the duration of her life. Elder also received $10,000 to pay legal expenses. An estimated four hundred people crowded into the room to hear the retirement announcement and the discussions of Elder's agreement with the trustees.[31]

The response of Southern Baptists to Elder's forced retirement were mixed. Moderate spokesman Bill Sherman was highly incensed, claiming that the whole episode was the result of a vendetta by Larry Holly and Robert Tenery. He called it an "abominable disgrace." Some, who apparently thought Elder's salary would come from Cooperative Program money, were openly critical of his "golden parachute." Mary Goodhue of Huntsville, Alabama, tried to set the record straight in a letter to the editor of the *Alabama Baptist* in May 1991. She pointed out that none of Elder's pension would come from CP money because the SSB was self-supporting. On the other hand, she noted, the called meeting of the EC in July 1990 to fire Al Shackleford and Dan Martin was paid for with about $60,000 in CP money, including the payment of armed guards to stand at the doors of the EC's executive session. Goodhue indicated her displeasure with the fundamentalist purges, saying:

> I have looked for integrity in the new leaders of the SBC and have only seen what Paul Pressler meant when he said that he was going for the jugular. I have looked to them for humility and have seen arrogance.
>
> In the SBC 'Baptist' has no meaning. I am no longer willing to give my tithe to support unbaptist decisions.[32]

During the time that Larry Holly carried out his successful campaign to oust Lloyd Elder, Judge Pressler was going after Al Shackleford and Dan Martin, Baptist Press's director and news editor, respectively. Baptist Press was formed in 1947. Its purpose was to serve the EC by disseminating news about Southern Baptists and their activities through Baptist state weeklies and other news outlets. By the time it became a fundamentalist target in the late 1980s it served four hundred outlets, including thirty-eight independent Baptist weeklies. Though headquartered in Nashville, BP had bureaus in Atlanta, Dallas, Richmond, and Washington, D.C. Even before Shackleford and Martin arrived on the scene, there was friction between BP and Judge Pressler. Shackleford's predecessor, Wilmer C. Fields, alleged that Pressler and others made a conscious effort to intimidate the media.[33]

In March 1987 Alvin Shackleford, longtime editor of the *Baptist and Reflector*, was elected to replace Fields, who had resigned. Paul Pressler and Adrian Rogers were opposed to Shackleford, who was the choice of EC president Harold Bennett. When Bennett nominated Shackleford, Pressler produced clippings from the nominee's paper that supposedly showed bias against the fundamentalists, but, not wishing to provoke an "angry confrontation," the judge did not present them. Still, Pressler and Rogers wanted David Simpson, editor of the *Indiana Baptist*, because he sympathized with the fundamentalist cause. State editors had announced their opposition to Simpson, claiming that he was short on experience. The EC accepted Bennett's recommendation and elected Shackleford by a vote of thirty-two to twenty-six. An editorial in the *Biblical Recorder* described the scene:

> Harold Bennett, chief executive, was treated rudely by some Executive Committee members as he carefully followed the stated procedure for nominating and electing the successor to W. C. Fields. Alvin C. Shackleford, his wife and younger daughter were subjected to the most embarrassing treatment we have observed at this level of Southern Baptist life. Apparently some committee members had been programmed to make motions they did not understand, wrangling took place and voting was

almost dead even. When the sound of voices and shuffled papers had ended, Shackleford was elected by a 32–26 vote. The corridors were filled with rumors he would be fired in September.[34]

Interestingly enough, Shackleford's theology was not in question. He even avowed inerrancy. He also promised to be fair and objective and asked the EC members for a year of grace while he proved that he could report the news without bias. Adrian Rogers indicated later that he did not know whether Shackleford's election was God's will or not, and Pressler said he would prayerfully support the new BP director and "carefully observe him." Very little time passed before Shackleford came under attack for "taking biased positions" on SBC actions "by initiating interviews that took opposing viewpoints." Such charges raised a critical issue: Was the business of BP to report the news, good and bad, or was it to promote Baptist causes? Was it proper to place the main emphasis on news or public relations? Some accused BP of overreporting the moderate view. Shackleford lamented that some of his most bitter critics were the people who had hired him. Had he forgotten that beginning with his first day on the job he already had twenty-six critics among EC members? He faced an uphill battle, and he knew it. Yet he vowed to hang on as long as he could, though he joked that he would probably not be around to retire at age sixty-five.[35]

At the same time Shackleford was being attacked by fundamentalists for supposedly favoring the moderates, he received high praise from his fellow professionals in the news business. After the San Antonio convention in 1988, Ed Briggs, president of the Religious News Writers Association and religion editor of the *Richmond Times-Dispatch*, gave Shackleford glowing marks. He asserted, "Baptist Press enjoys high credibility, if not the highest, when compared to news operations of other American denominations." At the San Antonio convention Judge Pressler had attempted to impose "new directives" on BP, and reports of the judge's efforts concerned Briggs, causing him to observe that a controlled and manipulated BP would result in only very slanted news being reported about the SBC's affairs.[36]

Shackleford really upset Pressler during the following year over the Bill Moyers incident. The judge asked the BP director not to publish the text of Moyers's fax letter to the EC on the ground that it was "ridiculous." BP went ahead and distributed the story with Moyers's accusations to the media. According to one EC source the committee backed away from hearing Moyers in Las Vegas "in the interest of peace and harmony" because "the media was planning to make this Moyers' thing a major event." Soon after the Las Vegas convention rumors circulated that Al Shackleford and Southwestern Seminary president Russell Dilday had been targeted for firing by fundamentalist EC members at the committee's September meeting. In August Pressler denied those rumors and was quoted as saying, "The conservative movement has never gone around firing people." The rumors also had it that Pressler meant to replace Shackleford with Louis Moore, formerly with the *Houston Chronicle* but more recently with the SBC's Christian Life Commission.[37]

As it turned out, Pressler did not have the votes to oust Shackleford and his right hand man, Dan Martin, until 1990. On June 13, 1990, during the convention at New Orleans, both men were promised six months severance pay if they resigned and left quietly. They refused, and on July 17, 1990, the Executive Committee met in closed session at the SBC headquarters building in Nashville. Armed off-duty city police officers stood guard outside the room where the EC met in executive session. The committee voted forty-five to fifteen to fire the two journalists. Pressler was conspicuous by his absence, being on a European tour at the time of the meeting.[38]

At a well-attended press conference after the EC purged Shackleford and Martin, the former told of several confrontations he had had with Judge Pressler over press releases that Pressler thought failed to praise the fundamentalist movement adequately. During one telephone conversation the judge told the BP director that he did not know with whom he was dealing and vowed to have Shackleford removed. The director responded that he would at least go with a clear conscience, if Pressler was successful in carrying out his threat.[39]

The news conference following the firing also became the forum for announcing the creation of a new news service to be called Associated Baptist Press. Several prominent editors of state Baptist journals were associated with its founding—Don McGregor of Mississippi, R. G. Puckett of North Carolina, and Bob Terry of Missouri. The announcement of this news service's creation was accompanied by a statement to the effect that the agency would report the news of all factions in an unbiased manner and would not be identified directly with any. Moderates, however, hoped that their views would be given wider coverage, and fundamentalists were convinced that the new agency would highlight the moderate cause.[40]

In the fall of 1990 the EC separated BP from SBC public relations. Mark Coppenger was hired as vice-president for public relations, while Herbert Hollinger was named vice-president for BP in the place of Al Shackleford. Not many state editors were impressed with Coppenger, although he had a master's degree from Southwestern Seminary and a Ph.D. from Vanderbilt University. It was suggested that Coppenger owed his new position to his loyalty to the fundamentalist cause. Hollinger, who had been editor of the *California Southern Baptist*, was readily accepted by the state editors. Not until 1991 was Dan Martin's vacancy filled by Art Toalston, Jr. Like Coppenger, Toalston had attended Southwestern Seminary, and Hollinger introduced him to the EC as a "highly respected journalist."[41]

Moderates, of course, were outraged over the firing of Shackleford and Martin, while fundamentalists defended the action. Alabama EC member Fred Wolfe, who voted to dismiss the two men, said that "vast numbers of grassroots Southern Baptists felt a deep conviction about the lack of balance" at BP under the fired journalists. Joy Dorsett, an EC member from Birmingham, commented that she supported the action "wholeheartedly." Dentist William Powell, another EC member from Birmingham, said that the BP colored stories so that they reflected badly on fundamentalists, but when he went to Nashville to deliberate on ousting Shackleford and Martin he thought "the timing was poor." Once at the meeting, however, he changed his mind and decided that "the problem had to be addressed." On the other hand, Philip Wise, pastor of the First Baptist Church of Dothan, Alabama, said he was "dismayed" that fundamentalist assurances that no one was going to be fired had been proven "false." Editor Hudson Baggett of the *Alabama Baptist* accepted the purge philosophically, saying that his fellow journalists were "casualties in a complex civil war." He further noted, "It is difficult to report a civil war without offending someone."[42]

While Shackleford and Martin were purged in an atmosphere of high drama, Foreign Mission Board president Keith Parks, who took a stand against the fundamentalists early on, was eased out gradually. Parks enjoyed so much respect among the majority of Southern Baptists and was so adept at compromising with his critics in some situations that ousting him was no easy matter. As early as 1984 Parks was admonishing Southern Baptists to choose SBC presidents whose churches supported the Cooperative Program and not men like Charles Stanley, whose church gave sparingly to the CP. Although he sympathized with men like Russell Dilday and Roy Honeycutt, Parks never used their tactics, which included attacking the fundamentalists head on. Even so, the pressure on the FMB president mounted as more and more fundamentalists were appointed to his board of trustees. That he held onto his position until 1992 was quite remarkable.

Removing Parks was not going to be easy, and the fundamentalists knew it. Hence, late in 1986 they struck an indirect blow at Parks and the FMB by organizing the Genesis Commission to establish their kind of churches in Mexico. The three leaders in founding the commission were Randy Best, a Houston layman, John Morgan, pastor of Houston's Sagemont Baptist Church, and Bill Darnell, former pastor of the Kirby Woods Baptist Church in Memphis, Tennessee. Paige Patterson was a member of the organization's board, which held its first meeting in November 1986 but did not announce its existence and purpose publicly until January 1987. Darnell said the group existed to found

Baptist churches and originally targeted "pioneer areas" where there were few Baptist churches. That idea was expanded, Darnell admitted, and Mexico became a prime objective. Finally the group decided to found churches and promote Christ wherever there was a need. The commission's leaders made clear that their emphasis would be on soul winning, not social service, and they would not use ordained women missionaries.[43]

Keith Parks contended that the Genesis Commission would be in competition with the FMB, but the Genesis leaders denied it. Patterson argued that such organizations were needed because of the restrictive policies of the FMB. The fundamentalist leader noted that would-be Southern Baptist missionaries were unacceptable to the FMB, regardless of training and credentials, if they had not spent at least one year at one of the six Southern Baptist seminaries. He warned, "If they [the FMB] persist in the present policy they had better get ready for a proliferation of organizations for appointing and sustaining missionaries, because if a man is called to foreign missions and the FMB says no, folks are going to find a way to go." Parks was joined in his public criticism of the commission by Carolyn Weatherford, the executive director of the Woman's Missionary Union. Although both were cautious and diplomatic in expressing their opposition, it was clear that they were not pleased.[44]

In 1988 and again in 1989 the FMB was caught up in controversy, first over the doctrinal views of a male missionary and then over the refusal to appoint an ordained woman to a foreign mission post. On July 21, 1988, Parks fired missionary Michael E. Willett for "doctrinal ambiguities." Willett held a doctorate from Southern Seminary and had once taught there. While training in Costa Rica for a mission assignment in Venezuela, he was accused by Mike McGinnis, a fellow missionary who held a doctorate from the independent Mid-America Seminary, of being doctrinally unsound. McGinnis made the accusations in a letter to Keith Parks, a letter in which he alleged that Willett did not believe in some of Christ's miracles, particularly his walking on water and turning water into wine. An investigation led to Willet's tendering his resignation on June 18, but when he concluded that he was being forced to resign because of an article he had written for *SBC Today* earlier that year, he withdrew the resignation. That article had criticized those who opposed women in the ministry. Parks informed Willett that it was not the article but the would-be missionary's "doctrinal ambiguities" that troubled Parks and his trustees. The FMB president told Willett on July 11 that he could be reevaluated if he would "affirm accepted Southern Baptist beliefs." Willett refused, and ten days later he was dismissed.[45]

After he was fired Willett defended himself, arguing that his views were consistent with the Baptist Faith and Message Statement of 1963. He asserted that missionaries would no longer feel safe because they would have to be forever on guard against attacks from fellow missionaries or pastors in the United States. He warned against the "prevailing winds of fundamentalism." Willett implied that Parks had caved in to pressure from fundamentalists, but the FMB president denied it, saying that Willett's dismissal was an isolated incident and was not the beginning of a purge of the FMB's missionary force.[46]

A year after the FMB dismissed Willett it stirred up controversy again by rejecting Greg and Katrina Pennington for mission posts in Scotland—presumably because the Northwest Baptist Church of Ardmore, Oklahoma, had ordained Katrina for the ministry. The church hired the couple in 1984 and ordained them in 1986. Greg served as minister of education, and Katrina as minister of preschool education. The Enon Baptist Association of which Northwest Baptist Church was a member withdrew fellowship from the church because of Katrina's ordination. When Greg and Katrina sought to go to Scotland under the auspices of the FMB, a board subcommittee recommended rejection. Northwest Baptist requested a hearing before the FMB trustees and circulated a three-page open letter to the trustees, to Baptist Press, and to the journals published by the state conventions. Both Paul Sanders, an Arkansas pastor who was chairman of the subcommittee that recommended against the Penningtons, and North Carolina pastor Mark Corts, who was the FMB board chairman, denied that Katrina's ordination was the issue. The position of the trustees, according to Corts, was that the Penningtons had caused divisions in Oklahoma Baptist circles and would likely cause them in Scotland.[47]

Predictably the FMB's rejection of the Penningtons resulted in an outpouring of criticism from the moderates, who decried the narrow biblical literalism of the fundamentalists and from women who were upset over the obvious gender discrimination championed by the fundamentalists. Editors Hudson Baggett and R. G. Puckett saw the FMB decision as a violation of two cardinal Baptist principles—the autonomy of the local church and the priesthood of the believer. Puckett called the action "more than a serious mistake; it is absolutely non-Baptistic." Glenn Turner, the moderate pastor of the First Baptist Church in Auburn, Alabama, would have none of Corts's explanation. He said it was all a matter of the fundamentalists doing "exactly what they said they would do." Alabama Baptist Shirley Woodke from Athens called the FMB's rejection of the Penningtons "a shame and a disgrace" and said she was "saddened and dismayed."[48]

The controversy over the Penningtons had hardly died down before Parks got into trouble with fundamentalists on his board over the appointment of William R. O'Brien as a "top special assistant to the president." Twenty-eight of the FMB trustees sent the president a strong letter of protest. Trustee Bob Claytor of Rome, Georgia, spoke for the twenty-eight. A major point raised against O'Brien was that he was openly identified "with the moderate faction in the Southern Baptist Convention." O'Brien, a former missionary to Indonesia, lived with his wife Dellana, who had recently accepted the executive directorship of the WMU, succeeding Carolyn Weatherford Crumpler. The WMU headquarters was in Birmingham, Alabama, while the FMB headquarters was in Richmond, Virginia. How could O'Brien work in Richmond and live in Birmingham? the dissenting trustees asked. Parks answered by saying that O'Brien's only open identification was "with the cause of foreign missions" and that because his job would require a great deal of traveling he could do it as well in Birmingham as Richmond.[49]

By the time of the New Orleans convention Parks was thoroughly frustrated with his board. Less than a month before the convention the FMB president circulated an open letter to Southern Baptists via the state journals. He called upon Southern Baptists to "rise above our controversy and recommit to sharing Christ with the whole world." He noted a decline in giving to missions through the CP and in the FMB's missionary appointments, and he blamed it all on the controversy. Some fundamentalist trustees accused their president of playing politics again, and former trustee chairman Mark Corts offered another possible explanation for the decline—the "soft national economy and troubled economic times"—and asserted that "we cannot separate our mission mandate from confidence in the integrity of the Word of God." For six years Parks had dodged fundamentalist arrows, but after the New Orleans convention his days were clearly numbered. He managed to hold on until March 1992 before he was forced into retirement in much the same way that Lloyd Elder had been. His retirement was short-lived. Before many months passed he hooked up with the Cooperative Baptist Fellowship, becoming that quasi-denomination's field director for missions.[50]

Just as the agency chiefs at the BJC, the HMB, the CLC, the SSB, BP, and the FMB ran afoul of the fundamentalist crusaders, so did two women who headed the WMU—first Carolyn Weatherford Crumpler and then Dellana O'Brien. The WMU was an auxiliary agency of the SBC working independently to raise money for Southern Baptist foreign missions work. Hence, there was little the fundamentalists could do about gaining control of the agency as long as the WMU had a strong executive director who would not knuckle under to fundamentalist pressure. Both Crumpler and O'Brien stood their ground against the fundamentalists, and no one was purged at the WMU. When the triumphant crusaders purged the leaders from other agencies, however, they were convinced that they were totally justified in doing so. By 1988 it was obvious to all perceptive observers inside the SBC and in the secular world, too, that the fundamentalists were in the process of driving supposed liberals from the SBC holy land.

Paul Pressler brushed all criticism aside, saying, "What we're doing here is basically returning the Southern Baptist Convention to the people." He called any "detrimental fallout in some areas" a "small price to pay."[51] This was the same man who said nearly two years later that the "conservative movement" did not go around firing people.

7

The Impact of the New Crusades on Southern Baptist Institutions of Higher Learning

IN A REAL sense the New Crusades were caused by a deep concern on the part of fundamentalists that liberal faculty members at Southern Baptist colleges and seminaries were destroying the faith of Baptist students, especially their belief in an inerrant Bible. Attention was focused on this issue first during the early 1960s by Professor Ralph Elliott's bitterly criticized book entitled *The Message of Genesis*. A few years later, during the fundamentalist crusade of the 1970s, M. O. Owens and his group were particularly critical of what was being taught at Southeastern Baptist Theological Seminary in Wake Forest, North Carolina, and at Wake Forest University in Winston-Salem, North Carolina. In their minds those two institutions were the fountainhead of the liberalism that permeated the ranks of North Carolina Baptists. Meanwhile, Paul Pressler was critical of liberalism in the Southern Baptist Convention from the early 1960s, but he was not spurred into launching the second fundamentalist crusade until he became alarmed in 1977 over what his "young people" were being taught at Baylor University in Waco, Texas. He soon became just as disturbed over the liberal views that he heard were being espoused at Southern Baptist Theological Seminary in Louisville, Kentucky. Once the second crusade was under way, other Southern Baptist institutions of higher learning came under careful scrutiny and heavy attack. There can be little doubt that the perceived failure of Southern Baptist schools to teach "historic Baptist beliefs," especially biblical inerrancy, was one of the catalysts of the fundamentalist crusades.

The crusaders' strategy for reforming the seminaries was exactly the same as it was for changing other agencies and institutions. By gaining control of the Committee on Boards through the president's appointive power, they could gradually fill the seminary boards with fundamentalist trustees, since all trustees were elected at the annual meetings from that committee's slate of nominees. (Staggered terms precluded the quick replacement of trustees.) Southern Baptists from throughout the Convention were eligible for nomination and election to any of the seminary boards.

That Owens and Pressler fixed upon Southern Baptist institutions of higher learning as a primary cause of the SBC's drift toward liberalism was not surprising. The first fundamentalists, those of the 1920s, had done the same thing. Those fundamentalists, most of whom were Northern Baptists, made a key point of the "school issue," warning of false teachers in Baptist colleges and seminaries. They condemned as dangerous and destructive "modernism in theology, rationalism in philosophy, and materialism in life." One leading Northern Baptist fundamentalist, Jasper C. Massee, asserted, "we must cease now to let Philistine teachers plow with our educational heifer, lest our denominational Samson, stripped of the goodly garments of his faith and virtue, fall under the witchery of a scholastic Delilah."[1]

Frank Norris and other Southern Baptist fundamentalists were in complete agreement with Massee, and, as has been noted earlier, there were occasional attempts by fundamentalists in the SBC to make an issue of what was being taught in the six seminaries owned and controlled by the SBC and the more than fifty colleges and universities owned and controlled by the various state conventions. The most dramatic episode was, of course, the Elliott controversy, but there was another confrontation over the issue at the 1969 convention in New Orleans. Thomas Simmons of Hope, Arkansas, introduced a motion that would have required writers of Sunday school and Training Union literature, along with teachers in Baptist colleges and seminaries, to sign a statement each year affirming their personal belief in "the authority, integrity, and infallibility of the entire Bible." The motion failed, but a substitute motion offered by President James Sullivan of the Sunday School Board passed. It called upon SBC agencies to make certain that their programs were carried out in a way that was consistent with the 1963 Baptist Faith and Message Statement.[2] For the time being the fundamentalist effort to insure the teaching of their theological perspective in Southern Baptist schools was stymied, but the issue would not go away.

Ten years later, with the election of Adrian Rogers to the SBC presidency, the school issue emerged again, and with the gradual change in the SBC power structure during the decade of the 1980s the fundamentalist educational agenda at last enjoyed an almost certain guarantee of being implemented. Although Rogers made an effort to disassociate himself from the methods of Pressler and Patterson, the new SBC president said right after his election in 1979 that he would favor an investigation of liberalism in the SBC seminaries, if it were carried out by a committee that was fair and balanced. He denied being in favor of any committee that would come "with blood in its eye to go on a witch hunt." He made it clear, however, that in his opinion the six seminaries had professors who did not believe in the inerrancy of the Bible. Rogers added that rank-and-file Southern Baptists already would have risen up if they knew what some professors believed. They did not know, he claimed, because the professors were "so good at semantics . . . that the rank and file" were kept in the dark. On another occasion Rogers was reputed to have said regarding alleged liberal professors, "If we believe pickles have souls and they can't teach it, then they shouldn't take our money."[3]

Thus, the first SBC president whose election was engineered by the fundamentalist crusaders made it clear immediately after being elected that Southern Baptist educational institutions were on the fundamentalist hit list. That became increasingly apparent as Paul Pressler attacked Baylor University and Southern Seminary, insisting that 95 percent of Southern Baptists "believe the Bible completely"—a belief some faculty members of those institutions allegedly denied. Like Pressler, Paige Patterson claimed to speak for mainstream Southern Baptists and announced in 1984 that he was keeping a "heresy file" on professors whose views departed from traditional Baptist beliefs.[4]

Moderates, of course, rushed to the rescue of the seminaries and other Southern Baptist schools. It was well known that the professors at all the seminaries signed some statement of faith. At Golden Gate, Midwestern, and Southwestern it was the Baptist Faith and Message Statement of 1963! What more could the fundamentalists want? The moderates were sure that they knew what the fundamentalists wanted. They wanted, according to Mercer University professor Walter Shurden, "static indoctrination," not creative education. He claimed that the fundamentalists "know *the* truth," and they wanted to impose it on people. He called the fundamentalists "butchers" of academic freedom who wanted to turn God's teachers and preachers into "mercenary stooges who teach/preach whatever the money dictates."[5]

The fundamentalists were condemned in many quarters for what amounted to anti-intellectualism. Joe Edward Barnhart, who wrote in the mid-1980s about the Southern Baptist "Holy War," noted that Paige Patterson was convinced that higher criticism of the Bible had been introduced into Southern Baptist life by an Englishman named Eric Rust, who became a faculty member at Southern Seminary in 1953. According to Barnhart, it was obvious that the "Inerrancy Party" wanted to return the seminaries "to the first part of the twentieth century, when higher criticism was not practiced among Southern Baptists." He argued further that what many inerrantists desired were "narrow enclaves of indoctrination with a thin veneer of education disguising their real interest."

Expressing similar sentiments was William W. Finlator, retired moderate (many would demand the adjective *liberal*) pastor of Pullen Memorial Baptist Church in Raleigh, North Carolina. The former pastor asserted that Southern Baptists in the 1980s sold out to conformity, uniformity, and orthodoxy, and that fundamentalists required all churches to look alike and be alike—as all McDonald's hamburger restaurants were alike. They demanded "totalitarian sameness." One way of achieving that, according to Finlator, was to change Baptist seminaries from "theological learning communities to centers of indoctrination and glorified Bible schools." There had been a time, Finlator observed, if you had told "an authentic Baptist what to believe, he would tell you where to go."[6]

Obviously the fundamentalists and the moderates held diametrically opposite views on the role of Southern Baptist institutions of higher learning. Claude Howe, a professor of church history at New Orleans Seminary, aptly summed up the matter:

> Conservative-fundamentalists desire that students be informed about destructive historical critical methodology only to defend the Bible against it. With few exceptions they interpret the Bible very literally. Moderates and denominational loyalists believe that the Bible should be studied critically as well as devotionally in order to so understand and apply it rather than simply defend it. Whereas an occasional student may be disturbed by this approach, many thousands learn from it and are enabled better to preach and teach the Bible in churches and schools around the world.

Since the fundamentalists abhorred genuine critical inquiry, they sought control of the seminaries and colleges to quash it. After becoming president of Southeastern Seminary, Paige Patterson told the author that Southeastern students should certainly learn about liberal and neo-orthodox theology, but they should also be shown why that "dog won't hunt." When Paul Pressler made his famous "going for the jugular" statement in 1980, Kenneth Chafin was convinced that the judge meant the seminaries, and he lamented that Southern Baptists were entering the "Dark Ages."[7] It was all a matter of perspective: To the moderates darkness was falling; to the fundamentalists a new day was dawning.

By 1985, when the fundamentalists prevailed in the great showdown at Dallas, trouble was brewing at four of the six seminaries. New fundamentalist trustees on the board at Southeastern began to demand more involvement in the hiring of faculty. Southern was being assailed by the fundamentalists because of Roy Honeycutt's call for a "holy war" against them a year earlier. At Midwestern, Professor Temp Sparkman, author of two controversial books entitled *Being a Disciple* and *The Salvation and Nurture of the Child of God*, was the focal point of a controversy. An attempt by fundamentalist trustees to oust Sparkman failed because the professor received the support of President Milton Ferguson and a majority of the board. Fundamentalists targeted Southwestern mainly in retaliation for President Russell Dilday's open attacks on them.[8]

Because the trouble at the seminaries obviously had a great deal to do with the friction between fundamentalists and moderates, the Peace Committee, which began its work in earnest during the early months of 1986, sent subcommittees to investigate charges that liberal theological views were being espoused at the seminaries. Chairman Charles Fuller promised that those subcommittees would neither "whitewash" the institutions nor conduct an "inquisition" while visiting them. In spite of his denials of an inquisition, the work of the subcommittees closely resembled an inquisition, since people were encouraged to appear before them to make charges in some cases and in others to defend themselves against charges if they wished. Larry Lewis, then president of Hannibal-LaGrange College, compared the subcommittees, incredibly, to accrediting teams! In any case, the Peace Committee's preliminary report at Atlanta in 1986 concluded that there was considerable "theological diversity" in the seminaries. Fundamentalists were pleased that the committee upheld their allegations that liberal views were being taught at Southern Baptist institutions of higher learning.[9]

Since Southern Baptist colleges and universities were owned and controlled by the state conventions and not by the SBC, fundamentalists had a more difficult time striking at them, but by the end of the 1980s momentous contests were under way in at least five states over Southern Baptist colleges and universities.[10] The struggle between fundamentalists and moderates to control the seminaries and colleges will be examined in some detail below on a case-by-case basis, beginning with the seminaries and concluding with the colleges and universities.

The flap at Midwestern Seminary in 1986 over Temp Sparkman and the Peace Committee's preliminary report in Atlanta were warning signs to the six seminary presidents. They knew that fundamentalist pressure would continue to build, and they attempted to compromise. In October of that year they met in New Mexico and issued the "Glorieta Statement," which affirmed that "the sixty-six books of the Bible are not errant in any area of reality." The presidents also agreed to enforce adherence to the seminaries' historical doctrinal statements. Their attempt to compromise delighted the fundamentalists and infuriated the moderates—especially seminary faculty members, according to Paige Patterson. In his interview with the author, Patterson expressed the belief that the attacks on the seminaries would probably have subsided if seminary faculty members had not been so vocal in their criticism of the "Glorieta Statement." Adrian Rogers called the statement the "strongest" he had heard—stronger than the Baptist Faith and Message Statement. He called for the Peace Committee to clear Southern, Southeastern, and Midwestern seminaries from further investigation. Other fundamentalists hailed the statement as a "breakthrough," while moderates called it a "breakdown." When the statement was drafted for the Peace Committee and approved by it, Cecil Sherman resigned from the committee, declaring, "What fundamentalists have wanted, the Peace Committee has helped them get." Contending that the statement would cause "serious" theological education to "wither," he asserted that the seminaries had taken "a long step toward their critics." The moderate spokesman warned, "What they have done will satisfy for a season, but fundamentalists will ask for more concessions from our educators." Sherman further contended, "Peace will not come from reconciliation and mutual acceptance, but peace will come when one group defeats the other and drives it from the field." While Sherman attacked the compromise, Robert Tenery was accusing the seminary presidents of backing away from it.[11]

During the next five years, tension mounted over the seminaries. Having the least trouble were New Orleans and Golden Gate. Landrum Leavell, the colorful president of the seminary at New Orleans, was moderately critical of both fundamentalists and moderates—the former for their "cheap worldly politics in the name of Jesus," and the latter for threatening to divert funds from the Cooperative Program. His criticism was never harsh enough to alienate either faction totally, and his seminary escaped being targeted for a radical overhaul by the fundamentalists. Golden Gate, like New Orleans, was basically a conservative institution, and it remained out of the line of fire until 1989, when its academic dean, Robert L. Cate, came under attack from fundamentalist trustees on the Sunday School Board. Larry Holly and others took offense at his article entitled "The Development of Monotheism," which appeared in the *Biblical Illustrator.* At their fall meeting held October 10–11, 1989, the president and trustees of Golden Gate Seminary affirmed Cate, noting that their academic dean had reaffirmed "that the Bible had 'truth without any mixture of error for its matter.' " With that resolution of the issue the controversy surrounding Cate's article blew over, and Golden Gate returned to business as usual.[12]

Midwestern Seminary had more trouble than New Orleans or Golden Gate, but far less than Southern, Southeastern, or Southwestern. The seminary's president, Milton Ferguson, managed to thwart the attempt to oust Temp Sparkman, but in 1990 he began to have serious trouble with new fundamentalist trustees. One of them wanted students to tape record class lectures and chapel services and argued with Ferguson about whether or not the Midwestern faculty had a "high view of Scripture."[13] This was a certain sign that Midwestern would hire faculty members in the future who were considerably more conservative, if the fundamentalist trustees had anything to say about it. But, as uncomfortable as Ferguson's position was, he was seldom under the kind of pressure that Roy Honeycutt, Randall Lolley, and Russell Dilday experienced.

Southern Seminary at Louisville, the SBC's oldest, was the first to come under heavy assault. As previously noted, when Duke McCall was Southern's president and William Hull its dean of theology, it was attacked in the early 1970s by Bill Powell. Attention was drawn to the seminary as never before, however, when Roy Honeycutt issued his call in 1984 for a holy war against the fundamentalists. Honeycutt's call was followed by demands for his resignation from such prominent fundamentalist pastors as W. A. Criswell and Homer Lindsay, Jr. The seminary president acted in part because of the Pressler-Durham episode mentioned earlier. Portions of the judge's taped telephone conversation with student J. Stafford Durham ended up in a story published by the *Houston Chronicle*. Durham's formal complaint to the Federal Communications Commission against Pressler for taping their telephone conversation without his permission ostensibly was made because, according to Durham, the *Chronicle* article was not accurately written. Dan Martin of Baptist Press reported Durham's complaint and the *Houston Chronicle* story in such a way as to provoke from Louis Moore, the *Chronicle*'s religion editor, charges that Martin was biased against Pressler and that he had misrepresented the story in the *Chronicle*.[14] The Pressler-Durham dispute, together with Honeycutt's throwing down the gauntlet to Pressler and Patterson, pointed to an all-out war between Southern Seminary and Southern Baptist fundamentalists.

After his call for a holy war, Honeycutt and the institution over which he presided remained under attack, but it was 1986 before there was another dramatic confrontation. In that year E. Glenn Hinson, a professor at Southern, was attacked for questioning the objectivity of the Gospel writers, and a new trustee, John Michael, expressed displeasure over Hinson's "doctrinal deviations." Besides Hinson, the Southern faculty member who attracted the most fire from fundamentalists was Molly Marshall-Green, who was accused of teaching universalism, the belief that all people will be saved ultimately. Questions were raised about the possible liberal views of ten other faculty members, but Honeycutt defended them all, saying that they were teaching in accordance with the Abstracts and Principles, a document that all Southern faculty were required to affirm.[15]

Tension at Southern continued to build. In 1987 new fundamentalist trustees were elected at St. Louis, but the following spring George Steincross, a moderate trustee and a member of the trustees' executive committee, led an unsuccessful attempt to deny them their seats on the board. Both fundamentalists and moderates knew that it was just a matter of time before the former would outnumber the latter. That time was at hand by 1990, and in April of that year the fundamentalists asserted themselves again. On the eve of the April board meeting Jerry Johnson, a twenty-five-year-old pastor from Colorado and a trustee, had a sixteen-page article entitled "The Cover-up at Southern Seminary" published in the *Southern Baptist Advocate*. Johnson specifically attacked Honeycutt and a number of faculty members—Glenn Hinson, Molly Marshall-Green, Frank Tupper, and Paul Simmons. He concluded that "one would have to be blind as a mole not to see that Dr. Honeycutt just does not believe the Bible," and accused the president of "political demagoguery" for calling Paul Pressler, Paige Patterson, and Charles Stanley "unholy" and "unscrupulous."[16]

At the board meeting later in the month the trustees debated a possible response to Johnson's article, but they voted to postpone action on the matter until the annual meeting in 1991. The fundamentalists did, however, flex their muscles by passing a resolution declaring abortion "the greatest moral issue faced by Christians today" and another allowing students to use tape recorders in seminary classes. The vote was thirty-two to twenty-four.[17]

Moderates were appalled by Johnson's attack on Honeycutt, and hundreds of letters supportive of the embattled president were sent to him. The Southern faculty immediately called for Johnson's resignation, and at the New Orleans convention in June messenger Lamar Wadsworth of Maryland moved that Johnson be removed as a trustee. Thousands of Southern Seminary supporters responded by giving Wadsworth a standing ovation, but his motion was ruled out of order because, according to SBC legal counsel, Johnson could not be removed without notice and a hearing during the SBC annual meeting. A second motion to refer the proposed action to the Southern board of trustees was approved by a show of hands. Johnson ultimately apologized to Honeycutt, the faculty members mentioned in the article, and the entire board of trustees. Supposedly reconciliation was effected, as all segments of the seminary community were "working hard to keep lines of communication open in order to build trust," but the trustees adopted new guidelines for hiring, tenuring, and promoting faculty. Henceforth all faculty members would be required to teach in accordance with the findings and recommendations of the Peace Committee report.[18]

The acrimonious confrontations at Southern Seminary in the spring of 1990 left one trustee, S. Ernest Vandiver, very distraught. Vandiver, a former governor of Georgia and a Baptist layman for sixty years, described the April 1990 meeting as one "dominated . . . from beginning to end" by the fundamentalist trustees. He reported that a young trustee offered Roy Honeycutt "a new car and a paid vacation if he would resign." The former governor said he was brokenhearted and saw little hope for Southern Seminary. Even if the moderates regained control, he was convinced that it would take ten years to repair the damage that had already been done.[19]

There was more damage to follow. On March 28, 1991, in order to avert a "crisis" at Southern, the trustees and faculty agreed to a document entitled "Covenant Renewal Between Trustees, Faculty and Administration." It called for a system of governance in which "trustees make policy, the President serves as chief executive and academic officer and the Faculty fulfill the implementing/teaching role." All pledged "to be sensitive to conservative viewpoints within the SBC" and agreed to seek balance in the faculty by hiring "conservative evangelical scholars for future openings." One trustee called the document "pretty much an inerrancy statement without using the term 'inerrancy.' "[20]

The signing of the "Covenant," which was endorsed by the faculty thirty-five to seven, was followed by several faculty resignations in 1991 and 1992. Bill J. Leonard, professor of church history, resigned to become chairman of the religion department at Samford University in Birmingham, Alabama. Glenn Hinson took a position at Baptist Theological Seminary in Richmond, Virginia—the new institution recently founded by the Southern Baptist Alliance. Loyd Allen left to become chairman of the religion department at Mississippi [Baptist] College in Clinton, Mississippi. Roy Honeycutt tried to remain optimistic about Southern's future, but Leonard and Hinson both called the seminary's future "bleak."[21]

After the New Orleans convention in 1990 Southern Seminary gradually became an institution dominated by fundamentalists, and Roy Honeycutt eventually had no recourse but to retire. Much the same fate befell Southeastern, where the man who ultimately emerged as president was none other than Paige Patterson. In August 1988 the author interviewed Alan Neely on the campus of Southeastern Seminary, at a time when Neely was cleaning out his office to move to the theological school at Princeton University. A little over four years later, on December 30, 1992, the author interviewed Paige Patterson on the same campus, a couple of months after Patterson's inauguration as the institution's new president. The departure of Neely, one of the founders of the Southern Baptist Alliance, and the subsequent arrival of Patterson, the theological guru of the fundamentalist cause, were events which indicated an unmistakable turn-around in Southeastern's orientation.

Southeastern had long been considered the most "progressive" of the SBC seminaries by moderates and the most "liberal" by fundamentalists. By the fall of 1987 a fundamentalist majority took over the board of the institution. At the October trustee meeting James Bryant, a new trustee attending his first meeting, offered a slate of executive committee officers in place of the slate offered by the nominating committee. All of Bryant's nominees were fundamentalists, and they were elected. The result was that the board's executive committee had eleven fundamentalists and one moderate. Thus, Southeastern became the first seminary to fall into the hands of the fundamentalist crusaders.[22]

During the following month Randall Lolley and Morris Ashcraft, Southeastern's president and academic dean, respectively, resigned along with four other key administrators, effective July 31, 1988. This did not disturb the fundamentalist trustees, who quickly announced that they would fill those posts and all future vacancies with people who believed in biblical inerrancy. Fundamentalist displeasure with Lolley went all the way back to 1970, when, as pastor of the First Baptist Church of Winston-Salem, North Carolina, he had allegedly offered the invocation for the formal opening of the Schlitz Brewing Company's new plant in that city. The fundamentalist trustees said they wanted Lolley to leave in January, but he refused. He argued that his departure in January would be disruptive to the school, and if he were forced to leave, he would say that he had been fired. Finally, an agreement was reached that allowed Lolley to remain until July 31, 1988, or until his successor was named, whichever came first. In March 1988 the trustees named Lewis A. Drummond, the Billy Graham Professor of Evangelism at Southern Seminary, as the new president of Southeastern. Drummond took office the following month with some fanfare, as Billy Graham addressed the audience while about sixty faculty and students staged a silent protest. The protestors wore yellow ribbons and passed out leaflets discussing what they regarded as the disaster that had befallen Southeastern.[23]

After Lolley's departure serious problems arose at the seminary. The Association of Theological Schools, an accrediting agency, questioned some of the seminary's policies. Then a condemnation of trustee policies in the student newspaper led to student unrest. Even more threatening to the seminary was a special study committee of the Southern Association of Colleges and Schools, another of the seminary's accreditors. That committee presented the trustees with a twenty-five page report that concluded that the seminary was "not functioning effectively as a scholarly community." The trustees called the report unfair. Potential loss of accreditation from two accrediting agencies was a serious matter, and Robert Crowley, the new trustee chairman, promised to do all he could to save the school's accreditation. Drummond, on the other hand, tried to downplay the threat, claiming he saw little or no chance that the seminary would lose its accreditation.[24]

The accrediting associations first took notice of the seminary because the new trustees assumed complete charge of hiring and firing faculty. New appointments under their regime were made by the president and approved by the trustees' "instruction committee." In the fall of 1988 this committee recommended that adjunct faculty members Mahan Siler and his wife Janice not be renewed for their adjunct teaching positions. Siler was pastor of Pullen Memorial Baptist Church in Raleigh, North Carolina—a church thought by many fundamentalists to be the most liberal in the state. Mrs. Siler was a marriage and family counselor. For six years the two had team-taught a marriage enrichment course at Southeastern. In a closed session in October 1988 the trustees upheld their instruction committee's recommendation not to continue the Silers as adjunct faculty members. Chairman Crowley announced the decision without giving any reasons. Some said that the Silers were dismissed because of something Mahan Siler had said outside his class. A number of seminary faculty members called for the reinstatement of the Silers, and the accrediting agencies continued to express concern about the unconventional direction of the institution. Mark Caldwell, a moderate trustee from College Park, Maryland, noted disapprovingly, "A new majority oriented toward fundamentalist and inerrantist theological views is now in control of Southeastern Seminary. The new majority feels it has a mandate from the Southern Baptist Convention to vigorously pursue a transformation of the school's historical character." He went on to warn that the "new ultra-conservative majority" was endangering the school's accreditation and creating a climate of secrecy, which was the "first step toward tyranny."[25]

In March 1989, over faculty objections, Drummond and the trustees hired as the seminary's new vice-president for academic affairs L. Rush Bush III, an associate professor of philosophy at Southwestern Seminary and a biblical inerrantist. This, along with other actions that deprived the faculty of a voice in personnel decisions, prompted the American Association of University Professors to report bluntly in June of the same year that "academic freedom at Southeastern has been placed in peril by a series of actions taken and statements made by its trustees and president."[26]

Fearful that the accrediting agencies would take action against the seminary, the trustees adopted on March 13, 1990, a compromise plan for hiring new faculty. The plan gave the faculty no more than a token voice. Henceforth a search committee consisting of the president, the vice-president for academic affairs, one trustee, and three faculty members would select new faculty members. No candidate could become a finalist without a two-thirds vote of the committee, and the trustees would ultimately elect a new faculty member on the president's recommendation. The president was not bound to recommend someone from the search committee's list. If he chose someone who was not on the list, he was required to tell the trustees that the faculty did not concur and explain to them the faculty's objections. Drummond claimed that this process gave the faculty a "significant role in faculty selection"! He called it "shared governance" and hoped it would "satisfy our accrediting agencies."[27]

To avoid the appearance of compromising their principles, the trustees adopted a doctrinal statement that was almost identical to the Peace Committee's statement on Scripture: "Southeastern Baptist Theological Seminary will endeavor to attract faculty candidates who reflect the viewpoint that where the

Bible speaks, the Bible speaks truth in all realms of reality, and to all fields of knowledge and that the Bible[,] when properly interpreted, is authoritative to all of life."[28]

The new process for hiring faculty satisfied the Association of Theological Schools, but not the Southern Association of Colleges and Schools. On December 12, 1989, SACS had warned the seminary that it must show improvement within two years in the areas of planning and evaluation, faculty selection, the role of the faculty on committees, and the role of trustees, or face possible loss of accreditation. In December 1991 Southeastern was put on academic probation by SACS. A few months earlier five professors, decrying the lack of academic freedom at the seminary, had resigned, effective at the end of the fall semester. Eight other professors were expected to resign or retire. Student enrollment had dropped from twelve hundred in the mid-1980s down to six hundred by the autumn of 1989. Although his leadership had been reaffirmed by the trustees in March, President Drummond announced his retirement, as some trustees advocated forgetting SACS accreditation in favor of creating a new agency to accredit only Southern Baptist seminaries. There were several exchanges of critical barbs between the Southeastern trustees and James T. Rogers, the executive director of SACS. Rogers bristled at the suggestion that SACS was not qualified to evaluate the seminary and vowed that he would not back down. At the end of 1992 Southeastern remained on academic probation by SACS, and the accrediting agency indicated that it would be at least one more year before the probation could be lifted.[29]

The trustees moved quickly to find Drummond's replacement. On April 20, 1992, Roger Ellsworth, the new chairman of the Southeastern trustees, told Baptist Press that Paige Patterson was the search committee's choice and that he would be recommended to the entire board on May 14. Presumably because excessive involvement in SBC politics had kept him from giving adequate attention to his job, Patterson had been fired on October 28, 1991, as president of Criswell College, but protests from students, alumni, and many SBC pastors had led to his reinstatement. Before being chosen for the Southeastern Seminary presidency, he had turned down an offer from Jerry Falwell to become president of Liberty University in Lynchburg, Virginia. The Southeastern trustees voted twenty-five to one on May 14 in favor of Patterson. When asked his position on academic freedom, he said it had to "be balanced with academic responsibility." He asserted that Southern Baptists were "conservatives" and that SBC institutions had a responsibility "to reflect their position."[30]

A few months later, in October, Patterson was inaugurated. Paul Pressler, to no one's surprise, was quite visible at the ceremony. To those two spearheads of the second fundamentalist crusade the capture of Southeastern no doubt meant that a liberal bastion had fallen to the crusaders, who could now turn it into a stronghold for biblical inerrancy. It meant something far different to Bill Self, a Southeastern alumnus and longtime pastor of Wieuca Road Baptist Church in Atlanta. He had earlier called the fundamentalists "theological vigilantes" and had accused them of trying to turn Southeastern into "a fundamentalist wind tunnel."[31] In October 1992, by which time he had given up his pastorate in frustration, Self undoubtedly thought that his worst fears had become reality.

The situation at Southwestern Seminary was far different from the ones at Southern and Southeastern. An evangelical spirit and a conservative theological stance had long been hallmarks of the seminary in Fort Worth, which was the world's largest theological training center. Most of the fundamentalists elected to the presidency of the SBC during the 1980s had attended Southwestern. The conflict probably would have had little effect on the institution if its president had not mounted a countercrusade against the fundamentalists in 1984 and if Professor H. Leon McBeth had not signed a contract to write the centennial history of the Baptist Sunday School Board. Even though the seminary attracted considerable attention, it was Russell Dilday, and not so much the institution, who became a target of the fundamentalists.

During 1989 Dilday came under attack by the board of trustees for his political involvement in the controversy. Although he had been criticized for such involvement since 1984, he had recently delivered an address entitled "Denominational Unity" at a symposium sponsored by Baptists Committed, and this offended trustee James Draper, the former SBC president. At its meeting on October 17, 1989, the board went into closed session for five hours to discuss the matter. There was considerable opposition to the closed session, but Draper said the board needed to deal with a "family matter." Five hours later trustee chairman Ken Lilly, a physician from Fort Smith, Arkansas, read a three-paragraph statement to about 250 people waiting outside. According to the statement the president and the board "affirm[ed] one another," and each side agreed "to cease and desist from making any statements, or writings, or engaging in any activities that could reasonably be interpreted as being intentionally political in nature." In other words, Dilday would keep silent and stay away from moderate meetings while the trustees, particularly Draper, would avoid fundamentalist gatherings. This was a compromise, since Draper had come prepared to take "whatever action was needed," meaning he had come to lead the trustees to fire Dilday.[32]

The compromise of October 1989 brought no more than an uneasy peace between Dilday and the trustees. In the spring of 1990 the fundamentalist tide continued to rise at Southwestern, as the trustees approved a motion condemning "any act of abortion, euthanasia, or any other act against God or against man who is created in God's image." The trustees also had considerable discussion before accepting Dilday's explanation of a conversation he had had in Nashville in February with SBC president Jerry Vines while the two men were attending a meeting of the SBC's Executive Committee. That conversation was about SBC politics. Finally, the trustees elected Draper as their new chairman without opposition.[33]

After the New Orleans convention later that spring Dilday remained under fire, although Draper tried to pretend that all was well. Tension continued to run high between Dilday and some trustees, particularly Draper. Since the latter had the votes to fire Dilday, many observers believed the axe would soon fall. Dilday's job was probably saved by two developments. First, the outspoken president was compelled to have heart-bypass surgery, and this forced him to limit his activities. Second, Draper was named as Lloyd Elder's successor at the Sunday School Board in 1991, and, when he assumed that position, he resigned as chairman of the seminary's board of trustees. Dilday remained president of Southwestern when Draper headed for Nashville, but he was much quieter and far less visible.[34] Like many moderates the Southwestern president had perhaps given up hope of ousting the obviously entrenched fundamentalists. His board of trustees had been the last to fall into their hands.

All that was required for the fundamentalists to gain control of the seminaries was the appointment of a majority of trustees on the seminary boards. That was accomplished in the relatively brief span of eight to ten years. Securing control of Baptist colleges and universities was a much more difficult task. Since the colleges and universities were tied to the state conventions, they did not answer to trustees elected by the SBC. If the fundamentalist crusaders were going to succeed in gaining control over Baptist colleges and universities, they would have to duplicate their seizure of the SBC in the various state conventions. That was a far more formidable task, although Judge Pressler said in 1987 that it would be done. As he put it, "We have to do the same thing in the states as we have done nationally." Noting that the struggle had already begun, he predicted that the fundamentalists would have success in the states "little by little."[35]

Indeed the struggle had begun. In fact, fundamentalist attacks on Baptist colleges and universities already had a long history. An attack in the early 1980s on Louisiana [Baptist] College by Ron Herrod, a fundamentalist pastor in the New Orleans area, backfired. Herrod, one of the college's trustees until 1984, assailed the school for having rock music groups on campus, for allowing Mormons to hold meetings, for having Catholics teaching at the school, and for giving an honorary doctorate to an Episcopalian who reputedly drank alcoholic beverages. The fundamentalist pastor resigned when his objections were ignored, but the president coaxed him to return by promising to implement new policies on both alcoholic beverages and the granting of honorary degrees. Herrod's tirades caused him to lose favor with many Louisiana Baptists.[36]

In 1986 and 1987 Samford University, Alabama's largest Baptist school, came under attack at the annual meetings of the Alabama Baptist Convention because of its "liberal direction." Leading the charge against Samford was Albert Lee Smith, a Birmingham insurance executive and prominent conservative Republican who served one term in Congress in the early 1980s. Smith's grandfather had been a faculty member and, for a brief time, acting president of Samford back in the days when it was known as Howard College. A thoroughgoing fundamentalist, Smith was convinced that Samford's religion department, as well as some other departments, harbored liberal faculty members. By 1988 the criticism of Samford began to abate somewhat because the university's new Beeson Divinity School had a sufficiently conservative faculty and dean, Timothy George, to satisfy the fundamentalists to some degree. At the end of that year, however, more criticism cropped up because the university's Cumberland School of Law invited Sarah Weddington, the noted attorney in the famous *Roe v. Wade* case, to speak. Her presence sparked an attempt to have the state convention ask its affiliated institutions to refrain from inviting prochoice speakers to their campuses. Samford's president, Thomas Corts, defended the right of the law students to invite speakers with opposing viewpoints as part of their academic freedom.[37]

Although Corts crossed the fundamentalists by standing firm for academic freedom, he reassured Alabama Baptists in 1990 that Samford would not follow the same path as other Baptist universities like Baylor, Furman, and Stetson, which had taken steps to eliminate control by their respective state conventions. A year later, as controversy continued to swirl around Baylor, Furman, and Stetson, Corts again asserted that he saw no problems developing between Samford and the Alabama Baptist Convention. He observed that in Alabama most people were more "focused on what they want[ed] to achieve" and had "a great revulsion to partisanship." Dean Timothy George added a perceptive comment: "Alabama Baptists are for the most part very conservative theologically. We have very few of what you would call left-wing liberal or moderate people in Alabama. There hasn't been that much to fight over. The essentially conservative theological nature of Alabama Baptists has been a unifying force."[38] Thus Alabama Baptists and Samford University avoided the bitter strife that plagued Baptists and their schools in other states, mainly because there was not "that much to fight over."

Georgia, Alabama's neighboring state, had a brief but bitter controversy over Mercer University, the Baptist school at Macon. In the fall of 1987 *Playboy* magazine listed Mercer as the nation's ninth best "party school." Lee Roberts, the fundamentalist layman and mortgage banker from Marietta, sent a sixteen-page "open letter" to Baptist pastors, Mercer faculty members, and the parents of Mercer students. In the letter Roberts said he had evidence of "filthy language, lewd photographs, heresies, student drunkenness, and sexually explicit material" on the Mercer campus. He called Mercer's president, Kirby Godsey, a heretic for writing that "any historical search to validate the deity of Christ is likely to fail." Roberts called for withdrawing the Georgia Baptist Convention's two-million-dollar annual appropriation to Mercer and for seeking the resignation of the trustees and replacing them with new ones selected by the state convention.[39]

Mercer students denied that Mercer was a party school, claiming that the opposite was true: it was "strict." They backed President Godsey, who asserted to student cheers, "This university will not be taken over by anybody." He noted that the trustees nominated future trustees and that a takeover was virtually impossible unless the trustees voted to change the charter—a highly unlikely prospect. Godsey labeled as "simply nonsense" the charge that his views were heretical. During the flap the First Baptist Church of Atlanta said it would stop supporting Mercer, while First Baptist Augusta promised to continue its support. The embattled president vowed that Mercer would learn to live without the state convention's annual appropriation, which amounted to less than 3 percent of the school's budget, if those funds were taken away.[40]

The Mercer students and the university's president were not the only ones irritated by the attack on the school. The *Atlanta Constitution* took sides with the institution, denouncing Roberts's attack as unfair. A *Constitution* cartoon showed a headless youth approaching the Mercer admissions desk with the admissions clerk telling a friend on the telephone, "Good news—I think the perfect fundamentalist just applied."[41]

Because Mercer University had a self-perpetuating board of trustees, the attempt to take it over went nowhere. At Mercer's sister institutions in Florida and South Carolina, matters proved to be more complicated because their ties with their state conventions were more binding. Stetson University in DeLand, Florida, moved in 1990 to reduce the Florida Baptist Convention's control over the institution. After a brief but bitter controversy a relatively amicable solution was worked out, one that virtually ended Stetson's relationship with the state convention.

At Furman University in Greenville, South Carolina, the struggle between that institution and the South Carolina Baptist Convention dragged on for two years. On October 15, 1990, the trustees at Furman voted eighteen to six to amend the school's charter in such a way as to make the board of trustees self-perpetuating. The change represented a sharp break with tradition, since the state convention had elected Furman trustees annually for 164 years. After a year of wrangling among South Carolina Baptists the state convention voted on November 12, 1991, to take Furman to court, thereby rejecting a pre-convention compromise that would have required 60 percent of the trustees to be South Carolina Baptists, 20 percent Baptists from outside the state, and 20 percent Christians but not necessarily Baptists. The messengers voted 2,011 to 1,973 to reject that compromise and sue the school. Before the case went to court thirty-four pastors led by four pastors with different theological perspectives were successful in bringing about a special convention "for the purpose of severing the legal and financial ties between [the] South Carolina Baptist Convention and Furman University." The proposal, made by the pastors on April 6, 1992, resulted in a special session on May 15, 1992, at which the messengers voted to dissolve legal and financial ties between Furman and the state convention. Before approving this motion, the convention rescinded its vote of November 1991 to seek legal action against the school.[42]

Reaction to the state convention's severing of ties with Furman was mixed. Hal Lane, a pastor from Greenwood, opposed the decision, saying it would "set a precedent for the loss of other Baptist institutions." He regretted the "retreat in the face of intimidation and controversy." On the other hand, Robert Shrum, a pastor from Rock Hill, said it was time for a "new relationship" between Furman and the South Carolina Baptist Convention. Furman's president, John E. Johns, liked the outcome because a costly lawsuit was avoided and the settlement enabled the university to turn all of its attention "to our real business of educating students."[43]

The struggles between fundamentalists and moderates over who would control Louisiana College, Mercer University, Stetson University, and Furman University had their moments of drama, but none of those battles was as intense and dramatic as the one over Baylor University in Waco, Texas. Baylor, the world's largest Baptist institution of higher learning, had a long history of being under the fundamentalist gun. As far back as the 1920s it had come under attack from one of its graduates, J. Frank Norris, who was as thoroughgoing a fundamentalist as ever appeared in the ranks of Southern Baptists. Norris was infuriated because a Baylor professor, C. S. Fothergill, allegedly taught evolution, and Norris lambasted his alma mater for years.[44]

When the fundamentalist tide began to rise again in the 1970s, Baylor came under heavy attack once more, this time from Paul Pressler and Zig Ziglar. As previously noted, it was Baylor's perceived liberalism that spurred Pressler into action and caused him to launch the second fundamentalist crusade. Some Baylor students from his "youth group" prompted the judge to visit the university in 1977. He reported his response to what he found as follows: "When I got up there and read their textbooks and found out what kind of garbage they were being fed, I promised the Lord I was going to do something about it."[45]

Three years later James Draper, then a Texas pastor and soon to be president of the SBC, attacked Baylor because H. Jackson Flanders was appointed head of the religion department. According to Draper, Flanders was a "liberal" and was especially culpable for publishing a work called *People of the Covenant*.[46]

A significant administrative change was made at Baylor in 1981 when Abner McCall was made chancellor and Herbert Reynolds, McCall's executive vice-president, became president. McCall had never concealed his moderate sympathies, but he had avoided fights with fundamentalists when possible. Reynolds was less reluctant to challenge the fundamentalists, and by 1984 he was in what amounted to a bareknuckle fight with them. In the *Baylor Line*, the institution's attractive publication, he lashed out at the fundamentalists, calling them a "little Baptist college of cardinals" and "a priestly class among us who feel they are endowed with special wisdom and special authority, when, in fact, they possess neither." He sneeringly called *inerrancy* a "code word" which some people were using as a vehicle "to gain power." Zig Ziglar had criticized Baylor for not teaching biblical inerrancy and for granting tenure to a Mormon who taught Spanish at the school. Reynolds saw nothing wrong with granting tenure to the Mormon professor, because he had pledged not to proselyte Baylor students.[47]

In 1986 there was more feuding. Paul Powell, a Baylor trustee and president of the Baptist General Convention of Texas, called upon Lee Roberts, the fundamentalist layman from Georgia, to apologize to Winfred Moore for accusing the Amarillo pastor and SBC presidential candidate of not believing in "truth." Roberts's response resulted in a quarrel between the two over whether or not both Powell and Moore, as Baylor trustees, had voted "to allow the continued showing of pornography depicting homosexuality, sadism, nudity, explicit sex, and the use of our Lord's name in vain" at Baylor. Roberts claimed that he obtained his information from Paul Martin, another Baylor trustee. As a result of the charges, there was considerable wrangling, as Reynolds explained to the trustees that the student officers of the Baylor Film Society had not followed orders from the faculty advisers to stop the showing of certain films. Assuring the trustees that he was opposed to pornographic films, Reynolds suspended the society until new guidelines could be worked out. Brad Blake, an honor student who had complained to the trustees about the films, was called by some moderates a "member of the Fundamentalist KGB."[48]

Early in 1988 a group calling itself United for a Better Baylor was organized. It was formed in response to a question raised in the *Southern Baptist Advocate:* "Are you mad about the liberal bent of the *Baylor Line?*" Among the leaders of this organization was Donny Cortimilia, a 1978 Baylor graduate and pastor of the First Baptist Church in Melissa, Texas. In August UBB attacked the Baylor Alumni Association and the school's trustees for allowing the university to become too liberal. Cortimilia called for a change of editorial policy in the *Baylor Line* to allow more fundamentalist representation. James Cole, the executive vice-president of the Alumni Association, responded, "These people have their own forum, the *Southern Baptist Advocate*." Cole called his association conservative, *not* liberal.[49]

Two months later UBB published an eight-page tabloid called *The Founder's Review* and criticized the university for straying from its original purpose. The charges made against the university included: (1) teaching evolution, (2) not chartering Campus Crusade for Christ as a student organization, (3) offering a yoga class in the division of continuing education, (4) allowing distribution of a planned parenthood publication, (5) permitting a Mormon to serve on the faculty, and (6) doing nothing about liberal statements made by professors in the religion department.[50]

Baylor became an issue at the annual meeting of the Baptist General Convention of Texas that year, but fundamentalist attempts to gain control of the convention's top offices failed. It was rumored at the convention that UBB would nominate an alternate slate of trustees for Baylor, but it did not. When Paige Patterson warned that the fight was not over, President Reynolds asserted that the Baylor administration had been sufficiently attentive to the concerns of the fundamentalists.[51]

Friction between Reynolds and the fundamentalists heightened each year, and in 1990 the spirited Baylor president took steps that led to a huge and bitter confrontation. Alarmed because fundamentalist trustees had gained control of the six seminaries' boards of trustees, Reynolds proposed in July 1990 that Baylor trustees consider establishing the George W. Truett Seminary at the university. Because of the SBC annual meeting in New Orleans the previous month, he decided that "things were just going to get much, much worse." Consequently, he "felt that we needed to send a message to the Presslerites who had been on the march since 1978 that while they might take over Southwestern, Southern, and the other seminaries, there existed a possibility of an alternative comprehensive seminary." The proposed seminary was incorporated in March 1991, and Reynolds hoped to begin the matriculation of students in 1994. He announced that he expected some support from the Cooperative Baptist Fellowship and expressed hope of raising an endowment of $25 million by 1997. Fundamentalists were not the only ones disturbed by the Baylor president's plans; moderate leader Russell Dilday saw the new seminary as a possible threat to his institution.[52]

Not long after announcing plans to establish the George W. Truett Seminary, Reynolds moved to take control of Baylor out of the hands of the Baptist General Convention of Texas. Fearing that the BGCT might soon fall under fundamentalist control, the Baylor president persuaded the Baylor trustees to amend the school's charter at a called meeting on September 21, 1990. The vote was thirty to seven with one abstention. The amended charter provided that Baylor would move from forty-eight trustees elected by the BGCT to a board of twenty-four regents by 1993, and only one fourth of the regents would be elected by the state convention. The other three fourths would be chosen by the regents themselves. The forty-eight trustees elected by the BGCT were to serve as liaisons between Baylor and the state convention.[53]

Trustee Dewey Presley of Dallas introduced the motion calling for the amendment. He and seven other outgoing trustees, including millionaire moderate spokesman John F. Baugh, were named to the new group of regents. The plan had been two years in the making. Reynolds and the school's attorney, Basil H. Thomson, worked with a team of lawyers, carefully planning every detail while informing only a few people of their actions. Reynolds said he worked out the plan and implemented it because "fundamentalists," who had a good track record of carrying out their intentions, had announced plans for seizing control of the BGCT.[54]

There were mixed reactions to the Baylor president's slick, clandestine maneuver. Many, including the board of directors of the Baylor Alumni Association, voiced their support. Fundamentalists, of course, expressed outrage, calling what Reynolds had done a "$750,000,000 jewel heist." Joel Gregory and James Draper were sharply critical, and Paige Patterson spoke of "a group of robber barons who were not happy with the way that Baptists, who were paying the bills all these years, were managing the university." Not all of the critics came from the fundamentalist camp. *Baptist Standard* editor Presnall Wood expressed opposition, as did Robert Naylor, a former president of Southwestern Seminary. Phil Lineberger, a moderate who was reelected in 1990 to a second term as president of the BGCT, said he wanted to see Baylor's governance returned to the trustees elected by the state convention so that the relationship that existed before September 21 could be reestablished.[55]

Fundamentalist chronicler James Hefley argued that Reynolds only imagined a fundamentalist takeover at Baylor, since moderates were in control of the BGCT. He contended further that many of the forty-eight Baylor trustees knew nothing of Reynolds's plan to amend the charter. At least five—John Baugh, Glen Diggs, Randall Fields, Winfred Moore, and Dewey Presley—were well informed. Ten trustees did not attend the September 1990 meeting, and the others walked in unaware of the plan. A motion to set aside the announced agenda passed, and Presley, seconded by Baugh, Diggs, and Fields, proposed amending the charter.[56]

When the BGCT met in November 1990, Baylor was a focal issue. Reynolds made it clear that he was tired of being second guessed and monitored by "fundamentalist extremists" and vowed to keep the university independent. His motive, he said, was not to remove Baylor from the lives of Texas Baptists, but to distance the school from the "extremist movement." Still, many Texas Baptists were not sympathetic with the Reynolds countertakeover strategy. Already the state convention was holding in escrow over $1 million of its 1990 appropriation for Baylor, and its messengers voted 1,995 to 1,966—by a margin of a mere twenty-nine votes—to do the same with the $6 million budgeted for Baylor in 1991.[57]

Besides placing in escrow funds appropriated for Baylor, the BGCT appointed a twenty-five-member committee to review the relationship between Baylor and the state convention. Robert Naylor, chairman of that committee, criticized Baylor for unilaterally amending its charter, claiming the action had created "much chaos." The former president of Southwestern Seminary pointed out that the BGCT had given Baylor $78 million over the past forty years. Herbert Reynolds's response was that Baylor was grateful for all the money given but that the university community would not "subject ourselves to the kind of focus that exists today just to save the money."[58]

A few weeks after the BGCT held its annual meeting at Houston in 1990 and voted to continue holding its funds for Baylor in escrow, the executive board of the state convention narrowly voted down a motion to ask the BGCT to release from escrow all convention scholarship funds allocated to the university. In the months that followed, negotiations went on between Baylor and the BGCT's special committee, as the opposing sides tried to reach a compromise. Naylor and others argued that the charter revision violated the BGCT's constitution, which required that all charter changes be approved by both the executive board and the state convention. The majority of Baylor's trustees, on the other hand, insisted that the board of trustees alone was responsible for such changes under Texas law. President Reynolds steadfastly maintained that the change was absolutely necessary because of the actions of Paul Pressler, who had been downgrading Baylor since 1978 at "strategy meetings" held at Felix's Mexican Restaurant in Houston. The Baylor president contended that Pressler had sought "to build a case" for taking over the university "to set things right," and that was what prompted and justified the action of the Baylor trustees to save the school. Quoting trustee John Baugh, Reynolds said that as far back as 1964 Pressler had vowed to rid the SBC of all liberals even if it split the Convention.[59] There can be little doubt that Reynolds was convinced that a fundamentalist takeover of the BGCT and Baylor University was possible and even likely.

On July 24, 1991, negotiations between Baylor and the BGCT's special committee ended in the announcement of a proposed agreement concerning future relations. The agreement recognized Baylor's independence, eliminated the school's "two-tiered system of governance" in favor of one board of twenty-four regents, offered the BGCT direct election of one fourth of the school's regents, and added to Baylor bylaws assurances that the school would remain "Baptist oriented." Signing the agreement for the BGCT were President Phil Lineberger, Robert Parker, chairman of the executive board, and George Gaston, chairman of the administrative committee. President Reynolds and the officers of the board of regents signed for Baylor. The agreement would go into effect after approval by the entire Baylor board and the BGCT at its annual meeting that November.[60]

After the proposed agreement was announced, a prominent Baylor graduate, Joel Gregory, pastor of First Baptist Dallas, preached a sermon in which he accused the Baylor trustees of stealing "the crown jewel of Texas Baptist life." Reynolds answered the charge by saying that ever since 1988 Gregory had been willing "to hammer his alma mater, his former professors, and me to establish his credentials as a bona fide fundamentalist." He accused Gregory of coveting the Dallas church's pulpit and working to prove his fundamentalism in order to obtain it. The Baylor president urged Texas Baptists to repudiate Gregory's attack. Gregory, on the other hand, vowed to do what he could to undo the action of the Baylor trustees. He called the action of the BGCT's executive officers in signing the proposed agreement "inexcusable and unprecedented" and promised to mail out five thousand copies of his sermon to rally support for his cause.[61]

Meanwhile, the "Presslerite confederates," according to Reynolds, were making plans to pack the annual state convention with their supporters. Reportedly, months in advance of the meeting at Waco they reserved motel and hotel rooms "*en bloc,*" leaving no rooms for moderates. The plan was thwarted, Reynolds revealed, by members of Baptist churches within a fifty-mile radius of Waco opening their homes to messengers who might need rooms. This was the situation Reynolds described in the *Baylor Line* on the eve of the state convention, and he urged Baylor alumni to attend the convention "in large numbers" in order "to preserve the Baptist General Convention and Texas Baptist work as we have known it."[62]

The showdown at Waco brought together the largest number of Texas Baptist messengers ever to attend an annual meeting of the BGCT—11,159. A "Baylor Restoration Committee" headed by Joel Gregory and other fundamentalist pastors from around the state urged the messengers to defeat the proposed agreement, claiming that its approval would doom Baylor to secularization. Houston pastor Edwin Young, who would soon become president of the SBC, offered a substitute plan, but it was defeated 5,976 to 4,714. The messengers then passed the original compromise 5,745 to 3,992. Some, including Dave Lucus who had formerly edited the *Southern Baptist Journal*, argued that a two-thirds majority was needed to approve the proposed agreement, but the chair ruled that the Baylor issue was unique and required only a majority vote.[63] And thus did the fundamentalist effort to thwart Herbert Reynolds and the Baylor trustees in their countertakeover maneuver go down to defeat.

Even so, the fundamentalists were not willing to admit final defeat. After they lost at Waco, Joel Gregory, Edwin Young, and about two hundred other pastors formed a "conservative fellowship" for the purpose of electing a fundamentalist president of the BGCT in 1992 and restoring Baylor's former relationship between Baylor and the state convention.[64] Their plan for Texas appeared to be a microcosm of the scheme Paul Pressler and Paige Patterson had successfully implemented on the national level over a dozen years earlier.

In launching what they regarded as their crusade for truth, fundamentalist Southern Baptists were spurred into action largely by Baptists institutions of higher learning, primarily because to them those institutions had become citadels of liberalism. Their solution was to gain control of the schools, fire liberal faculty members, and hire in their places teachers who affirmed biblical inerrancy and other "fundamentals" of the faith. Achieving their objective was not easy. It took about a decade to capture Southeastern and Southern seminaries and whip the other four seminaries into line. Their efforts at the state level all ended in failure, as four top Baptist universities—Baylor, Furman, Mercer, and Stetson—in effect declared independence of the respective state conventions that were their ostensible owners. In Alabama, President Thomas Corts of Samford University successfully steered a middle course acceptable to moderates and most fundamentalists. Pressler predicted that the fundamentalists would succeed little by little in the states. Perhaps he should have added that they would succeed except in their attempts to secure control of Baptist colleges and universities, since achieving that looked highly doubtful at the close of 1991.

8

Issues Other Than Inerrancy Raised by the Fundamentalist Crusades

ALTHOUGH PAUL PRESSLER and other crusaders consistently maintained that biblical inerrancy was *the* issue in the struggle between the fundamentalists and the moderates, it quickly became obvious that this was not the case. An inerrant Bible was certainly an issue, and, perhaps to many it was the main issue, but there were clearly other issues. Some of the other issues were contested at least as bitterly as was the inerrancy issue. Among them were such women's issues as abortion and the ordination of women as deacons and ministers, freedom of the press, and denominational involvement in politics. Besides the social issues involving women there were others such as pornography and homosexuality, issues on which fundamentalists and many conservatively inclined moderates agreed, as they did on the abortion issue. There was little agreement, however, on the ordination of women. This issue, plus freedom of the press and political involvement, drove a wedge between fundamentalists and moderates that divided them—permanently it would seem—as much as did the inerrancy issue.

As society at large accepted an expansion of the role of women, largely because of the gigantic contribution women made to the defense effort during World War II, fundamentalists, including Southern Baptist fundamentalists, clung tenaciously to the notion that women should not depart from their traditional roles. Nor should they make life-and-death decisions, even regarding the unborn who grew in their bodies, for life-and-death decisions were the prerogative of males who dominated the society.

Fundamentalists, whether Baptist or other, seemed to believe that God had ordered it so, and to challenge male dominance, they apparently thought, was tantamount to challenging God. The *Roe v. Wade* decision, handed down by the United States Supreme Court in 1973, was to many fundamentalists a sign that evil forces were at work to undermine the social order decreed by God Himself. When fundamentalists began to gain control of the SBC in 1979 and during the years that followed, they made numerous attempts to use the denomination to stem what they viewed as the satanic tide of social change. Exactly how much support they had on the abortion question was not clear. A survey taken by Nancy Ammerman revealed that just over 50 percent of those she sampled were willing to allow abortions under certain circumstances—rape, incest, and saving the life of the mother. Well over 50 percent of the fundamentalists who responded said that they opposed abortion under all circumstances except to save the mother's life.[1]

Beginning in 1979 and continuing throughout the decade of the 1980s, resolutions against abortion were offered at the annual meetings of the Convention. At the New Orleans meeting in 1982 Alabama pastor Calvin Kelly presented a resolution on abortion and infanticide. It affirmed that "all human life, both born and pre-born is sacred" and "not subject to personal judgments as to the 'quality of life.' " An attempt by moderates to amend the resolution by reaffirming "positions taken by previous Conventions" failed. Two years later at Kansas City the messengers adopted another resolution opposing abortion except to save the life of the mother. At Dallas in 1985 the SBC Calendar Committee, dominated by fundamentalists, recommended a Sanctity of Life Sunday to be observed by Southern Baptist churches in January, the anniversary month of the *Roe v. Wade* decision. Realizing that such an observance in January would symbolically tie the SBC to the Right to Life movement, Foy Valentine, director of the SBC's Christian Life Commission, attempted to have the convention designate a Sanctity of Life Day in April, but the Calendar Committee's recommendation was overwhelmingly adopted.[2]

Valentine's weak stand on abortion and his refusal to support a human life amendment to the Constitution of the United States irked fundamentalists. At the Atlanta convention in 1986 John F. Wilder, Jr., a messenger from Florida, moved that the convention censure the CLC director for publishing a tract on abortion and not mentioning "past pro-life resolutions" adopted by the SBC. Wilder called for all tracts published by the CLC to be destroyed and "new ones published which reflect and incorporate our strong published pro-life resolutions." The motion was not passed; instead it was referred to the Convention's Executive Committee.[3]

There was almost no let up in the struggle over abortion at the annual SBC meetings. It was alleged at the 1986 convention that four West Virginians were summarily rejected for trusteeships because they were "pro-abortionist." At the Las Vegas convention in 1989 Resolution No. 3 was presented. It called upon all messengers to "strongly urge the fifty state legislatures and the Congress to enact legislation to restrict the practice of induced abortion." Wayne Bartee, a messenger to that convention from Missouri, spoke against the motion. At that point

Mark Coppenger, who was serving as chairman of the Committee on Order of Business, "shared the committee's rationale" with the convention, and his motion to adopt Resolution No. 3 carried.[4]

Before the next annual meeting it was revealed that the Annuity Board had switched its insurance carrier to the Prudential Insurance Company, a company that became a sponsor of the organization Planned Parenthood, a leading defender of abortion rights. This development brought forth a resolution at New Orleans in 1990 which called upon all SBC entities and individuals "to carefully examine the charitable contributions of corporations they patronize."[5]

When Richard Land assumed the directorship of the CLC, the minds of the fundamentalists were set at ease. He fought on behalf of prolife policies in the nation's capital. The thoroughly prolife director called upon Southern Baptists to deliver "a massive outpouring of Southern Baptist support" of the prolife family planning rules under attack in Congress by "proabortion fellow travelers." Land was not alone among agency heads in fighting for the prolife cause. Larry Lewis had led the trustees of the Home Mission Board to take a stand "supporting the sanctity of human life" at its meeting in February 1990.[6]

Besides the struggle over abortion at the national level, several state conventions focused a great deal of attention on the issue. Florida Baptists held a special session of the Florida Baptist Convention on September 8–9, 1989, the first such session ever called to deal with a moral and social issue. The meeting, held at Downtown Baptist Church in Orlando, had the air about it of a prolife rally. Its 1,708 messengers adopted a statement opposing abortion in an attempt to influence an upcoming special legislative session that had been called by Governor Bob Martinez for October 10–13. Martinez, a Roman Catholic, wanted the legislature to pass a more restrictive abortion law. He addressed the Baptists' special session and was cheered.[7]

Alabama Baptists followed approximately the same course as their Baptist neighbors to the south. At the 1989 state convention in Huntsville the messengers passed a strongly worded resolution "urging Baptists to take the fight into the legislature." A prolife group of pastors who had organized a group called Alabama Baptists for Life announced their intention to participate in a "massive anti-abortion march in Montgomery on January 23, 1990." There was little doubt, judging by the consistent support of the prolife cause at state convention meetings, that the abortion forces among Alabama Baptists were outnumbered, although there were moderates who argued otherwise and some who forthrightly defended a woman's right to choose. For example, Dan Ivins, who helped found Citizens for Choice and Clergy for Choice, claimed that his organizations had taken a statewide poll that showed that 63 percent of Alabamians were for choice and only 31 percent were advocates of prolife. He in effect argued that the votes in the state convention turned out as they did only because fundamentalist leaders who were prolife were so vocal that they could sway the vote. Letters on the issue printed by the editor of the *Alabama Baptist* came from both sides, but the greater number came from prolifers. An atypical letter from one prochoice writer argued that the Bible did not condemn abortion and that the "notion that the fetus is fully human at the moment of conception" first became "church dogma at the Vatican Council of 1869." The prolife position held sway among most Alabama Baptists, however, and on February 15, 1990, the Christian Life Commission of the Alabama Baptist Convention issued a public statement in favor of a strong antiabortion law for Alabama.[8]

Creating nearly as much tension and division between Southern Baptist fundamentalists and moderates as the abortion issue was the issue of ordaining women both as deacons and ministers. Again the crux of the matter was dominance in church affairs. As far as fundamentalists were concerned God had made clear in his inerrant word that men controlled the church. In the late 1970s and early 1980s a number of churches began ordaining women, first as deacons and then as ministers. On January 16, 1983, the First Baptist Church of Oklahoma City voted 232 to 167 to allow women to become deacons. According to Baptist tradition, which had always gloried in local church autonomy, the decision should have been nobody's business but that of First Baptist Church. That was not the case, for its action set off a controversy in the Capital Baptist Association. Bailey Smith, immediate past president of the SBC, was among those who condemned First Baptist Church for ordaining women as deacons. It was soon discovered that Parkview Baptist Church of Tulsa had taken the same action in 1980, and University Baptist Church in Shawnee had done likewise in 1979. Moreover, there were reports that the First Baptist Church of Norman had taken the same step.[9] Apparently it was the cumulative effect of several churches ordaining women deacons over four years, plus the fact that the fundamentalists were riding the crest of a conservative national tide, that stirred Oklahoma fundamentalists to react in 1983.

Later that year, when the SBC met in Pittsburgh, fundamentalists were given further cause for concern when Southern Baptist women who had been ordained as ministers met prior to the convention to organize officially as Southern Baptist Women in Ministry. At that meeting it was reported that there were 175 ordained "clergywomen" already in the SBC and that there were hundreds more awaiting ordination. After that meeting the convention made an attempt to pay tribute to Southern Baptist women by adopting a resolution that expressed gratitude for contributions made by women in various forms of ministry and praised them as homemakers. It also called for "fairness" in compensating women and in offering them opportunities for advancement. Debate on the resolution became intense when Joyce Rogers, wife of Adrian Rogers, attempted to amend the resolution by adding, "Be it finally resolved this resolution should not be interpreted as endorsing the ordination of women." During the debate Adrian Rogers attempted to speak only to be greeted by cries that he was out of order. Ultimately President James Draper ruled that Rogers was indeed out of order. Mrs. Rogers's amendment was defeated, and the original resolution was approved by a sizable majority.[10]

Perhaps the fundamentalists were caught unawares on the women's issue at Pittsburgh, but that was not the case at Kansas City in 1984. The fundamentalists were firmly in control and adopted a strongly worded resolution against ordaining women as deacons and pastors. Specifically the resolution encouraged the service of women "in all aspects of church life and work other than pastoral functions and leadership roles entailing ordination." The rationale for the resolution was that women must submit to men because man was created first and woman was first in the Edenic fall. Thus were women blamed for bringing sin into the world, a deed for which they were condemned to be forever subservient to men. The resolution passed by a vote of 4,793 to 3,466. One of the opponents of the resolution was Wayne Dehoney, a former SBC president, who stated that the resolution dealt with "something that is the affair of the local church entirely." Bill Leonard, then a professor of church history at Southern Seminary, soon suggested that the Convention's opposition to women's ordination, which he too believed threatened the autonomy of the local church, could become "the catalyst which ultimately brings schism to a diverse and increasingly disoriented denomination."[11]

The issue of women in the ministry created a stir again in 1987 when Prescott Memorial Baptist Church of Memphis, a small church of only 235 members, appointed Nancy Hastings Sehested as its pastor. Mrs. Sehested was the first woman pastor of a Southern Baptist Church in Tennessee and one of only a few in the nation. The church that called her to the pastorate was soon expelled from the Shelby Baptist Association. Sehested, who was from Texas and who was the daughter and granddaughter of Southern Baptist ministers, had previously served as the associate pastor of the Oakhurst Baptist Church in Decatur, Georgia. Those who voted to disfellowship her new church argued that Eve's behavior in the Garden of Eden made women ineligible to head congregations. Her response was that people often used the Bible to support their "own cultural biases and prejudices."[12]

In spite of the barriers erected in their pathway, Southern Baptist Women in Ministry persisted in their cause. That they knew what they were up against was clear from the following statement, which appeared in the summer issue of *Folio* (the publication of Southern Baptist Women in Ministry) in 1989: "No immediate change in status of SBC women is likely as long as the overall theological and political climate is male-dominated and paternalistic." Still, they were convinced that logic and even Baptist tradition was on their side, as was indicated by another statement: "If we accept the doctrine of the priesthood of the believer, then anyone, regardless of gender, can be called to minister."[13]

The very next issue of *Folio* reported on the case of Katrina and Greg Pennington, which has already been noted. As previously indicated, spokesmen for the Foreign Mission Board claimed that the decision to deny the Penningtons an appointment as foreign missionaries had nothing to do with the ordination of women. Nor, according to them, did pressure from the Enon Association, which had disfellowshiped the church in which the Penningtons served. The evidence suggests otherwise, for the FMB subcommittee that recommended against the Pennington appointment cited as its reason the "divisive" manner in which the Penningtons "dealt with the issue of ordination in the climate of the local association." Also, two letters from the Enon Association were sent to the FMB urging rejection of the pair because "It is our conviction that the ordination of Mrs. Pennington violated clear Bible teaching."[14]

Offering strong support to Southern Baptist Women in Ministry was the Southern Baptist Alliance. On a small budget, the Alliance granted the women's organization $5,000 per year. After the Alliance changed its name to Alliance of Baptists in March 1992, it continued to be the primary financial supporter of SBWIM. By that time the organization was also receiving some support from the new Cooperative Baptist Fellowship.[15]

Just as the abortion issue spilled over into the state conventions, so did the issue of ordaining women. One Arkansas Baptist, Michael Trammell of Jonesboro, became very upset when the *Arkansas Baptist Newsmagazine* gave space in the paper to the advocacy of "radical views on issues such as the ordination of women." There was such an acrimonious debate over the issue at the 1987 Alabama Baptist Convention that President Steve Tondera had to admonish the messengers to remember what they were doing and settle down. In the end the convention voted 748 to 684 to take no action on a resolution that would have commended women for their services in vocational ministries. A few weeks before the convention the Calhoun Baptist Association had withdrawn fellowship from the First Baptist Church of Williams, Alabama, for ordaining two women as deacons. Meanwhile, in Kentucky, a month before the Calhoun Association took that step, the Mount Zion Baptist Association had expelled the First Baptist Church of Corbin for doing the same thing.[16]

At the same time Southern Baptists fought it out over women's issues, they also raised the issue of freedom of the press and quarreled mightily over it. There were two arenas in which this battle was waged, Baptist Press and the papers published by the state conventions. Fundamentalists were convinced that the Baptist news media in Nashville and in the states slanted their coverage in favor of the moderates. Since much of the news published in the state papers was furnished them through releases issued by Baptist Press, the way to correct the problem, the fundamentalists concluded, was to put fundamentalists or their sympathizers in charge of Baptist Press. That is why Al Shackleford and Dan Martin were fired—to make way for people who would report the news in a manner satisfactory to the fundamentalists. Although the purging of the two journalists was discussed in a previous chapter, it needs to be examined here in the context of an issue that went far beyond a single religious group to the very core of American liberty. That issue—freedom of the press—was first raised in America by the famous trial of John Peter Zenger in New York City in 1735. In the minds of many, Southern Baptist fundamentalists raised it again at Nashville in the summer of 1990, and their decision flew in the face of the one handed down in the Zenger case 255 years earlier. At the press conference following his dismissal, Dan Martin said that the Executive Committee, which was clearly dominated by fundamentalists, wanted a "minister of communication" or "spin doctor" who would put a fundamentalist spin on the news. Quite a few people in the room responded in such a way as to indicate their agreement with the remark.[17]

There was plenty of evidence that the fundamentalists did want a good deal more than "fair and objective" reporting; they wanted reporting that was slanted in their favor. To them, "fair and objective" meant reporting "the truth." Dave Lucus, who edited the independent *Southern Baptist Journal* in the late 1980s, wanted Baptist Press to tell "people that we are in a classic struggle between the liberals and conservatives." At the 1987 convention in St. Louis he made a motion to investigate the "objectivity and fairness" in Baptist Press news reporting from 1978 to 1987. The motion was referred to the Executive Committee. Instead of investigating Baptist Press, the EC generally affirmed it, but urged restraint in reporting "sensitive controversial issues" for the sake of peace and harmony.[18]

Fundamentalist displeasure with Baptist Press went back a long way. There was bad blood between Paul Pressler and Wilmer C. Fields, Shackleford's predecessor as BP director, and the judge was even less happy with Shackleford. Like Shackleford, Fields had been accused of publishing stories that were biased against the fundamentalists. Baptist Press was sharply criticized at the 1983 and 1984 conventions, while Fields was still its director. Whether or not Fields slanted his coverage is open to debate, but there can be no doubt that he had little use for fundamentalists. After he announced his retirement, he reportedly referred to them as an "evil force" from "the Abyss" who had wrecked the "golden age" of Southern Baptists. He called what had happened to the SBC "an unrelenting, shameless takeover by a narrowly-partisan political group."[19]

Even if Fields did the fundamentalists no harm in his coverage, it is highly doubtful that he did them any favors. Shackleford, on the other hand, was as conservative in his theology as the fundamentalists, and, by all accounts except those of the fundamentalists, he was evenhanded in reporting the news about Southern Baptists. On the eve of the July purge he said that he and Martin were asking for the right to focus on the "real issue, and that is the Baptist right to know." He reported that no one had told him what the EC's "criticisms are directly," and he noted that out of 1,298 stories BP reported in 1989, he had received criticism on fewer than ten. Martin said that he and Shackleford had always sought to "present fair, balanced and accurate stories." The fundamentalists, of course, did not agree. Fred Wolfe, a member of the EC, said the issue was not a free press but "a fair press." The Mobile pastor said he believed that the two journalists would have been "fired on the spot" if the matter had come up at the convention in New Orleans.[20]

Evenhandedness was obviously not what the fundamentalists desired. It is clear that Shackleford and Martin were highly regarded by the vast majority of their peers. There were, however, a few journalists who found fault with them. The fundamentalist editors Dave Lucus and Robert Tenery constantly complained, and David Simpson of the *Indiana Baptist* called for addressing the issues "straight on factually" and for presenting fundamentalist opinions. Louis Moore, when he was still with the *Houston Chronicle*, charged that "the moderate-controlled Baptist news media" had become "so politicized and partisan in their coverage that they can't be relied on any longer for a fair presentation of the issues." On the other hand, Shackleford and Martin were highly praised by J. B. Fowler, president of the Southern Baptist Press Association, the Associated Church Press, Bill Moyers, and syndicated columnist Paul Greenberg among others.[21]

Those who applauded the work of Shackleford and Martin spoke glowingly of the two journalists, who together had over thirty years of journalistic experience. As rumors ran rampant of the impending purge, J. B. Fowler, who edited the state Baptist paper in New Mexico, said that the BP director and news editor had "bent over backwards to be fair in reporting Baptist news." Donald Hetzler, executive director of the Associated Church Press, an ecumenical agency representing 195 periodicals of a variety of denominations (Roman Catholic and Eastern Orthodox as well as Protestant), wrote President Morris Chapman of the SBC and expressed alarm that "responsible and respected journalists" were about to be "penalized and dismissed for their proper reporting of the news."

He noted that the incident was especially regrettable because of BP's "credibility and trust among secular press agencies for its open, balanced reporting of controversial matters." Bill Moyers, a lifelong Southern Baptist, urged Baptist editors to challenge the "vindictive act and the bully who is responsible. . . . I mean of course Paul Pressler, who has just shamelessly engineered the firings." The television journalist further asserted that Pressler "rules the Southern Baptist Convention like a swaggering Caesar, breaking good men when it pleases him." In a syndicated story in the *Los Angeles Times* Paul Greenberg said, "let's not pretend that this is anything but censorship," and charged that "the new Southern Baptist powers want to manage the news." He concluded that the EC's explanation for firing Shackleford and Martin sounded "like something Torquemada might have said on behalf of the Spanish Inquisition if he had had a good PR man."[22]

While news media professionals were in effect accusing the SBC's fundamentalist leadership of undermining the cherished right of a free press, some moderates were throwing up their hands in frustration and abandoning the struggle. One who did was Terry L. Davis, pastor of the Ocean City Baptist Church in Maryland. A member of the Executive Committee, Davis resigned following the committee's vote of forty-five to fifteen to fire Shackleford and Martin on July 17, 1990. He said upon leaving that his resignation would be welcomed by some leaders as the departure of one more moderate member. He also predicted that there would be more purges in the future, declaring, "If you don't toe the line, if you don't do what present leadership says, you are going to be gone."[23]

Moderates were quick to charge that BP would soon be used to spread fundamentalist propaganda. Sam Pace, chairman of the EC, denied that the committee had any plans to use BP as a "propaganda tool." Hardly anyone outside fundamentalist circles was reassured by Pace's statement, as was evidenced by the fact that on the same day Shackleford and Martin were fired—even at the same press conference following that episode—the formation of an alternative press service called Associated Baptist Press was announced. Nashville attorney Jeff Mobley, who announced it, said, "Associated Baptist Press will be neither the servant nor savior of any group among Southern Baptists. A guiding principle for Associated Baptist Press will be to tell Southern Baptists the facts and to trust them with those facts. Associated Baptist Press will not serve as a 'press agent' of any political group or groups among Southern Baptists."[24]

Fundamentalists were skeptical, to say the least, of Mobley's assertions. When the new Associated Baptist Press published its first edition by facsimile machine on September 26, 1990, Dan Martin was serving as interim editor, and Al Shackleford was a member of the ABP's board.[25] More than ever fundamentalists were convinced that ABP had but one purpose, which was to promote the cause of the moderates.

Like Shackleford and Martin, Jack U. Harwell, editor of the Georgia Baptist Convention's *Christian Index* for twenty-one years, became a martyr to the cause of a free press during the fundamentalist crusade. Fundamentalists, led by the outspoken Lee Roberts, put Harwell under heavy pressure during the mid-1980s. Their campaign against his editorials led in October 1987 to the establishment of a review board to monitor his subsequent editorials. This prompted Harwell to announce his retirement as of December 31, 1987, saying he could no longer work under the group's restrictive policies. At the November 1987 meeting of the Georgia Baptist Convention the messengers voted to dismiss the review board and to ask Harwell to stay on as editor of the *Christian Index*. He said he was willing, but the convention's executive committee voted fifty-seven to fifty-four against a motion allowing him to continue as editor. When Harwell had announced his retirement in October, Bill Self, the moderate pastor of Wieuca Road Baptist Church, remarked, "They finally got him; they've been trying to get him 15 years." Another Atlanta-area pastor, Tom Conley, called Harwell's departure "another notch in the fundamentalists' gun."[26]

On January 15, 1988, Smoke Rise Baptist Church, of which Harwell was a member, held a testimonial banquet for him. About five hundred people attended, and the former editor was praised by *Biblical Recorder* editor R. G. Puckett as a "martyr for the cause of truth, freedom, and integrity." Floyd Roebuck, a former president of the Georgia Baptist Convention, called him a "great servant-leader" and a "prophet." Harwell announced that he was considering twenty job offers. He ended up assuming the editorship of *SBC Today* in place of Walker Knight, who remained with the paper as publisher.[27]

Harwell's ouster in Georgia was well publicized in Southern Baptist circles and condemned by many as a blow against freedom of the press, but it did not command nearly as much attention as the July purge at Nashville two-and-a-half years later. The dramatic dismissal of Al Shackleford and Dan Martin by the SBC's Executive Committee in the summer of 1990 brought the new fundamentalist leaders in the Convention more negative publicity than anything they had done up to that time. Outrage was expressed within the denomination and all over the country. On the national scene the people who were outraged were among America's most articulate—news media professionals—and they had the means to bombard the fundamentalists with damaging publicity. In their minds, the fundamentalist crusade had gone beyond a quarrel over theology and a power struggle for control of the SBC to an attack on one of America's most cherished freedoms, and there was a flood of protest and criticism.

Meanwhile, the fundamentalists were accused of other activities that also damaged their image at the national level. Some of their most visible leaders were active in right-wing political causes, and they were charged over and over with promoting the cause of the informal movement called the New Religious Political Right and trying to turn the SBC into a political agency of the Republican party. Those charges were not entirely unfounded.

As far as many moderates were concerned the fundamentalist crusaders were as fully committed to promoting a right-wing political agenda as they were to promoting fundamentalist Christianity. By the end of the 1980s few moderates doubted this conclusion. In 1989, missionary Richard Horn, pastor of Tokyo Baptist Church in Tokyo, Japan, wrote to Dan Ivins of the Southern Baptist Alliance, "I am disheartened by the unholy wedding of our convention with the agenda of the political right wing in America." Three years later, Collinsville, Alabama, Baptist Stephen M. Fox, perhaps the most outspoken of Alabama moderates during the years of conflict, attacked President George Bush for hoisting the family value flag, calling it a ploy to hold on to "his core constituency, the religious right, of which the Southern Baptist Convention is now a major flank."[28]

Exactly how much of a "wedding" there was between the SBC, the New Religious Political Right, and the Republican administrations of Ronald Reagan and George Bush is debatable. That they all had similar interests and goals and sometimes worked together to promote them is beyond question. Traditionally Southern Baptists, as a denomination at least, had remained aloof from direct political action. Southern Baptists as individuals were politically active, of course, but the SBC did not take political stands—until the fundamentalists began "to get out the vote" and dominate the annual meetings. How the fundamentalist leaders became bedfellows with adherents of the New Religious Political Right is an interesting story, but given the fundamentalist mindset, the fact that it happened was not surprising.

While many Southern Baptists were not fundamentalists, the vast majority of Southern Baptists were undeniably conservative on nearly all religious, moral, and social issues—in spite of the fact that the fundamentalists accused most moderates of being liberal and, sometimes, left-wing. In a national poll taken in the late 1970s, the only religious group to register above 80 percent in giving consistently conservative answers on religious, moral, and social questions were Baptists. Lutherans, Methodists, and Presbyterians responded conservatively on just under 80 percent of the questions, while less than half the Episcopalians and Jews who answered gave conservative responses. Such responses, however, did not mean that most Southern Baptists joined the ranks of the various organizations which were found under the umbrella of the NRPR at the end of the 1970s. The largest of the NRPR organizations was Moral Majority, founded and headed by independent Baptist Jerry Falwell. One survey of Southern Baptist ministers revealed that less than 4 percent of the respondents were members of Moral Majority, and less than 50 percent sympathized with that organization. Almost 47 percent said they opposed Moral Majority. Even though Southern Baptist pastors did not join Moral Majority in large numbers, they apparently did join the Republican party. One report said that the proportion of Southern Baptist ministers in that party increased from 29 percent in 1980 to 66 percent in 1984![29]

Jerry Falwell entered the political arena reluctantly, it would appear. In the 1960s he eschewed political involvement, but by 1976 he was organizing "I love America" rallies on the steps of state capitols all over the nation. His efforts meshed with those of other organizations (altogether about ninety) that wanted to restore prayer and Bible reading in the public schools, obtain equal time for teaching "scientific creationism" alongside evolution in the classroom, overturn the *Roe v. Wade* decision with a constitutional amendment, and in general restore a "Christian America." Before Moral Majority, however, there appeared several right-wing political organizations established by the "gang of four"— Paul Weyrich and his Committee for the Survival of a Free Congress, Howard Phillips and his Conservative Caucus, Richard Viguerie and his RAVCO (Richard A. Viguerie Company), and John "Terry" Dolan and his National Conservative Political Action Committee. Three of these organizations were formed in the mid-1970s (after *Roe v. Wade*), and Viguerie's group dated back to the mid-1960s. While these organizations did not start out with a religious purpose, they soon sought to tie into the emerging Christian Right groups like Moral Majority and then the Religious Roundtable. They set out to change American politics by placing politicians on "hit lists" after judging them by "moral report cards" and "Christian political action manuals." These people, called "Christian Stalinists" by some, were comfortable working with all kinds of religious conservatives, including "morally conservative" Catholics, Mormons, and Conservative and Orthodox Jews, as well as Protestants. It was to be a marriage of the political right and the religious right for the purpose of restoring the nation's Christian heritage and family values.[30] One is left to wonder how the NRPR leaders thought they could enlist Jews to work toward restoring America's *Christian* heritage.

In step with the organizations already mentioned were some that had a particular interest in straightening out the public schools. Among these were Phyllis Schlafly's Eagle Forum, Beverly LaHaye's Concerned Women for America, Pat Robertson's National Legal Foundation, Mel and Norma Gabler's Educational Research Analysts, and Citizens for Excellence in Education, the activist arm of the National Association of Christian Educators. The people associated with these organizations appeared to believe that the public schools should teach their sectarian views and not encourage students to think critically and independently.[31]

The fundamentalist leaders of the "conservative resurgence" and an undetermined number of Southern Baptists fell in line behind these right-wing political and religious groups. Playing a part in their activities were Paul Pressler, Paige Patterson, Adrian Rogers, Bailey Smith, James Draper, and Charles Stanley, among others, but the man who provided the most direct link between the SBC and the NRPR was a layman, Ed McAteer, who was a member of Bellevue Baptist Church in Memphis. McAteer, born in Memphis in 1927, was a decorated soldier of World War II and a former golden gloves middleweight boxer. He worked for the Colgate-Palmolive Company in various marketing positions for twenty-eight years. In 1979 he founded the Religious Roundtable to work with other NRPR organizations "to defend the free enterprise system, the family, and Bible 'morality.' " The Roundtable was organized around an eleven-member board of directors and a "Council of 56." Among those on the board of directors with McAteer were Paige Patterson, Adrian Rogers, and Charles Stanley. W. A. Criswell, Bill Powell, and Jesse Helms were on the council, along with Jerry Falwell and Tim LaHaye. The Roundtable's message, McAteer declared, was that America should get back to family values and away from its "national sin" of "killing [its] own babies." He proposed that the organization "reach into the Southern Baptist Convention . . . as well as other conservative denominations."[32]

McAteer attended the 1980 meeting of the SBC in St. Louis and tried to secure adoption of a resolution "concerning involvement of Southern Baptists in the United States governmental process." His proposed resolution was not referred to the Resolutions Committee because McAteer was not a duly elected messenger. He continued his activities on other fronts during that year by lobbying, with the support of Adrian Rogers, for Senator Jesse Helms's bill to reinstitute prayer in the public schools, and by registering in the *Southern Baptist Advocate* his condemnation of "debating everything, critically re-examining every precept and concept, including the Ten Commandments." He lamented that "there are no longer any eternal truths."[33]

When McAteer attended the 1982 SBC meeting in New Orleans, he played a significant, behind-the-scenes role by "counseling" Norris Sydnor, chairman of the Resolutions Committee. Sydnor, identified as a "black bivocational pastor" from Maryland, was attending his very first annual meeting of the SBC. Yet he was appointed by President Bailey Smith to the chairmanship of an important committee. Smith knew Sydnor only through McAteer. The Memphis layman's top priority was a strong resolution in support of Israel. He failed to secure its adoption, but he was successful in gaining approval of resolutions condemning abortion, supporting prayer in the public schools, and advocating the teaching of "scientific creationism."[34] Obviously the NRPR was beginning to "reach into the Southern Baptist Convention."

Earlier in 1982 Bailey Smith had revealed his sympathy for the NRPR agenda through an incident involving Tim LaHaye, who directed an organization in California called Family Life Seminars. LaHaye was convinced that he had been lured into an intellectual ambush at Southwestern Seminary by Joe Haag of the SBC's Christian Life Commission. After the encounter he wrote to both Haag and Smith to complain. LaHaye condemned Haag for deceiving him and getting "that angry liberal ... to do a hatchet job on me." He added, "you gave him a platform from which he could vent all his frustrations at me, the Moral Majority, conservatism, fundamentalism, slavery, and even history— without benefit of response." Exactly who the "angry liberal" was is not clear, but that LaHaye was infuriated by the incident is quite clear. On February 24, 1982, he wrote to Bailey Smith, "Last night I had the dubious honor of being a target for the 'theological humanists' at Southwestern Seminary."[35]

Although Smith showed no inclination to do anything about what had happened to LaHaye, he was definitely sympathetic. In his response he revealed a great deal about his own views. He wrote that he was "horrified" over what had happened to LaHaye at Southwestern Seminary. "There is no room in Southern Baptist Institutions for humanism or evolution," Smith declared. He closed by saying, "I am so sorry you were set-up by the Christian Life Commission. That group definitely needs a good Holy Ghost Revival."[36]

Other evidence of Smith's very conservative sympathies is that he was on the board of governors of the American Coalition for Traditional Values, along with James Draper, Adrian Rogers, Charles Stanley, Jerry Falwell, and Jimmy Swaggart. The board was headed by Tim LaHaye. President Ronald Reagan was a forthright supporter of the organization, which was included in the NRPR network and was well known for its ultraconservative political orientation.[37]

By 1987 it was clear that Paul Pressler and Paige Patterson were connected to the NRPR. In an interview with Bill Moyers that year, Pressler admitted to being a member of the Council on National Policy, a network organization for top leaders of the NRPR. The judge allegedly was also connected with a fringe group called the Reconstructionists who reportedly sought to turn the United States into a theocracy. In August 1987 Pressler, Patterson, and Howard Phillips of the Conservative Caucus joined Joseph and Holly Coors in hosting a one-thousand-dollar-per-couple reception at a ranch near Dallas. Coors was notorious for his reactionary political stance. At the San Antonio SBC meeting in 1988 Patterson admitted to belonging to the Council on National Policy, but he denied any involvement with Reconstructionism "in theology." In a letter to the author in 1994 he asserted that neither he, Judge Pressler, nor the council had any ties to Reconstructionism. While he was being assailed for his NRPR connections during the late 1980s, he contended that he was concerned about the direction of the United States and that the council had "educational programs" to which he could go for information.[38]

There were lesser lights among Southern Baptist fundamentalists who became involved in right-wing political activities. At the Pittsburgh convention in 1983 Samuel Currin of North Carolina was elected to the SBC's Public Affairs Committee, and he became its chairman. He soon tried to convey the idea to the Senate Judiciary Committee, chaired by Senator Strom Thurmond, that Southern Baptists supported President Reagan's proposed prayer amendment, but twelve other members of the PAC sent Thurmond a letter saying that Currin did not speak for them. Currin had sent Thurmond a copy of the 1982 New Orleans resolution calling for such an amendment, while the twelve who demurred sent a copy of the 1983 Pittsburgh resolution, which softened the Convention's stand.[39]

Another outspoken second-level Southern Baptist fundamentalist who worked for right-wing causes was Albert Lee Smith of Alabama, a former Republican congressman. Smith, a member of Southside Baptist Church in Birmingham, took an active part in the affairs of the SBC. During the 1960s he had been an active member of the John Birch Society. His wife, Eunice ("Eunie") Waldorf Smith, headed Alabama's Eagle Forum. Both Smith and his wife were greatly disturbed over the teaching of "secular humanism" in the public schools, and at the 1986 convention in Atlanta the ex-congressman offered an awkwardly worded resolution urging all Southern Baptists "to oppose censorship of the Judeo-Christian heritage as a historical fact from our public school textbooks" and "to encourage city, county, and state boards of education not to accept textbooks that have censored the Judeo-Christian heritage." A few months later, at the annual meeting of the Alabama Baptist Convention, he called upon President Thomas Corts of Samford University to comment on rumors that Karen R. Joines, a Samford faculty member since 1967, did not believe in hell or an afterlife.

By the end of the 1980s Smith had replaced Samuel Currin as chairman of the SBC's PAC. Under the former Alabama congressman's leadership in 1990 the PAC gave its "Religious Liberty Award" to Senator Jesse Helms, the ultraconservative North Carolina senator who was a lifelong Southern Baptist. In 1991, when the PAC was absorbed by the Christian Life Commission at the Atlanta convention, Smith made the final report of the PAC, urging Southern Baptists to "wake up to the fact we have the responsibility to be salt and light in all facets of life. We should be active in the political arena." Soon after that he attacked secular humanism and called upon the public schools to resume "value setting."[40] By "value setting" Smith presumably meant teaching fundamentalist Christianity.

Ronald Reagan and George Bush, the two Republican presidents of the 1980s, were usually great favorites of Southern Baptist fundamentalists. Reagan's popularity never faltered with them, but Bush did stumble at one juncture. Apparently Bush initiated the idea of his speaking to the convention at New Orleans in 1990 but later backed away after being criticized in Southern Baptist fundamentalist circles for his recognition of gay and lesbian groups and for having them at the White House. A few Southern Baptist leaders suggested "disinviting" the president to speak to the convention, and Richard Land, as director of the Christian Life Commission, wrote the president a letter on April 30, 1991, and said, "The White House should not be giving its sanction and implicit approval to such groups."[41]

Because of the fundamentalist crusade to seize the SBC holy land and destroy the liberalism that fundamentalists believed had corrupted it, Southern Baptists became, for the first time in their denominational lives, directly involved in secular politics. The politics of choice among the fundamentalist crusaders were unmistakably right-wing in orientation, sometimes far right-wing. Although Paige Patterson denied it, this issue became a serious one between moderates and fundamentalists. Fundamentalists found right-wing political groups more attuned to their highly conservative social and political views (which went along with their highly conservative theological views) and gravitated toward the Republican party, which was led during the 1980s by two avowedly conservative presidents.

Some moderates regarded Reagan, Bush, and their supporters as extremists who held rigid positions and appeared not to know the meaning of the word "flexibility," a word moderates cherished and lived by. They wanted no part of political figures they regarded as reactionary, and fundamentalists were just as opposed to politicians with "liberal" views as they were to theologians and denominational officials who held "liberal" views. The moderates adamantly opposed the Convention's shift to the political right, and the fundamentalists just as adamantly, perhaps more adamantly, insisted upon it. In assessing Southern Baptist ties with the NRPR, Ellen Rosenberg has written, "The New Right is like the Old Left; tolerance and democracy are not on their agenda." Historian Richard Hofstadter once wrote of the right that it "tolerates no compromises, accepts no half measures, understands no defeats." When interviewed by the author in 1988, Alan Neely indicated that he viewed the right in exactly the same way as Hofstadter and Rosenberg. He called right-wingers "extremists," and he was appalled that they were in power in Washington and that their religious counterparts were in power in Nashville.[42]

In the beginning, the rallying cry of Southern Baptist fundamentalist crusaders was biblical inerrancy, but in just a few years it became obvious that nonfundamentalist Southern Baptists could incur the disapproval of the new fundamentalist leaders in ways other than rejecting inerrancy. They could do it just as quickly by being prochoice on the abortion issue, by advocating that women be ordained as deacons and ministers, by failing to report the news in a way that flattered fundamentalist efforts, and by not supporting the right-wing political agenda of the incumbent Republican presidents and the network known as NRPR. The term *liberal* was constantly redefined and expanded by the fundamentalists until many who held conservative theological views, even some who believed in inerrancy, were tarred with the liberal brush because they were inclined to be flexible on social and political issues and did not applaud the entire fundamentalist agenda.

9

After New Orleans

The Crusaders Consolidate Their Power, 1990–1991

IF THERE HAD been any doubt before the New Orleans convention in 1990 that the fundamentalists were in control of the SBC, all doubt was removed during that annual meeting and the months following it. Fully in charge after a bitter conflict of more than a decade, the new leaders moved to consolidate their power. Those who stood in the way of the fundamentalists' implementing their agenda were silenced or removed. Al Shackleford and Dan Martin, the two journalists who believed that they were simply doing their job and doing it in an unbiased manner, were the first upon whom the axe fell as the fundamentalists moved to oust their perceived enemies. Then Lloyd Elder was forced out at the Sunday School Board, and James Draper was chosen as his successor. Harold Bennett, though not forced out, announced his retirement as president of the EC, and Morris Chapman was elected in his place. Throughout 1990 and 1991 fundamentalist pressure was brought to bear more and more on Keith Parks, and early in 1992 he gave up the struggle and announced his early retirement. While many moderates and moderate sympathizers remained as employees of the SBC in lower level positions and a few upper level ones, most of the important and strategic agencies were headed by fundamentalists at the end of 1991.

Writing in 1991, James Hefley aptly summed up what had happened to that point:

> The first stage in the [conservative] resurgence, which brought control of the boards, is now complete. The second—installation of agency executives who will incorporate the renewal into teaching, publications and programs—is well under way. The third stage—extending the renewal into state conventions, associations and local churches—is also in process and will accelerate as greater change comes to national agencies. This will take many years.
>
> Conservative board policy in agencies and institutions, for the most

part, has been not to fire, but to wait for resignations and retirements. The most notable firings to date have been at Baptist Press.[1]

Hefley, of course, failed to note that some of the resignations and retirements were helped along by fundamentalist pressure.

The fundamentalists were unquestionably in charge of America's largest Protestant denomination by mid-1990, and the SBC holy land they had struggled for almost a dozen years to gain was no small domain. There were thirty-six state conventions, 1,208 associations, 37,974 churches, and 15,044,413 recorded members that, collectively, made up the Convention. The denominational agencies consisted of the seventy-seven-member Executive Committee, four general boards, eight institutions, seven commissions, and four associated organizations, although ties with one of the associated organizations—the Baptist Joint Committee on Public Affairs—would be severed the following year, and an acrimonious quarrel would break out with another—the Woman's Missionary Union. Not to be overlooked, too, was the fact that Southern Baptists contributed nearly $4.6 billion in 1990 (nearly 365 million of it being channeled through the Cooperative Program), and the property owned by the Convention and its affiliated churches was worth nearly $22.5 billion. The SBC holy land was a huge religious empire.[2]

What had happened to it during the years between 1979 and 1990 was that its fundamentalist members and moderate members had experienced a reversal of roles. As more than one observer noted in the latter stages of the conflict, those who had led the denomination for so long—the moderates—were on the outside looking in, while those who had been largely excluded from the decision-making process—the fundamentalists—were in a dominant position. Some Alabama Baptists representing both parties described what had taken place, but their perceptions were entirely different. Looking back on the 1979 convention and before, Fred Wolfe said, "I felt we always went to the convention 4,000 votes down, and that we were always going to lose. I'm sitting here today amazed at how quickly and decisively things have changed."[3]

Wolfe, of course, was delighted with the change, but the moderates were appalled and crestfallen. George Bagley, who retired as executive secretary-treasurer of the Alabama Baptist Convention in 1984, said that no one "realized that they [the fundamentalists] could pack the convention, bus people in, and control the vote." Like others, he had thought the movement would "run its course in a couple of years and would swing back." By September 1991 he had concluded that it was not going to swing back. Bagley denied that moderates had ever sought to control the agencies or politicize the presidency of the Convention. "We never tried to pack boards," he asserted. Howard Reaves, former pastor of Mobile's First Baptist Church, and Lamar Jackson, former pastor of Southside Baptist Church in Birmingham, agreed with Bagley, but Wolfe, along with Birmingham pastor Doug Sager, insisted that an insider, good-old-boy network of "liberals" made the decisions in the SBC before 1979.[4] By 1991 there was a new network of decision makers, and the people who comprised it had little intention of including moderates.

Many Southern Baptist fundamentalists had remained in the SBC for years when theirs was a minority voice. Some had left, becoming independents and maintaining fellowship with an informal network of fundamentalists. Those who remained were not at ease in Zion, as they griped and criticized and longed for the day when the Convention would alter its course and take a direction more in line with their views. At last their patience and long-suffering had paid off. Would the ousted moderates follow a similar course and become the loyal, albeit disgruntled, opposition? The answer to that question was obvious immediately after the New Orleans convention, when moderate leaders issued a call for a "national consultation" to be held at Atlanta in August 1990.

As noted in a previous chapter, that meeting at Atlanta in August suggested that a new denomination was in the making. Dan Vestal, the moderate who had been defeated for the SBC presidency by Morris Chapman in New Orleans, called the meeting, declaring that "many of us" left New Orleans "crushed in spirit." He implied that his patience was exhausted when he said that he had not left the SBC; instead the SBC had left him. The primary purpose of the Atlanta meeting was that of finding ways to provide financial support for SBC agencies not under the control of the fundamentalists and to withhold money from those that were. In other words, the moderates wanted to designate their contributions in such a way as to bypass the fundamentalist-dominated EC, which designed the denomination's budget. The word was out that a host of Texas churches were inclined to take action, including the First Baptist Church of Midland, which had given more than one million dollars through the CP in 1989—more than any other Southern Baptist church. Its pastor, James Denison, went to the Atlanta meeting "with an open mind." Churches from all over Texas —Waco, Plano, Amarillo, San Angelo, Dallas, and San Antonio—moved to designate their gifts or to hold them in escrow. Thirty-one churches in North Carolina announced that they were excluding some SBC agencies from their giving, and the number was growing. Similar developments occurred in Virginia.[5]

When the number attending the meeting swelled from an expected five hundred to over three thousand, questions naturally arose as to whether or not a new denomination was in formation. Dan Vestal did not clear the matter up by saying, "We are not out to create a new denomination. We are not out to reconcile with fundamentalists." A Columbia, South Carolina, moderate pastor named Marlon Aldridge implied that he was tired of the struggle and wanted out. He said, "The fundamentalists will do whatever they want, whenever they want, however they want without any concern for . . . moderates." Until the New Orleans convention and the firings at Baptist Press he had thought something could be done about the SBC power structure, but by the time of the Atlanta meeting he had come to realize "that's a fantasy." He apparently thought the "national consultation" might find a way out.

Former SBC president Jimmy Allen chaired the meeting, for which 3,155 registered. Out of the deliberations in Atlanta came "an alternative funding mechanism" called the Baptist Cooperative Mission Program, which was to receive designated funds from individuals, churches, and state conventions. Those funds were to be sent to designated SBC agencies or institutions and even to non-Baptist entities. An interim steering committee of about sixty people was established to administer the vehicle and to devise plans for the future based on suggestions made at the meeting. Those who took a leading role, either as members of the interim steering committee or as members of the BCMP board of directors, made up a list that sounded like a who's who of the moderate leadership—Dan Vestal, Duke McCall, Randall Lolley, Grady Cothen, Carolyn Weatherford Crumpler, Steve Tondera, John Baugh, Larry Baker, Foy Valentine, and Darold Morgan, former president of the SBC Annuity Board. The only sitting SBC agency head present at the meeting in Atlanta was Keith Parks.[6]

Parks apparently left Atlanta fearing that there would be a split in the Convention, a prospect that would not bode well for the work of the FMB over which he presided. He soon expressed alarm and appealed for "dialogue" and continued support of the CP. SBC president Morris Chapman was quoted as saying that the moderates had made it clear that they had "no desire to cooperate with mainstream Southern Baptists." He viewed the "consultation" as the first step toward withdrawal from the Convention and said that the impetus for dialogue would have to come from the moderates. Dan Vestal responded, saying he had "been dialoguing for 12 years" in order to promote reconciliation, but it could not be achieved without a willingness on the part of the fundamentalists to allow the moderates to share in decision making. He alleged that the fundamentalists did not want the moderates, only their money. He also contended that the moderates could no longer use the CP in good conscience as a mechanism to support God's work because the fundamentalists had a stranglehold on it and denied the moderates a voice. The moderates fully intended, through the new funding mechanism they established in Atlanta, to make sure that none of their gifts went to the Executive Committee, the Christian Life Commission, the Public Affairs Committee, and Southeastern Seminary.[7]

The Woman's Missionary Union was not long in putting its stamp of approval on the moderates' alternative funding mechanism. On September 22, 1990, the WMU held an executive board meeting in Richmond, Virginia, and approved mission donation programs that might bypass the CP. Dellana O'Brien, the WMU's executive director, said, "We affirm the right of individuals, churches, and state conventions to choose other plans for cooperative mission giving." The national executive director, all state executive directors, national leaders like former presidents Christine Gregory and Dorothy Sample, and former national executive directors Alma Hunt and Carolyn Weatherford Crumpler enthusiastically endorsed the action of the executive board. O'Brien denied that the WMU was involved in the SBC controversy and expressed regret for any appearance of such involvement.[8] The WMU action, which fundamentalists interpreted as that organization's endorsement of alternative funding by the moderates, was actually an attempt to straddle the fence, even if many prominent women in the organization did sympathize with the moderates. WMU wanted all missionary activity funded and did not want to lose the contributions of either faction. The organization's leaders apparently shared Keith Parks's apprehensions.

The prospect of losing moderate money had a sobering effect on the fundamentalists. At its September 1990 meeting the EC rallied to the support of the CP by adopting a resolution calling for cooperation from all Southern Baptists. Keith Parks warned that cooperation could not be brought about by passing resolutions. He said that trust had to be restored in the SBC. The other agency heads present endorsed the resolution.[9] Parks's warning apparently was ignored.

Atlanta was just the beginning for the moderates. During a series of meetings in 1991 and on into 1992 they took steps that appeared to be leading toward the creation of a new denomination. By the end of 1991 they had already formed a quasi-denomination that had all the earmarks of the Methodists within the Anglican Church during the late eighteenth century (before the Methodists formally broke away and established their own separate church). Even so, whether the moderates would take the final step remained to be seen. In March 1991 the steering committee, named seven months earlier in Atlanta, formed the "Baptist Fellowship" and called it a "loose coalition" of moderate Baptists. That action was expected to receive a favorable vote at the next moderate convocation scheduled for Atlanta on May 9–11, 1991, and it did, with slight modifications. At the May convocation over six thousand moderates voted on a new constitution and bylaws that formally established the Cooperative Baptist Fellowship. Still, moderates denied that they were laying the groundwork for a new denomination. As of that time only two hundred churches were redirecting their gifts from the CP to the CBF mechanism, but the new organization certainly looked like a denomination in the making. John Hewett was elected moderator, or presiding officer. Earlier he had been quoted as saying that the New Orleans convention "spelled the end of efforts to fight the fundamentalist movement in the convention," for he saw no sign that the fundamentalists would ever "be more inclusive."[10]

Among those present for the May convocation was Timothy George, the conservative dean of Samford University's Beeson Divinity School. Although many identified George with the fundamentalist cause, he professed to be neutral, and he attended the Atlanta meeting strictly as an observer. His observations caused him to conclude that the moderate group constituted a new denomination, but he noted that those present were divided between "eager beavers" and "reluctant campers"—those who wished to break away completely and those who wished to remain at least "emotionally tied" to the SBC. He believed that most moderates would remain in the SBC. Even so, he contended that the new Cooperative Baptist Fellowship was the "third major split from the Southern Baptist tradition since 1900." The other two were the Landmark Baptists, who established a separate body, and Frank Norris's followers, many of whom opted for independence. Agreeing with George that the CBF looked like a new denomination was R. Albert Mohler, Jr., the young man who had replaced Jack Harwell as editor of the *Christian Index* and who would, before very long, be named Roy Honeycutt's successor as president of Southern Seminary.[11]

Also attending the May convocation in Atlanta was the outspoken moderate president of Baylor University, Herbert Reynolds. In an interview some time after the meeting he made comments implying that the CBF might become a new denomination. He asserted that the SBC would never again be the same, since the fundamentalists were "firmly in control" and would be for at least twenty to twenty-five years. Even though Reynolds refused to say forthrightly that a new denomination would come out of the CBF, he remarked, "I think we can come up with something that could become the permanent home for about half the Baptist people—maybe even a larger percentage than that." He went on to say that he favored a "centrist" course, but did not explain what he meant. At the same time, however, he affirmed that Baylor was proceeding with plans to establish the George W. Truett Theological Seminary in case the six SBC seminaries began teaching ideas that were out of harmony "with our history, our heritage, and historic Baptist principles."[12]

Little was said in Atlanta to indicate that the moderates would ever again make common cause with the fundamentalists. One speaker, Jim Johnson, pastor of the First Baptist Church of Sarasota, Florida, spoke very disparagingly of the soon-to-be-held 1991 meeting of the SBC in Atlanta, a meeting that featured

George Bush and Oliver North on the program. Johnson said, "That segment of Baptists will be here for a group think-session in a couple of weeks, and pretend that the earth is flat, that women exist for birthing babies and satisfying their men, that pablum prayers will stem the tide of secularism, and that God is a white, Anglo-Saxon, Protestant, card-carrying Republican who must surely look a bit like Oliver North."[13]

A few weeks after CBF's Atlanta convocation, Baptists Committed to the Southern Baptist Convention, heretofore the largest moderate opposition group, disbanded on June 1 and became part of the CBF. The Southern Baptist Alliance, on the other hand, announced its intention to continue as a separate organization, but promised to work in cooperation with the CBF. During the following year the SBA would drop "Southern" from its name and choose the new designation of Alliance of Baptists.[14]

The chasm between moderates and fundamentalists widened further in the summer of 1991 when a group of the former, reacting against the strict conservative stance of the Christian Life Commission, announced on July 30 the formation of the Baptist Center for Ethics in Nashville. The new BCE was to fill "a vacuum in Southern Baptist life." Robert M. Parham resigned as associate director of the CLC to become director of the BCE. It was announced that the BCE would be an "ethics resource" for Southern Baptists and that its agenda would include issues like hunger, substance abuse, racism, and so forth. It was hoped that the BCE could eventually establish a relationship with the CBF, but for the time being the new organization would seek contributions from churches and individuals to pay its way. A twenty-one-member board was formed to guide the BCE's positions on policies and issues. The board consisted of Nancy Ammerman, Emory sociologist and author of several studies dealing with the SBC controversy, Carolyn Weatherford Crumpler, Bill Sherman, and eighteen others identified with the moderate cause.[15]

Two months after the creation of the BCE, in September 1991, the CBF took a momentous step by announcing that it would search for a full-time coordinator. James Slatton was named chairman of the search committee, which set a November 1 deadline for applications. When hired, the coordinator would serve the CBF as chief executive officer and would be responsible for the "advocacy of the CBF and its missions and for the management of the CBF office." He or she would report to the administrative committee of the CBF's coordinating council. Slatton noted that his committee was in search of a person "with extensive experience in Baptist causes in the United States." That search ended with the appointment early in 1992 of Cecil Sherman who was then serving as pastor of the Broadway Baptist Church in Fort Worth, Texas. Sherman, who was sixty-four years of age, was hired at a salary "not to exceed $100,000 per year." He was required to move to Atlanta, where the CBF maintained its headquarters.[16]

The CBF publicly announced that its mission was "to lead people to a saving knowledge of Jesus Christ and to carry out the Great Commission by an inclusive global mission in which all Baptists can participate." *Inclusive* was the key word, of course. One CBF pastor, Charles Wade of Arlington, Texas, said: "We just want to do the work of God with whatever group [that] wants to work with us." Among the causes for which the CBF announced support were some SBC agencies, including the Foreign and Home Mission boards, in addition to Ruschlikon Baptist Theological Seminary in Switzerland and Associated Baptist Press.[17]

Within a few months of the founding of the CBF numerous disenchanted Southern Baptist missionaries contacted moderator John Hewett to ask if they could "switch over" to the Fellowship's sponsorship and support. Hewett declared that those who had inquired were not "liberals who deny the Scriptures" but "God-called Christian ministers." By the time these inquiries were made, Keith Parks was moving steadily toward a showdown with his board of trustees, and Hewett held out the possibility of the CBF's hiring Parks if he became available. "If Dr. Parks wants to continue to shape a Baptist mission force in the world, he can certainly do that with Cooperative Baptist Fellowship," Hewett was quoted as saying.[18]

As 1991 faded into 1992 the CBF picked up momentum. In the spring of the latter year the organization held a three-day general assembly in Fort Worth, Texas. Three thousand people attended. By then 950 churches (almost five times as many as the previous year) were sending funds through the CBF. Still there was no admission that the organization was a new denomination. Bill Leonard, moderate spokesman and author of a book on the SBC controversy, claimed that CBF supporters were "living between the times," having "one foot in the old SBC . . . and another foot thrashing around for some solid ground, some hope and vision for the future." Hewett, who was completing his term as moderator, called the CBF an "enduring" organization, but said he did not know if it would take the shape of a "convention."[19]

Fundamentalist leaders in the SBC were upset with the moderates for founding the CBF, but they appeared to believe that the damage to the SBC— even if the churches supporting the CBF withdrew—would not be great. SBC president Morris Chapman asserted that a "funding program designed to go around the Cooperative Program" was "unacceptable to mainstream Southern Baptists." He warned that it might well "lead to a permanent break from the convention." HMB president Larry Lewis called the CBF "the Uncooperative

Program," but said that it posed no serious threat to the CP. Paige Patterson predicted that not more than five hundred churches would leave the SBC for a new denomination and that maybe two or three hundred more would dually align with the two denominations. He argued that the CP would not lose more than 10 percent of its contributions and that "conservative churches" would make up the losses by "giving around the state conventions and directly to the national convention." By the end of 1992 Morris Chapman, then in a new position as president of the Executive Committee, would invite the CBF to withdraw from the SBC, because that organization was "a denomination in the making."[20]

In spite of moderate actions that threatened to reduce SBC income and possibly split the Convention, fundamentalists proceeded with their agenda, stubbornly refusing to make any concessions to the fed-up moderates. The fundamentalists continued to consolidate their power and to attack head-on what they regarded as liberalism. There was no indication at any time during 1991 that the fundamentalists intended to budge on a single issue. Nor did 1992 bring any change in attitude or action. In the spring of 1991 former SBC president Jerry Vines nominated Paige Patterson for the presidency of the Sunday School Board. Although James Draper, and not Patterson, received the appointment, it is noteworthy that the position, with all its prestige and power, remained in fundamentalist hands. Fundamentalists were clearly in control, and they all but taunted the moderates and dared them to do something about it. Two months before the Atlanta convention and one month before the moderate meeting in Atlanta at which the CBF was formally established, Morris Chapman said that the moderates had chosen to "disassociate themselves" from the majority of Southern Baptists, that they had not (as they had alleged) been driven out, and that they had "no one to blame but themselves." He claimed that their organization would come to "an uneventful end." After the creation of the CBF Chapman said he believed in local autonomy, the priesthood of the believer, and that "each Southern Baptist is free to make his or her own choice." What he meant, however, was that those who did not believe certain doctrines, particularly that the Bible was "God's perfect Word," could choose to leave the SBC. He said that the CBF was not a split, but more like "a splinter, even if they choose to leave." He observed that only about 125 churches out of nearly 38,000 would depart.[21]

The 1991 SBC meeting in Atlanta demonstrated that the fundamentalists had little regard for the concerns of moderates. It resembled a conservative political rally more than a convention for doing a religious denomination's annual business. Patriotism was a major theme. Among the featured speakers were President George Bush, Oliver North, a key figure in the Iran-Contra scandal, and Charles Colson, a convicted felon from the Watergate scandal of the mid-1970s. Bush shed tears during his speech as he reiterated his support for a voluntary public school prayer amendment to the Constitution, parents' rights in choosing their children's schools, and a bill to provide tax vouchers for parents who wished to send their children to private religious schools. Rumors circulated that Oliver North was being paid $20,000 to $25,000 for speaking. Tim La-Haye addressed the Pastors' Conference and called on Christians to become more involved in political affairs. He condemned the public schools as sources of deception and called for more churches to start Christian schools. Jerry Falwell appeared "unexpectedly" at the Pastor's Conference. He was introduced as a "Southern Baptist who just doesn't know it," and was asked to speak, despite the fact that he was not on the program. The scheduled events prompted one speaker to remark, "I have never spoken to a Republican convention before."

It was a heady experience for the fundamentalist leaders and apparently most of the messengers, too, but not for all. Charles Hannah, a high school English teacher from Opelika, Alabama, wrote to the *Alabama Baptist* and condemned the Atlanta convention as "a political pep rally." He called the "slashing comments" by Bush, North, and LaHaye on public education "particularly uninformed and upsetting." The son of a Southern Baptist minister and lifelong Southern Baptist himself, Hannah concluded, "If the convention leaders and the boards of trustees who have replaced honest scholarship and debate with Orwellian control in our convention, at our colleges, and at our seminaries represent a true majority of our convention, then they have created a new denomination perversely different from the one which raised me. This convention has made me feel as if I were an alien in my own home. I pray I am not alone in opposing the destruction of our denomination." The Opelika English teacher was undoubtedly in a minority at the Atlanta convention, but he was not alone in opposing what happened there. Wilder E. Barnes of Decatur, Alabama, condemned North's convention speech, calling him an "unrepentant criminal" who did not "know right from wrong."[22]

Besides tying the annual convention to secular politics in an unprecedented way, the fundamentalists proceeded to pass numerous resolutions on human sexuality, abortion, and religious freedom that were sure to antagonize many moderates. Premarital sex and homosexuality were condemned outright. An antiabortion resolution allowing for abortion only to save the life of the mother passed. Also, a resolution condemning the United States Supreme Court for a decision purportedly infringing on religious freedom and another resolution attacking the National Endowment of the Arts for supporting obscene and offensive art were adopted. The fundamentalist majority further amended Bylaw 16 so that moderates would have almost insurmountable difficulty in substituting nominees for those submitted to the Convention by the Committee on Nominations, and they *totally* defunded the Baptist Joint Committee on Public Affairs.[23]

The fundamentalists were in charge, and they made that point with an exclamation mark in Atlanta.

At that convention Paul Pressler ended seven years on the SBC's Executive Committee. Soon afterward the judge announced that he would not seek reelection in 1992 to the Fourteenth Court of Appeals, saying he wanted to spend more time with his family and "follow other pursuits." If anyone jumped to the conclusion that the judge regarded his work in the SBC as done and that he would quietly fade from the scene, that person was sadly mistaken. In less than a year Pressler would be nominated as a trustee on the Foreign Mission Board, an action that produced an outcry from moderate quarters. Also in July 1991 the trustees of the Sunday School Board met and elected James Draper to become the eighth president of the BSSB. A unanimous vote was prevented by the abstention of Memphis dentist Leon Bolton, who had some questions about Draper's management skills. Upon election Draper noted that he had a "high view of Scripture" but would not require a writer of literature for the BSSB to be an avowed inerrantist as long as the writer was comfortable with words like "God-breathed," "perfect," or "infallible" as descriptive terms for the Bible. "We are people who believe the Bible," Draper proudly stated.[24]

As the summer of 1991 moved into fall, the fundamentalist juggernaut moved relentlessly forward. In June the Convention had already taken all funds away from the BJC, and at its September meeting the EC voted to terminate SBC participation in that committee's activities. The door was left open, however, for Richard Land and the CLC to relate to the committee "in any manner it may deem appropriate." It is unlikely that James Dunn expected to hear from Land anytime soon. Later in 1991, at Southeastern Seminary's October board meeting, that institution's trustees voted to include a commitment to biblical inerrancy in the school's new statement of purpose, thus becoming the first SBC seminary to adopt an explicit endorsement of inerrancy. Much of the business at that meeting was conducted behind closed doors. The board also "tentatively" approved a "faculty profile" requiring all new teachers to affirm their belief in inerrancy. All of this was done in the face of the faculty's being reduced to about half its former size "by a rash of recent resignations and retirements."[25]

An opportunity for the fundamentalists to gain an even tighter grip on the SBC came late in 1991 when Harold Bennett, president of the EC, announced his retirement effective the following year. There was no evidence that Bennett was forced out or even that he left because of disenchantment with fundamentalist iron-handedness. It appears that he somehow maintained a neutral stance throughout the controversy and left in almost everybody's good graces. The EC was not long in finding his successor. A search committee chaired by Julian Motley, a pastor from Durham, North Carolina, had a recommendation for the

EC when it met for its regular meeting in February 1992. The person recommended was Morris Chapman, who had been reelected president in Atlanta
without opposition. Paige Patterson was the search committee's second choice.
Elected unanimously for the job, which paid $120,000 per year in addition to a
housing allowance, Chapman said, "I'm trusting God will bring spiritual awakening through Southern Baptists to this nation." It was announced at the same
meeting that the SBC had experienced in the past year a growth in membership
of 1.3 percent, bringing the total number in the Convention to 15.2 million.[26]

The fundamentalists were in position to do whatever they wanted. All that
the moderates who had any fight left in them could do was criticize, and an
occasion to do that presented itself late in 1991. In October the trustees of the
Foreign Mission Board voted thirty-five to twenty-eight to withdraw the FMB's
1992 contribution from the budget of the Baptist Theological Seminary in
Ruschlikon, Switzerland, because the trustees disagreed with the seminary's
"theological stance." The FMB had agreed in 1978 to fund the seminary
through 1992, allocating $365,000 annually to it. That action was reaffirmed in
1988. Keith Parks urged the trustees to honor their commitment, but they declined, citing the seminary's persistence in pursuing a "liberal direction" as jus-
tification for the withdrawal of support. In particular the trustees disapproved
of the seminary's allowing Professor Glenn Hinson (still with Southern Seminary but not for long) to teach at Ruschlikon for four months while he was on
sabbatical. California trustee Ron Wilson declared that the trustees viewed Hinson as one who held "liberal views of Scripture," while Hinson insisted that he
was not a liberal. European Baptist leaders were dismayed and said that the
withdrawal of funding would hamper future relationships with the FMB. Statements opposing the "breach of trust" were soon forthcoming from Germany,
England, France, Italy, Finland, and Norway. Trustee Wilson defended the defunding, arguing that it would restore the "Southern Baptist Conservatives'
confidence" in the FMB.[27]

A storm of protest followed the defunding decision. A month after its announcement the various state conventions held their annual meetings. Messengers in at least nine states and the District of Columbia adopted resolutions opposing the FMB's decision and urged that it be reconsidered. Virginia Baptists
went a step further, approving $100,000 for the school if the FMB's decision was
not reversed. North Carolina Baptists voted to send $30,000 immediately. In Ar-
kansas a motion of support for the seminary was defeated. Twice in Louisiana
maneuvers to forestall a resolution of support for the seminary were defeated
before that convention finally passed such a resolution. Two attempts were made
in the Georgia Baptist Convention to divert funds to Ruschlikon, but they were

ruled out of order by convention officers on the advice of the parliamentarian. So much flack was generated by the defunding decision that Bill Hancock of Kentucky, chairman of the FMB's board of trustees, called a meeting for December 5–6, 1991, to allow leaders from Europe and the United States to air their views. That action was followed by a decision to mail out forty thousand copies of a ten-page letter to explain the decision. All pastors, state conventions, Baptist journals, and people who contacted the FMB on Ruschlikon's behalf were sent a copy. The letter explained that the seminary's hiring Glenn Hinson for a brief teaching stint was only the latest in a long line of events that proved to the trustees that the institution was too liberal and too expensive.[28]

At the meeting called by Hancock for December 5–6 a committee of the FMB discussed the matter with Karl Heinz Walter, general secretary of the European Baptist Federation, Wiard Popkes, chairman of Ruschlikon's trustees, and John David Hopper, Ruschlikon's missionary president. Hancock offered to recommend to the full FMB restoration of the $365,000 for 1992 provided that (1) European Baptist leaders agreed to "acknowledge their insensitivity to the conservative concerns," (2) they alerted FMB trustees in advance of the selection of professors to teach there, and (3) they accounted for funds received from American sources other than the FMB. Walter and Popkes declined to accept the terms, and the committee voted thirteen to ten not to recommend restoration of the $365,000 when all the trustees would meet a few days later. Popkes noted that European Baptists feared involvement with "militant fundamentalism" because it reminded them of the situation they had recently rid themselves of in "some of the communist countries." Morris Chapman bristled at that remark and sharply replied that such fears misrepresented all Southern Baptists about whom he knew anything. Paige Patterson also took offense. He denied that the trustees were asking anybody to "walk in lock step with us." Even so, he contended that Southern Baptists could not be expected to "support those things that call into question the veracity and truthfulness of the Word of God."[29]

Moderator John Hewett of the Cooperative Baptist Fellowship responded to the defunding of Ruschlikon Seminary with a scathing attack. He asserted:

The trustees have broken a covenant with European Baptists. They have broken faith with Southern Baptists.

Against the recommendations of (FMB) President Keith Parks and the entire European staff, despite the protests of Woman's Missionary Union and thousands of mission-minded Southern Baptist churches, and with utter contempt for the sensitivities of European Baptist leaders, they've let the political agenda of Presslerism overrule common sense and negate solemn oaths. They've set Baptist work in Europe back 45 years.

Hewett called for all "free and faithful" Baptists to restore the $365,000 taken away from Ruschlikon by funneling gifts to the seminary through the CBF's office in Atlanta. Gifts soon began arriving daily. On January 11, 1992, the coordinating council of the CBF offered to fund Southern Baptist missionaries in Europe "who resign from the Foreign Mission Board." The motion to take that action was made by Cecil Sherman, who would soon become CBF's coordinator. Hewett denied that CBF's action was tantamount to announcing itself as a new denomination. He claimed the decision should be compared to parachurch organizations that supported missions work.[30]

The defunding of Ruschlikon by the FMB trustees not only brought strong protests from moderates, it put the board and its president, Keith Parks, on a collision course. When two key FMB administrators, G. Keith Parker and Isam Ballenger, announced their resignations in the wake of that decision, Parks lamented their decision, calling their resignations an "incalculable loss to our mission cause." The trustees, on the other hand, moved to send Parker and Ballenger immediately on their way. Trustee Ron Wilson, who had introduced the motion to defund Ruschlikon, spoke disparagingly of Parks. He said the president did not have to agree with the board, but he did have to carry out its decisions. He noted that for "some reason" Parks had "chosen to go with the liberals." Wilson added that "conservatives" had been disturbed about Ruschlikon for many years and were finally doing something about it, now that they were in the majority on the board.[31]

As early as February 1992 it became obvious that some FMB trustees would push to move up Parks's retirement from the presidency. Rancor precipitated by the defunding decision lingered, and at a retreat held behind closed doors on March 19–20 in a hotel near the Dallas-Fort Worth airport (attended by seventy-eight trustees and twelve FMB staff members), Parks announced that he was moving up his retirement date from 1995 to October 1992. He said he would make an official announcement of his decision at the April board meeting.[32] Another denominational leader, and a very important one, who had resisted the fundamentalist agenda had been squeezed out of office.

The fundamentalists paid a heavy price financially for forcing Parks out. In response to Parks's "retirement," Baptist philanthropist J. Harwood Cochrane wrote the FMB out of his will, a decision which deprived the board of an inheritance amounting to tens of millions of dollars. Cochrane and his wife, Louise, had already given the board $9,000,000, and it was estimated that they would leave it $30,000,000 more at their deaths. The seventy-nine-year-old Baptist millionaire was a member of the Tabernacle Baptist Church in Richmond, Virginia. He hinted that he might support the CBF, but that he was not enthusiastic about it. He was sure of one thing; he would no longer support the FMB because its trustees were trying "to recycle everyone and make a fundamentalist out of them." He added, "I don't like it a bit."[33]

Even though the fundamentalists were in complete control of the SBC and charged ahead, sometimes to their detriment, in 1991, there was some evidence of dissension in their ranks. Leading crusader Paige Patterson was fired as president of Criswell College on October 28, 1991, ostensibly for spending too much time and energy on SBC politics to the school's injury. Protests from students and some fundamentalists, along with the resignations of twenty-five members of the school's financially supportive board of regents, led to Patterson's reinstatement. He promised to work on alleviating the concerns of the college's trustees.[34]

Earlier in 1991, on the eve of the SBC annual meeting in Atlanta, there had been another spat among the fundamentalists. A Kansas City layman named Ken Cochran, who managed a Christian radio station, was nominated by the Committee on Nominations as a trustee for Midwestern Seminary. Before the convention, Missouri fundamentalists worked to have Cochran removed from the slate, but top SBC leaders, including Judge Pressler, insisted that he be elected, and he was. Cochran was known to be an outspoken critic of the seminary, having attacked it for liberalism and homosexuality among faculty and staff members. So strong were Cochran's allegations that the school considered taking legal action against him. Bill Dudley, a pastor from Golden, Missouri, condemned Cochran's nomination, saying it played into the hands of "liberals." He charged that Cochran was guilty of child abuse, spouse abuse, assault on a police officer, divorce, and failure to pay child support. Cochran was divorced, and his stepson was taken away from him and put in a foster home, but the embattled nominee denied all other charges. Several other ministers who knew Cochran and his wife confirmed the charges made by Dudley.[35] Although the fundamentalists showed no signs that the quarrels among themselves would severely damage their cause, the squabbles over Patterson and Cochran did indicate that there were some dents, if not chinks, in their armor. Could they maintain a united front and keep the Convention together for as many years as the moderates had, especially if they continued to lose millions of dollars by forcing people like Keith Parks out of the denominational bureaucracy?

There were other ominous signs that the fundamentalist crusaders might stumble in their quest to consolidate their gains. The capital of the holy land, Nashville, was firmly in their grasp, but some of the outlying areas, the state conventions, remained in doubt. In the fall of 1991 four state conventions—Florida, Missouri, South Carolina, and Tennessee—elected presidents identified as fundamentalists or supported by fundamentalists. Arkansas, Louisiana, Maryland, North Carolina, Texas, and Virginia elected presidents identified as or supported by moderates. Georgia reelected its moderate president by the thinnest of margins—50.7 percent of the vote. The moderate candidate in Louisiana won by just 50.9 percent. Only in Arkansas, Florida, Maryland, and Virginia did the elected presidents receive more than 55 percent of the vote. In North Carolina moderate candidate Glen Holt, pastor of the First Baptist Church in Fayetteville, defeated his fundamentalist opponent, Billy Cline of Asheville, by a vote of 2,583 to 2,441—a margin of only 142 votes. Holt had made it clear before the election that he "did not share the views of those who are in leadership of the Southern Baptist Convention at this time." He had gladdened the hearts of moderates when he declared on the eve of the convention, "I am committed to Baptist principles, including a conservative theology, belief in the inspiration and authority of the Bible, a commitment to responsible freedom, support for missions and evangelism, the priesthood of all believers, the importance of the laity, and a recognition that God calls and equips both men and women to serve."[36] Thus the moderates still held important enclaves of power, albeit by narrow margins in some states. When or if the fundamentalists could wrest them away remained to be seen. James Hefley probably conjectured accurately when he said it would take years.

Although by late 1991 it was painfully obvious to most Southern Baptists on both sides that the fundamentalists held the SBC firmly in their grasp, there were a few conciliatory people who still believed the Convention could be brought back together. One of them was country comedian Jerry Clower who announced in the fall of 1991 that he would nominate Jess Moody, pastor of the Shepherd of the Hills Baptist Church in Chatsworth, California, and an avowed neutral in the conflict, for president of the SBC at the 1992 convention in Indianapolis. Clower contended that Moody could "heal the rift" between the two factions, but the California minister stated that he would reluctantly allow his name to be placed in nomination and would "not lift a finger" to help his election prospects. Moody said he was like an old uncle who wanted to stop the family from fighting and bring it back together. He added that he was proud of the fundamentalists for "keeping true to the Word of God" and of the moderates for "keeping true to Baptist polity." He wanted no part of "divorce," however, and called upon the moderates to dismantle organizations like the CBF that could lead to a new denomination. Moody indicated early that he would bow out if there was "no groundswell" for his candidacy. Enthusiasm for his candidacy did not develop, but he remained in the race and won the second highest number of votes. Unfortunately for him and those who wanted to bring the Convention back together, Moody's vote count amounted to less than 22 percent of the total.[37]

After more than a year of almost total fundamentalist control of the SBC, it was not clear how the denomination was bearing up with regard to its finances and to its progress in various areas. Although there was growth, the rate of growth, compared to earlier years, had definitely slowed. Baptisms in 1991 were up 3 percent over 1990, contributions throughout the Convention were up an equal amount, Sunday school enrollment was up just over 2 percent, membership was up slightly more than 1 percent, and the number of churches had grown by less than 1 percent. Cooperative Program receipts were down slightly, as were designated gifts, indicating that the efforts of the CBF were having a deleterious effect on SBC finances.[38] The denomination was certainly not growing at the rate of previous years, but it appeared to be holding its own, even if barely. CBF's negative impact upon SBC finances, though noticeable, appeared to be minimal.

Looking back over 1990 and 1991 it was obvious that the fundamentalist crusaders had won the struggle at the national level and were fully in charge. All moderates had been driven from the seats of power in Nashville or soon would be. They were beaten and they were well aware of it. Many of them, having fought in the trenches for a dozen years, did not even bother to attend the convention in Atlanta. They looked more and more to the CBF to give them opportunities to carry out the mission of Baptists as they understood it. Meanwhile, the fundamentalists, despite a fracas or two among themselves, proceeded to consolidate their power over the SBC. They held firm in pressing their agenda, even in the face of the withdrawal of financial support by the moderates. The denomination showed no serious signs of breaking apart, since less than a thousand churches sent funds to the CBF and many of those churches supported both the CBF *and* the CP.

Epilogue

BY 1992 IT was obvious that the SBC would never be the same again. A preponderance of moderates had given up, and fewer and fewer of them were attending the annual conventions. Another fundamentalist, Edwin Young, pastor of the Second Baptist Church of Houston (a church that gave a meager 2.35 percent of its budget to the CP), won the presidency at the convention in Indianapolis with 62 percent of the vote. One of his opponents was Georgia fundamentalist pastor Nelson Price, who received just over 16 percent of the vote. The two fundamentalist candidates together garnered an impressive 78 percent, while the candidate of reconciliation, Jess Moody, received a mere 21.66 percent. The moderate cause was dead and buried, and the moderates knew it. A meeting resembling a funeral for the cause was held at Mercer University in October 1992. Historian Walter B. Shurden called the meeting, and those who had led the moderate faction were there to lament their defeat and acknowledge the demise of the cause. Cecil Sherman, Alan Neely, James Slatton, Jimmy Allen, Duke McCall, and Dan Vestal were all there, along with many others. Sherman, the first of the moderate leaders, said he had no regrets. "We did not win. But we were right. And we did all we could at the time when it could have made a difference," he was quoted as saying. To preserve the history and memory of their moribund cause, the moderates at the Mercer University meeting formed "The William H. Whitsitt Baptist Heritage Society" and designated the Mercer University Library to house the archives of the Cooperative Baptist Fellowship. Dan Vestal went so far as to suggest that the CBF might become a denomination when it had two thousand participating churches.[1]

What brought on the meeting at Mercer was a 1992 that looked a great deal like 1991, a year in which the fundamentalists had flexed their muscles and demonstrated conclusively that they were in charge and that they would insist upon the implementation of their entire agenda. At its February meeting the EC took a strong stand against homosexuality, after announcements had been made that Pullen Memorial Baptist Church in Raleigh, North Carolina, was considering recognition of a "same-gender union," and Olin T. Binkley Memorial Baptist Church in Chapel Hill, North Carolina, planned to license a homosexual to preach the gospel. Fundamentalists and many moderates as well expressed strong opposition to same-sex marriages and homosexual preachers, but the two churches proceeded with their plans and were read out of their local associations, the North Carolina Baptist Convention, and the SBC. The EC offered changes in the SBC constitution and bylaws at the 1992 SBC meeting to exclude from participation at the annual meetings any churches approving homosexuality. An amendment providing for such exclusion was approved and became part of the constitution in 1993.[2]

More fundamentalist muscle flexing occurred early in 1992 at the Baptist Sunday School Board. Not long after he became the board's president, James Draper nominated Ray Clendenen, chairman of the Old Testament and Hebrew department at Criswell College, to be general editor of *The New American Commentary,* a forty-volume reference work being published by Broadman Press. Clendenen, whose nomination was supported by Paige Patterson, had "impeccable" academic credentials, according to Draper. Robert Sloan, an associate professor of religion at Baylor University, either disagreed with Draper regarding Clendenen's credentials or feared that the reference work would turn into a thoroughgoing fundamentalist commentary, and he resigned as a consulting editor and writer for the project.[3]

Controversy erupted again when Larry Holly went on a crusade against the Masonic Order in the spring of 1992. The Beaumont physician mailed letters to five thousand SBC leaders asking them to take a stand against membership in the Masonic Lodge. His mailout included a fifty-eight-page booklet contending that Freemasonry was of pagan and ultimately satanic origin. Many were appalled by Holly's charges, and one irate Alabama Baptist, Vernon L. Lowe of Lillian, responded to them with the angry words, "That's a lie!" Lowe went on to say that it appeared Southern Baptists had run out of something to fight about and wondered what the SBC had "come to as an organized religion?" At the convention in Indianapolis the matter was referred to the Home Mission Board for study and a possible recommendation at the Houston convention in 1993. Holly expressed his disappointment and said, "I'm just going to pray and trust the Home Mission Board will deal with it."[4]

The 1992 SBC meeting was similar to the meeting in Atlanta the year before. Vice-President Dan Quayle, who would shortly go down to defeat with George Bush in the 1992 election, addressed the messengers on the subject of family values, and his words seemed to please the vast majority of those in attendance. Numerous conservative statements were made and made emphatically by the Convention. The messengers voted to break with the Baptist Joint Committee on Public Affairs finally and entirely. After voting for a constitutional amendment to exclude churches that "affirm, approve, or endorse homosexual behavior," the Convention withdrew fellowship from Pullen Memorial Baptist Church and Olin T. Binkley Memorial Baptist Church, as noted above. Highly conservative resolutions were passed on a number of social issues, and a feeble attempt to prevent Paul Pressler from becoming an FMB trustee was turned back by about a four-to-one vote.

Although the Convention affirmed its "historical relationship" with the WMU at the meeting in Indianapolis, it was noted that there was apprehension concerning the WMU's ties with the CBF. Executive Director Dellana O'Brien regarded the SBC action as a veiled threat and let it be known that the WMU would remain complementary to, and not a part of, the SBC. She noted that the WMU could no longer ignore and remain silent about the SBC controversy because it had had a negative impact on mission work. "It's not WMU's fault that the controversy has changed our convention," she said.[5]

Meanwhile, significant changes were in the making at three of the six seminaries. Russell Dilday, though still president of Southwestern Seminary, was silent—at least publicly—but tensions between him and his board of trustees pulsated beneath the surface. In January 1992 Southwestern's accreditation was renewed by both the Association of Theological Schools and the Southern Association of Colleges and Schools. Like the other five SBC seminaries, Southwestern was losing student enrollment, but Dilday predicted that the Convention's seminaries would not go into decline. In fact, he declared that Southwestern's best days lay in the future, not the past.

By this time the future of Southern Seminary was in grave doubt, as many expected that "something terrible" was coming, perhaps even the demise of the seminary. Roy Honeycutt put the best face he could on the situation, but the end of his presidency was clearly visible on the horizon, as was a fundamentalist overhaul of the Convention's "flagship seminary."

And at Southeastern in 1992 Paige Patterson would be elected president by the board of trustees in May and inaugurated in October. Judge Pressler and Morris Chapman were both present to say what a great day October 12, 1992, was in the life of Southern Baptists.[6] Thus, Southern and Southeastern seminaries, long considered the SBC's most liberal, were on their way to being transformed into fundamentalist citadels of instruction, and the once outspoken moderate president of Southwestern had been silenced.

Perhaps the most glaring sign in 1992 that fundamentalists would settle for nothing short of total victory was that they began to speak openly of taking over the state conventions. Through the efforts of "consensus men" who guided the Alabama Baptist Convention after 1984, Alabama Baptists had largely kept the national fight over inerrancy out of their annual meetings. That promised to change as early as May 1992, when Fred Wolfe announced that a number of "conservative" pastors intended to seek the election of Fred Lackey, a fundamentalist pastor from Athens, because he had "fully supported the Baptist Faith and Message, the SBC's Peace Committee report, and biblical inerrancy." Although Lackey lost, he was defeated by only a handful of votes. That the fundamentalists would try again to win control of the Alabama Baptist Convention was a foregone conclusion.

A few months after the 1992 SBC meeting the fundamentalists met in Memphis and plotted strategy for extending their control over all the state conventions. At the meeting of the Baptist General Convention of Texas that November there was another acrimonious showdown between moderates and fundamentalists, and the moderates prevailed again. Before 1992 ended the Baptist General Association of Virginia appeared on the verge of a split over whether to send part or all of its money to the CBF.[7]

The two years that followed were no better. Edwin Young was reelected president of the SBC in 1993, and there were no signs of any closing of the breach between the two sides. In fact, at times it appeared that they were ignoring each other. The CBF pursued its objectives virtually unnoticed, while the SBC lumbered on. Except for each side's hurling an occasional barb at the other, a moratorium prevailed. That changed on March 9, 1994, when the board of trustees at Southwestern Seminary fired President Russell Dilday, who had been a target of the fundamentalists for a decade. Dilday did not go quietly. His dismissal received a great deal of media attention, being covered thoroughly by the secular press as well as the journals of the state Baptist conventions. The ousted president attended the annual meeting of the SBC in Orlando three months after his firing, and it was reported that his presence was felt.[8]

A month before the Orlando convention the Cooperative Baptist Fellowship held its annual meeting May 5–7 in Greensboro, North Carolina. Because of Dilday's ouster, the moderate group debated a motion to exclude CBF financial support from all Southern Baptist seminaries. The CBF's administrative committee supported the motion, but only about a third of the gathering voted for it. Another proposal, less stringent than the defeated one, did pass. It called upon churches dissatisfied with Southern Baptist seminaries to send their CBF contributions to the group's Vision 2000 budget, which already excluded SBC educational institutions in favor of the CBF's own efforts in theological education. Apparently CBF leaders felt greater alienation from the SBC in the wake of the Dilday firing than did many of the lay people, for Cecil Sherman, the CBF's chief executive, stated in an interview about the time of the Greensboro meeting that the moderates might establish their own denomination. He was quoted as saying: "If the Southern Baptist Convention continues with the same attitude it has displayed in the last year or so, the fellowship will move toward being a convention."[9]

Many who still longed for reconciliation between the moderates and the fundamentalists thought they saw a glimmer of hope as a result of the presidential election at the 1994 SBC in Orlando. Jim Henry, pastor of Orlando's First Baptist Church, won the presidency over Fred Wolfe, who was numbered among the earliest fundamentalist crusaders and who had the endorsement of the SBC's most visible fundamentalist leaders. Some called Henry a moderate and declared that the pendulum was swinging back toward moderation in the Convention. That was hardly the case. The Orlando pastor, a closet fundamentalist from the beginning, had come out of the closet in 1990 to support Morris Chapman's election to the presidency as well as to applaud the Texas pastor's plan to determine the Bible issue once and for all in favor of the inerrancy view. Wolfe had been a weak candidate in 1990 when he withdrew his name from consideration, and he offered no stronger credentials in 1994 than he had four years earlier. Perhaps Henry was more amiable and more gregarious than Wolfe, and he certainly had the advantage of standing for election on his own home ground, but he was no less a fundamentalist than Edwin Young, Morris Chapman, Jerry Vines, Adrian Rogers, James Draper, Charles Stanley, or Bailey Smith. The SBC was still firmly in the grasp of the fundamentalists in the summer of 1994, and their determination to rid the denomination of lingering moderates was dramatically demonstrated in August when President Albert Mohler of Southern Seminary forced Molly Marshall to resign her tenured position as associate professor of Christian theology. Before the month was out Jack Brymer, editor of the *Florida Baptist Witness*, resigned, apparently because of pressure from fundamentalist members of the newspaper's governing board, who criticized Brymer for using stories furnished by Associated Baptist Press. The fundamentalist critics insisted that ABP's releases were slanted in favor of the moderates.[10]

What did it all mean? Counting the failed first crusade and the successful second crusade of the fundamentalists, there had been nearly a quarter of a century of fighting. Throughout those years the fundamentalists asserted that they were out to cleanse the SBC of the liberalism that permeated the Convention's agencies and institutions, particularly its educational institutions, and put the denomination back on the path of theological truth, the linchpin of which was biblical inerrancy. Denying that there was a significant amount of true liberalism in the SBC, moderates insisted that they believed in biblical authority (some of them even in inerrancy) and that the fundamentalists had manufactured a bogus issue to camouflage a bid for political power. There was truth in both contentions. First M. O. Owens, Jr., and William A. Powell, Sr., and later Paul Pressler and Paige Patterson fully intended to seize control of the Convention (Pressler and Patterson's denials to the contrary notwithstanding) in order to put it

on the straight-and-narrow path of biblical inerrancy. There could be no impo-
sition of theological truth without conquest.

The moderate accusation that fundamentalists sought political power over
the Convention was accurate, but the insistence by moderates that the fundamentalists were deceptive in stating their motives is open to grave doubt. In
spite of the fact that Paige Patterson once referred to the "inerrancy thing" in
such a way as to imply that it had been used simply as an emotional rallying
cry[11] and in spite of the fact that there were several kinds of inerrantists, there
is little reason to doubt that the fundamentalists were sincere in their belief
about the doctrine of inerrancy, as they defined it. Their bid for power was undoubtedly rooted in a desire to revamp the SBC according to a fundamentalist
blueprint, but that plan, grandiose as it was, had a theological base. They often
tried to conceal their sweeping designs by claiming that they merely wanted to
return the Convention to the grass-roots Southern Baptists who "believed the
Bible" and to achieve "parity" in hiring seminary professors. In view of what
happened after New Orleans, they obviously had concealed a considerable part
of their plan for the denomination. That the fundamentalists intended a total
overhaul of the SBC was, by 1992, quite clear to the moderates who remained in
the Convention in hopes that the two sides could reconcile and somehow learn
to live and work in harmony.

A surprising number of scholars—anthropologists, historians, philoso-
phers, political scientists, and sociologists—have investigated the Southern Baptist conflict, and a wide variety of interpretations have emerged. The controversy has been viewed as an antibureaucratic movement opposing modern ways
of organizing, a mask to cover racism and sexism, a bid for prestige and respectability, a reaction against modernity, and, of course, an ideological struggle.
While it cannot be denied that economic, political, and social developments fig-
ured prominently in the emergence of the SBC conflict, it was, in the final analysis, "deeply ideological," just as Timothy George has rightly argued. Yet, while
George's explanation concerning the cause of the conflict is correct, many of his
other conclusions about it are suspect, since he ultimately becomes an apologist
for the fundamentalists.

It was the fundamentalists who insisted that their movement was a struggle
on behalf of theological truth; they just did not bother to reveal what else it was
—an effort to promote male control over religion and society by denying women
access to ordination and abortion, a rejection of the time-honored American belief in a free press (at least within the Southern Baptist family), and the promotion of a right-wing political and social agenda. Therefore, the moderates told
the whole story for them, pointing out that the fundamentalist movement was

a power grab carried out by people who employed secular political tactics to promote a religious and social conformity rooted in fundamentalist theological and social dogma. They, too, were right, but they also erred by refusing to admit that the fundamentalists acted out of a genuine desire to return the SBC to the path of theological truth that, they believed, it had abandoned.

One serious flaw in all the studies up to this point has been the failure of those who have examined the conflict to explore fully the movement started by M. O. Owens, Jr., and its connection to the later Pressler-Patterson movement. After all, it was Owens who started the Baptist Faith and Message Fellowship and hired Bill Powell as the editor of that organization's newspaper, *The Southern Baptist Journal*, and it was Powell who first devised the strategy that Pressler and Patterson successfully used in their bid to control the SBC, beginning at Houston in 1979.

In rejoicing over their definitive victory at New Orleans and in proceeding headlong with their agenda, the fundamentalists overlooked the possibility that their program might well doom the SBC in the long run, or certainly drastically reduce it in size. They always argued that the vast majority of Southern Baptists (perhaps 90 percent of them!) believed, as they did, in biblical inerrancy. A survey by Nancy Ammerman in the mid-1980s placed the figure at around 80 percent. While it is conceivable that such a high percentage of Southern Baptists may have believed in some form of inerrancy, probably 60 percent or less were committed to the fundamentalist agenda.

If Ammerman's survey accurately reflected Southern Baptist opinion in 1985, then apparently the number of Southern Baptists believing in inerrancy shrank significantly by 1992. In the spring of that year the Princeton Religion Research Center took a survey that revealed that 60 percent of Southern Baptists, compared with 32 percent of Americans in general, believed the Bible to be the literal word of God. "Only in the South does a plurality of 46 percent of the adult population continue to believe in the literal truth of the Bible," the report of the Princeton survey concluded. Nationally, belief in the Bible as totally reliable had dropped from 65 percent to 32 percent since 1965, and less than 50 percent of the general population in the South believed it in 1992.[12]

If confidence in the Bible was declining, what might happen to an SBC led by fundamentalists who insisted that loyalty to the denomination depended upon a belief in biblical inerrancy? By seizing the SBC holy land the fundamentalists not only drove out those who had guided it for so long, they also insisted upon a dogma that might repel many who might otherwise want to enter the denomination and declare their allegiance to it. The SBC was theirs to lead forward or to saddle with a narrow theological perspective and a reactionary political and social stance. Whether or not they could make it grow and progress as the moderates had for so many years was an open question at the end of 1992.

Two years later the picture would not be much clearer. Paul Pressler, Paige Patterson, Morris Chapman, and other fundamentalist leaders exuded confidence in the SBC's future, while many moderates could see only disaster looming. Others, not quite sure what the future might bring, waited and watched.

The events of 1994—the firing of Russell Dilday at Southwestern Seminary, the opening of the George W. Truett Seminary at Baylor University (which soon appointed Dilday as a faculty member), the announcements that Mercer University and Wake Forest University would establish their own divinity schools, too, and the sudden and unexpected decision of Samford University's board of trustees in September to adopt a new charter making the board self-perpetuating—pointed more clearly than ever toward a lasting division between the fundamentalists and the moderates. On the other hand, those events also indicated that out of the turmoil of nearly a quarter of a century could come good in the form of expanding opportunities. Some of those opportunities could be found even beyond the denomination's boundaries. For example, T. Furman Hewitt, who resigned from the Southeastern Seminary faculty in 1992, became the director of a Baptist-studies program at Duke University. He suggested that Southern Baptist seminaries would not want the kind of students he had at Duke because they would ask questions and cause trouble. Hewitt viewed the Baptist world as "flying apart," but he observed that paradoxically the upheaval was both "tragic" and "healthy."[13]

Church realignments and the establishment of new theological institutions with which the vanquished moderates could be comfortable offered all sorts of possibilities. A small percentage of Southern Baptist churches could turn the Cooperative Baptist Fellowship into a new, fledgling denomination and support the new institutions. On the other hand, the CBF could remain in the SBC as the quasi-denomination it already was, and its moderate supporters could play the role of disgruntled critics, as the fundamentalists did for many years before their ascendance to power beginning in 1979. Since the conflict had spawned new institutions of a moderate bent, there were places for Southern Baptists of both persuasions. If the moderates chose to stay and play the part of the disenchanted, it was conceivable that the rancor that lingered from the conflict might ebb with the passage of time. The events of 1994, however, pointed more toward schism than eventual reconciliation.

Notes

1. SBC Origins and Development to 1979: An Overview

1. James Leo Garrett, Jr., "Who Are the Baptists?" *Baylor Line* 47, no. 3 (June 1985): 11–13; David T. Morgan, "The Great Awakening in North Carolina, 1740–1775: The Baptist Phase," *North Carolina Historical Review* 45, no. 3 (Summer 1968): 267–83.

2. Garrett, "Who Are the Baptists?" 13–14; Walter B. Shurden, "The Erosion of Denominationalism: The Current State of the Southern Baptist Convention," speech delivered at the annual meeting of the South Carolina Baptist Historical Society, November 12, 1984, 3. Copy in Special Collections, Samford University Library, Birmingham, Ala.

3. Grady C. Cothen, *What Happened to the Southern Baptist Convention?* (Macon, Ga.: Smyth & Helwys Publishing, 1993), 54–56; Walter B. Shurden, "The Southern Baptist Synthesis: Is It Cracking?" *Baptist History and Heritage* 16 (April 1981): 5–8.

4. Robert A. Baker, *The Southern Baptist Convention and Its People, 1607–1972* (Nashville: Broadman Press, 1974), 208–19; Garrett, "Who Are the Baptists?" 13–14; James Leo Garrett, Jr., E. Glenn Hinson, and James E. Tull, *Are Southern Baptists Evangelicals?* (Macon, Ga.: Mercer University Press, 1983), 133–34; Gordon H. James, *Inerrancy and the Southern Baptist Convention* (Dallas: Southern Baptist Heritage Press, 1986), 64; H. Leon McBeth, *The Baptist Heritage* (Nashville: Broadman Press, 1987), 447–61.

5. Home Mission Board Report, quoted in William W. Barnes, *The Southern Baptist Convention, 1845–1953* (Nashville: Broadman Press, 1954), 92–93.

6. George M. Marsden, *Understanding Fundamentalism and Evangelicalism* (Grand Rapids, Mich.: Eerdman's, 1991), 36–61 passim; Ernest R. Sandeen, *The Roots of Fundamentalism: British and American Millenarianism, 1800–1930* (Chicago: University of Chicago Press, 1970), ix–xix.

7. John Lee Eighmy, *Churches in Cultural Captivity: A History of the Social Attitudes of Southern Baptists* (Knoxville: University of Tennessee Press, 1989), 9; Robison B. James, ed., *The Takeover in the Southern Baptist Convention: A Brief History* (Decatur, Ga.: SBC Today, 1989), 4–5.

8. Garrett, Hinson, and Tull, *Are Southern Baptists Evangelicals?* 10–12, 99–104.

9. Ibid., 102; George M. Marsden, *Fundamentalism and American Culture* (New York: Oxford University Press, 1980), 160–62; James J. Thompson, *Tried as by Fire: Southern Baptists and the Religious Controversies of the Twenties* (Macon, Ga.: Mercer University Press, 1982), 91–95.

10. Eighmy, *Churches in Cultural Captivity,* 126–27; Garrett, Hinson, and Tull, *Are Southern Baptists Evangelicals?* 11, 15–16; Marsden, *Fundamentalism,* 171–75, 184–85.

11. Nancy Tatom Ammerman, *Baptist Battles: Social Change and Religious Conflict in the Southern Baptist Convention* (New Brunswick, N.J.: Rutgers University Press, 1990), 48–49; Norman F. Furniss, *The Fundamentalist Controversy, 1918–1931* (Hamden, Conn.: Archon Books, 1963), 126 (published originally in 1954); Garrett, Hinson, and Tull, *Are Southern Baptists Evangelicals?* 15–16; Bill J. Leonard, *God's Last and Only Hope: The Fragmentation of the Southern Baptist Convention* (Grand Rapids, Mich.: Eerdman's, 1990), 49–51; Ellen Rosenberg, *The Southern Baptists: A Subculture in Transition* (Knoxville: University of Tennessee Press, 1989), 139.

12. Barnes, *The Southern Baptist Convention,* 256, 259–60.

13. David O. Beale, *In Pursuit of Purity: American Fundamentalism Since 1850* (Greenville, S.C.: Unusual Publications [of Bob Jones University], 1986), 251–69; Eighmy, *Churches in Cultural Captivity,* 124–25; Garrett, Hinson, and Tull, *Are Southern Baptists Evangelicals?* 50; Marsden, *Understanding Fundamentalism and Evangelicalism,* 68–76.

14. Eighmy, *Churches in Cultural Captivity*, 74–76; James Carl Hefley, *The Truth in Crisis*, 5 vols. (Dallas: Clarion Publications, and Hannibal, Mo.: Hannibal Books, 1986–1990), 1:49–52; James, *The Takeover*, 15–16; Rosenberg, *The Southern Baptists*, 139–40.

15. Hefley, *The Truth in Crisis*, 1:54–58; James, *The Takeover*, 16; Rosenberg, *The Southern Baptists*, 139–40; *The Southern Baptist Journal*, special 1973 convention issue, 1–2.

16. Hefley, *The Truth in Crisis*, 1:54–58; James, *The Takeover*, 16; audiotape of an early meeting of the Baptist Faith and Message Fellowship in possession of M. O. Owens, Jr., and made available to the author at an interview in Salisbury, N.C., on December 29, 1992; William A. Powell, Sr., biographical sketch in M. O. Owens, Jr., Papers, along with *Southern Baptist Journal*, special 1973 convention issue, 1–2; December 1973, 7; February/March 1976, 1; July 1977, 1, boxes 2 and 3; Paul Pressler to David T. Morgan, September 30, 1992; Rosenberg, *The Southern Baptists*, 139–40.

17. *Annual of the Southern Baptist Convention* (Nashville: Executive Committee of the SBC), 1939, 28–29; 1980, 80; Hefley, *The Truth in Crisis*, 2:179–80; Leonard, *God's Last and Only Hope*, 53–58; Rosenberg, *The Southern Baptists*, 56–57; Thompson, *Tried as by Fire*, 215.

18. *Annual of the SBC*, 1979, 5.

19. *Alabama Baptist*, May 4, 1989, 1, 7–8; November 2, 1989, 11; *Annual of the SBC*, 1979, 5; 1981, 2; minutes, Executive Committee of the SBC, September 16–18, 1985; Hefley, *The Truth in Crisis*, 1:139; James, *The Takeover*, 9–10, 11–13; interview with Mrs. William A. Powell, Sr., and James A. Pate, July 1, 1993; Rosenberg, *The Southern Baptists*, 54–55, 95.

Concerning the allotment of messengers, Article III of the SBC constitution stated in 1979: "The Convention shall consist of messengers who are members of missionary Baptist churches cooperating with the Convention as follows: 1. One (1) messenger from each such church which is in friendly cooperation with this Convention and sympathetic with its purposes and work and has during the fiscal year preceding been a bona fide contributor to the Convention's work. 2. One (1) additional messenger from each such church for every two hundred and fifty (250) members; or for each $250.00 paid to the work of the Convention during the fiscal year preceding the annual meeting. 3. The messengers shall be appointed and certified by the churches of the Convention, but no church may appoint more than ten (10). 4. Each messenger shall be a member of the church by which he is appointed" (see *Annual of the SBC*, 1979, 5).

In 1993 Article III was amended to include the following statement: "Among churches not in cooperation with the Convention are churches which act to affirm, approve, or endorse homosexual behavior" (see *Annual of the SBC*, 1993, 4).

20. Interview with Paige Patterson, December 30, 1992.

2. The First Crusade: A Scarcity of Funds and Followers, 1969–1979

1. Résumé of Milum Oswell Owens, Jr. Copy in author's possession made available by M. O. Owens, Jr. Much of what appears on the résumé is confirmed by the many letters and other papers contained in the Owens Papers at the Southern Baptist Historical Library and Archives, Nashville, Tenn.

2. David T. Morgan, "Upheaval in the Southern Baptist Convention, 1979–1990: Crusade for Truth or Bid for Power?" *Journal of Religious History* 17, no. 3 (June 1993): 323–24; Interview with Paige Patterson, December 30, 1992.

3. Paul Pressler to David T. Morgan, September 30, 1992.

4. Interview with Paige Patterson, December 30, 1992; interview with Mrs. William A. Powell, Sr., and James A. Pate, July 1, 1993.

5. Morgan, "Crusade for Truth or Bid for Power?" 322–23; interview with M. O. Owens, Jr., and Gerald Primm, December 29, 1992; interview with Paige Patterson, December 30, 1992.

6. James C. Hefley, *The Conservative Resurgence in the Southern Baptist Convention* (Hannibal, Mo.: Hannibal Books, 1991), 217–18; Paul Pressler to David T. Morgan, September 30, 1992.

7. Paul Pressler to David T. Morgan, September 30, 1992.

8. Paul Pressler to M. O. Owens, Jr., November 12, 1969, Owens Papers, box 1.

9. Ibid.

10. M. O. Owens, Jr., to Fellow Pastors, January 28, 1969; Clark Pinnock to William W. Bell, February 5, 1969; M. O. Owens, Jr., to Clark Pinnock, February 6, 1969; Clark Pinnock to M. O. Owens, Jr., April 7, 1969, Owens Papers, box 1; M. O. Owens, Jr., to David T. Morgan, November 1, 1993.

11. Clark Pinnock to Paul Pressler, May 7, 1969, Owens Papers, box 1. In January 1974 Pinnock wrote Owens, declining an invitation to go to North Carolina because he felt "out of touch with S. B. concerns." Clark Pinnock to M. O. Owens, Jr., January 18, [1974], Owens Papers, box 4.

12. Johnnie Bradley to M. O. Owens, Jr., May 16, 1969; B. C. Tschudy to M. O. Owens, Jr., May 20, 1969; M. O. Owens, Jr., to Fellow Pastors, May 21, 1969, Owens Papers, box 1.

13. Lynwood Walters to William W. Bell, May 11, 1969, Owens Papers, box 1.

14. Memo from M. O. Owens, Jr., October 28, 1969, Owens Papers, box 1; *Sword and the Trowel*, August 1969, 3.

15. Forrest L. Young to M. O. Owens, Jr., November 13, 1969; Robert M. Tenery to M. O. Owens, Jr., November 21, 1969; Robert M. Tenery to Paul Pressler, November 21, 1969, Owens Papers, box 1.

16. Interview with M. O. Owens, Jr., and Gerald Primm, December 29, 1992; Gerald C. Primm to M. O. Owens, Jr., November 29, 1969, Owens Papers, box 1.

17. Gerald C. Primm to M. O. Owens, Jr., December 13, 1969, Owens Papers, box 1.

18. C. O. Vance to M. O. Owens, Jr., January 19, 1970, Owens Papers, box 1. Vance was pastor of Greenway Baptist Church in Boone, North Carolina. He enclosed two dollars in this letter. Owens received many letters that were remarkably similar to this one.

19. Victor Trivette to M. O. Owens, Jr., February 12, 1970; J. C. Caruthers to Gerald C. Primm, October 20, 1970; M. O. Owens, Jr., to Fellow Baptists, September 15, 1972; J. C. Caruthers to M. O. Owens, Jr., December 29, 1972, Owens Papers, box 1; *Sword and the Trowel*, special pre-Southern Baptist Convention issue, May–June 1972, 2, 4–5.

20. M. O. Owens, Jr., to Virginia York, November 12, 1970; M. O. Owens, Jr., to W. M. Haskins, December 10, 1970, Owens Papers, box 1.

21. *Baptist Program*, May 1972, 7; interview with William E. Hull, June 16, 1993; interview with M. O. Owens, Jr., and Gerald C. Primm, December 29, 1992. Hull was more than a little skeptical of Owens's contention that equal space in *Baptist Program* for a fundamentalist response to his views might have satisfied the fundamentalists and dissuaded them from pursuing their aims.

22. *baptists United News*, March 15, 1972; Neil J. Armstrong to M. O. Owens, Jr., September 30, 1971; William W. Leathers, Jr., to M. O. Owens, Jr., October 1, 1971; M. O. Owens, Jr., to Fellow Pastors, October 26, 1971; J. S. Larrimore to M. O. Owens, Jr., November 1, 1971; Marion D. Lark to Julian Hopkins, November 16, 1971, Owens Papers, box 1; *Sword and the Trowel*, special pre-Southern Baptist Convention issue, May–June 1972, 2. See also Julian Hopkins, "A Defense of the Proposed Owens' Amendment to the Constitution of the Baptist State Convention of North Carolina," brochure made available to the author by Gerald C. Primm. The brochure is in possession of the author.

23. J. C. Caruthers to M. O. Owens, Jr., December 3, 1971; M. O. Owens, Jr., to James E. Johnson [of Arlington, Tex.], December 16, 1971; M. O. Owens, Jr., to W. Ross Edwards, January 6, 1972, Owens Papers, boxes 1 and 2.

24. M. O. Owens, Jr., to Joe T. Odle, December 16, 1971; M. O. Owens, Jr., to D. Scott Gore, January 12, 1972; M. O. Owens, Jr., to Mrs. D. L. Jordan, January 26, 1972, Owens Papers, boxes 1 and 2.

25. M. O. Owens, Jr., to Maude P. Jordan, March 2, 1972; Mrs. Zelle M. Browning to John

R. Roberts, June 16, 1972; Richard Batchelor to Bennett Cook, June 24, 1972; Richard Batchelor to M. O. Owens, Jr., July [?], 1972; Mark Corts to M. O. Owens, Jr., August 4, 1972; M. O. Owens, Jr., to Raymond Crook, August 22, 1972, Owens Papers, boxes 1 and 2.

26. *Baptists United News*, October 16, 1972, 1; J. Ned Beatty, Sr., to M. O. Owens, Jr., August 28, 1972; Eugene E. Johns to M. O. Owens, Jr., August 29, 1972; Blaine H. Grose to M. O. Owens, Jr., September 7, 1972; M. O. Owens, Jr., to Marse Grant, September 21, 1972; Yates W. Campbell to M. O. Owens, Jr., November 15, 1972; Robert L. Clark to M. O. Owens, Jr., November 16, 1972; also numerous other letters to and from Owens with a variety of correspondents, as well as a newspaper article entitled "Immersion Rule Is Null, Official Says," Owens Papers, box 2.

27. Audiotape of an early meeting of BFMF in Atlanta in possession of M. O. Owens, Jr., who lent it to the author on December 29, 1992; interview with M. O. Owens, Jr., and Gerald C. Primm, December 29, 1992; Joe T. Odle to M. O. Owens, Jr., October 5, 1972; Howard H. Carlton to M. O. Owens, Jr., October 27, 1972; M. O. Owens, Jr., to Henry Kinkeade [of Irving, Tex.], June 29, 1973, Owens Papers, box 2.

28. Homer G. Lindsay, Jr., to M. O. Owens, Jr., January 25, 1973; M. O. Owens, Jr., to Homer G. Lindsay, Jr., February 16, 1973, Owens Papers, box 2.

29. Adrian Rogers to M. O. Owens, Jr., February 7, 1973; Jerry Vines to M. O. Owens, Jr., February 9, 1973; M. O. Owens, Jr., to David N. Freeman, June 28, 1973; M. O. Owens, Jr., to John K. Roberts, July 13, 1973, Owens Papers, box 2.

30. Wendell F. Wentz to M. O. Owens, Jr., January 23, 1973; Wendell F. Wentz to M. O. Owens, Jr., March 13, 1973, Owens Papers, box 2. In 1994 Wendell Wentz was a minister and columnist residing in Clinton, Missouri. He had abandoned the fundamentalist views he held in the 1970s.

31. M. O. Owens, Jr., to Laverne Baker, February 17, 1973; M. O. Owens, Jr., to Byram H. Glaze, February 18, 1973; M. O. Owens, Jr., to Herbert M. Pierce, March 9, 1973, Owens Papers, box 2.

32. "Conservative Baptists Form a New Fellowship," *Baptist Bible Tribune*, May 4, 1973; M. O. Owens, Jr., to J. Harold Smith, February 12, 1973; M. O. Owens, Jr., to Bob Estes, November 7, 1973; M. O. Owens, Jr., press release, March 1973, Owens Papers, box 2; *Southern Baptist Journal*, special 1973 convention issue, 1–2.

33. Articles of incorporation of BFMF, provided to the author by Gerald C. Primm and in the author's possession; W. A. Powell to M. O. Owens, Jr., October 8, 1973; By-Laws, The Baptist Faith and Message Fellowship, Inc.; BFMF's Statement of Objectives, Owens Papers, box 3.

34. A. V. Rose, Jr., to M. O. Owens, Jr., March 30, 1973; LeRoy Cooper to M. O. Owens, Jr., April 25, 1973; BFMF Officers to Whom It May Concern, April 26, 1973; Robert M. Jaye to M. O. Owens, Jr., May 1, 1973, Owens Papers, boxes 2 and 3.

35. John H. McCoy to M. O. Owens, Jr., [February 1973]; J. Wallace Little to M. O. Owens, Jr., June 7, 1973; Joe T. Odle to M. O. Owens, Jr., June 20, 1973; M. O. Owens, Jr., to Samuel F. McLamb, July 3, 1973, Owens Papers, boxes 2 and 3.

36. Jerry Wilcox to M. O. Owens, Jr., November 13, 1973; William Boheler to M. O. Owens, Jr., November 16, 1973; Kenneth W. Veazey to M. O. Owens, Jr., November 19, 1973; M. O. Owens, Jr., to Jerry Wilcox, November 21, 1973; Kenneth W. Veazey to M. O. Owens, Jr., November 30, 1973; M. O. Owens, Jr., to John Thornbury, December 28, 1973, Owens Papers, boxes 2, 3, and 4.

37. Biographical sketch of William Audrey Powell, Sr., Owens Papers, box 2; interview with Mrs. William A. Powell, Sr., and James A. Pate, July 1, 1993.

38. M. O. Owens, Jr., to Worth Grant, June 26, 1973; M. O. Owens, Jr., to William H. Rose, June 26, 1973; M. O. Owens, Jr., to "Fellow-workers," July 3, 1973; R. Dean Ramey to M. O. Owens, Jr., [October 1973]; M. O. Owens, Jr., to R. Dean Ramey, October 31, 1973; financial report, December 31, 1973, Owens Papers, boxes 2 and 3; William A. Powell to Arthur B. Rutledge, October 1, 1973, in possession of Mrs. William A. Powell, Sr., and made available by her to the author; *Southern Baptist Journal*, December 1973, 7.

39. *Baptists United News,* October 24, 1973, 1; *Biblical Recorder,* November 3, 1973, 15; William A. Powell to M. O. Owens, Jr., November 19, 1973; report clipped from *Word & Way,* December 6, 1973, Owens Papers, boxes 2 and 3.

40. A manuscript copy of this essay can be found in the Owens Papers, box 3. The published version is in *Sword and the Trowel,* Winter 1973, 11–15.

41. Budget study for 1974; financial report, March 1974; Status Report—The First Eleven Months, Owens Papers, boxes 3 and 4; interview with Mrs. William A. Powell, Sr., and James A. Pate, July 1, 1993.

42. Audiotape of the conference in Louisville, made available to the author by M. O. Owens, Jr.; interview with William E. Hull in Birmingham, Ala., on June 16, 1993; Duke K. McCall to William A. Powell, November 21, 1974, Owens Papers, box 4; Duke K. McCall to William A. Powell, April 1, 1974; William A. Powell to Duke K. McCall, December 12, 1974, Owens Papers, copies in the author's possession.

43. William A. Powell to Charles Stanley, December 14, 1974, Owens Papers, box 4; Bill Powell to R. G. Puckett, June 6, 1974; William A. Powell to M. O. Owens, Jr., July 12, 1974; M. O. Owens, Jr., to R. G. Puckett, July 19, 1974, Owens Papers, copies in the author's possession.

44. Interview with M. O. Owens, Jr., and Gerald C. Primm, December 29, 1992; James F. Cole to Bill Powell, March 12, 1974, Owens Papers, box 4. In an editorial Cole referred to Owens and his followers as "infallible critics of the Convention." See *Alabama Baptist,* November 15, 1973, 4.

45. *Baptists United News,* June 28, 1974, 2; M. O. Owens, Jr., to W. A. Criswell, May 14, 1974, Owens Papers, box 4.

46. *Baptists United News,* September 30, 1974, 1–2; November 27, 1974, 1, 4.

47. Ibid., December 29, 1975, 3.

48. Hefley, *The Truth in Crisis,* 1:75–76; *Southern Baptist Journal,* March/April 1975, 4–5; February/March 1976, 1; July 1977, 1.

49. "Creedalism Is Not a Danger to Baptists," manuscript by M. O. Owens, Jr., Owens Papers, box 4; *Southern Baptist Journal,* September 1979, 2.

50. *Baptists United News,* July 18, 1975, 3; March 29, 1976, 3.

51. *Maryland Baptist,* June 26, 1980, 1–2; M. O. Owens, Jr., to David T. Morgan, September 16, 1992; interview with Mrs. William A. Powell, Sr., and James A. Pate, July 1, 1993; *Southern Baptist Journal,* September/October 1985, 1–4. Bill Powell's "terminal illness" was Alzheimer's disease. As of July 1, 1993, he was still alive but institutionalized in a nursing facility.

52. Interview with Paige Patterson, December 30, 1992; interview with Mrs. William A. Powell, Sr., and James A. Pate, July 1, 1993; Paul Pressler to David T. Morgan, September 30, 1992.

3. The Second Crusade: In the Trenches, 1979–1984

1. Hefley, *The Conservative Resurgence,* 40.

2. *Southern Baptist Advocate,* May–June 1981, 4.

3. Rosenberg, *The Southern Baptists,* 65.

4. Paul Pressler to David T. Morgan, September 30, 1992; "Interview with Judge Paul Pressler," *Theological Educator,* 1985 special issue, 17–18.

5. *Baptists United News,* May 30, 1979, 1; interview with Mrs. William A. Powell, Sr., and James A. Pate, July 1, 1993; interview with Paige Patterson, December 30, 1992; Walter B. Shurden, ed., *The Struggle for the Soul of the SBC* (Macon, Ga.: Mercer University Press, 1993), ix.

6. Hefley, *The Truth in Crisis,* 1:67–68; Claude L. Howe, Jr., "From Houston to Dallas: Recent Controversy in the Southern Baptist Convention," *Theological Educator,* 1985 special issue, 33–37; minutes, Executive Committee of the SBC, September 17–19, 1979, SBHLA; Rosenberg, *The Southern Baptists,* 65.

7. *Annual of the SBC,* 1980, 63–64; *Biblical Recorder,* July 10, 1982, 9; James, *The Takeover,* 9.

8. Minutes, Executive Committee of the SBC, September 17–19, 1979; February 18–19, 1980; September 18–19, 1980; February 16–17, 1981. See especially minutes, Executive Committee, Addendum A: Registration Irregularities at Houston Convention—1979, September 17–19, 1979.

Although Paige Patterson stated in a letter to the author that Lee Porter was "constrained" to confess that a complete investigation had revealed few voting irregularities and that there were not enough of them to have influenced the outcome of the election, Lee Porter told the author in a telephone interview that he had never repudiated his report to the Executive Committee. Porter did, however, acknowledge that both sides were guilty of irregularities. Paige Patterson to David T. Morgan, April 7, 1994; telephone interview with Lee Porter, April 19, 1994.

9. *Baptist and Reflector,* June 20, 1979, 1; *Baptists United News,* October 15, 1979, 5–6.

10. *Baptists United News,* October 15, 1979, 2–3; Paige Patterson to David T. Morgan, April 7, 1994. In another letter, dated May 3, 1994, Patterson did acknowledge that Judge Pressler was an illegal messenger at the Houston Convention.

11. Paige Patterson to David T. Morgan, April 7, 1994, and May 3, 1994.

12. *Annual of the SBC,* 1979, 31–33, 45, 56, 58; *Arkansas Baptist Newsmagazine,* June 21, 1979, 3, 5; Hefley, *The Truth in Crisis,* 1:69–71.

13. *Arkansas Baptist Newsmagazine,* June 21, 1979, 3.

14. David T. Morgan, "Upheaval in the Southern Baptist Convention, 1979–1990: The Texas Connection," *Perspectives in Religious Studies* 19, no. 1 (Spring 1992): 53–54.

15. Morgan, "Crusade for Truth or Bid for Power?" 335.

16. Ibid., 326–27.

17. Firestorm Chats with Judge Paul Pressler. Audiotape in the Southern Baptist Historical Library and Archives; "Interview with Judge Paul Pressler," 22, 24.

18. *The Fayetteville* [North Carolina] *Observer,* August 4, 1990, A9; Hefley, *The Truth in Crisis,* 1:15, 86–87; *Southern Baptist Journal,* SBC Pittsburgh special edition, June 14–16, 1983, 1; Vaughn W. Denton to Charles Stanley, October 17, 1984, Charles F. Stanley Papers (presidential), box 2, SBHLA.

Morris Chapman's statement smacks of bibliolatry, and the author has seen a number of such statements by other fundamentalists, but Paige Patterson strenuously denied the charge of bibliolatry. To the author he wrote, "Nobody preaches any more diligently than we that salvation is appropriated by the Grace of God through faith alone. While that is not unrelated to propositional facts, it is our belief that a person could be right on every propositional fact and still die and go to Hell. . . . I have known many persons who did not believe in the inerrancy of scripture who were, to the best of my human ability to determine such a thing, saints of God, washed in the blood and saved by His grace. It is not belief in a theory of biblical inspiration but belief in a crucified, resurrected Lord that saves." In still another letter he emphasized, "I repeat again, however, that inerrancy is not necessary to salvation." Paige Patterson to David T. Morgan, April 7, 1994, and May 3, 1994.

19. *Baptists United News,* April 30, 1984, 5; Hefley, *The Truth in Crisis,* 1:30–31, 82–83; Paige Patterson to Friends, May 2, 1980, with attachment called "A Reply of Concern," in possession of Professor Fisher Humphreys, Beeson Divinity School, Samford University, Birmingham, Ala.; *Southern Baptist Advocate,* March/April 1981, 6; Fall 1981, 7; May 1986, 3. The debate between Patterson and Sherman was held at the Burkemont Baptist Church in Morganton, N.C. At the time, Robert Tenery was pastor of that church.

20. James, *Inerrancy,* 26–27, 103–4, 119–67 passim; Robison B. James, ed., *The Unfettered Word: Southern Baptists Confront the Authority-Inerrancy Question* (Waco, Tex.: Word Book Publisher, 1987), 78; *Southern Baptist Journal,* March 1980, 6. See also *Alabama Baptist,* January 5, 1989, 9, and *Southern Baptist Journal,* July/August 1976, 6.

Of special interest are two papers, "What Is Biblical Inerrancy?" and "Parameters of Biblical Inerrancy," that Clark Pinnock presented at the Ridgecrest Conference on Biblical Inerrancy in 1987. Paige Patterson responded formally to the former paper and Adrian Rogers to the latter. In his comments, Patterson remarked that when considering Pinnock's views on inerrancy one had to ask which Pinnock—"early," "middle," "late," or "contradictory?" Adrian Rogers noted that he agreed entirely with Pinnock—the Pinnock of 1968 who had written that "God is bypassing many of the great denominations today because they refused to maintain a pure testimony to the truth." See *The Proceedings of the Conference on Biblical Inerrancy, 1987* (Nashville: Broadman Press, 1987), 73–106.

21. James, *Inerrancy*, 79.

22. Ibid., 30, 68–69, 72–78; James, *The Takeover*, 16–18; Michael Lienesch, "Right-Wing Religion: Christian Conservatism as a Political Movement," *Political Science Quarterly*, 97, no. 3 (Fall 1982), 404; *Southern Baptist Advocate*, September 1980, 2.

23. *Annual of the SBC*, 1981, 35, 45, 66; Hefley, *The Truth in Crisis*, 1:83–84; 2:23; James, *Inerrancy*, 94–95; minutes, Executive Committee of the SBC, September 22–24, 1980; Morgan, "Crusade for Truth or Bid for Power?" 329; *Southern Baptist Advocate*, January/February 1981, 8–9.

24. *Alabama Baptist*, August 4, 1988, 7; Baptist Press release, May 30, 1990, 1; *The Bell* [congregational paper of Snyder Memorial Baptist Church, Fayetteville, N.C.], July 13, 1990, 1–2; James W. Watkins, "Stop the Takeover," a tract located in the files on the SBC controversy, SBHLA; *Western Recorder*, May 20, 1981, 1.

25. *Alabama Baptist*, October 18, 1990, 3–4; Hefley, *The Truth in Crisis*, 4:73; Hope for Reconciliation: A Dialogue at Samford University, Birmingham, Alabama, October 11, 1990. The participants were Paul Pressler, David Montoya, Wayne Dorsett, and Randall Fields. The author was present, and some of the information cited is from his notes.

26. *Baptist Beacon*, May 22, 1980, 1; *Baptists United News*, May 23, 1980, 7; Hefley, *The Truth in Crisis*, 1:80–81; Jean Caffey Lyles, "Creeping Creedalism in the Southern Baptist Convention," *Christianity Today*, July 2–9, 1980, 691.

27. *Baptist Standard*, April 23, 1980, 2; "Evidences," circulated by Paige Patterson with a rebuttal from Fisher Humphreys; *The Maryland Baptist*, May 15, 1980, 1; Paige Patterson to Friends, May 2, 1980, with an attachment called "A Reply of Concern."

28. Hefley, *The Truth in Crisis*, 1:78–80; Paul Pressler to Bailey Smith, June 18, 1980; Bailey Smith to Paul Pressler, July 8, 1980, Bailey Smith Papers (presidential), box 1, SBHLA.

29. *Baptist Beacon*, July 3, 1980, 1; Hefley, *The Truth in Crisis*, 1:78–80.

30. Hefley, *The Truth in Crisis*, 1:81–82; Cecil Sherman, "An Overview of the Moderate Movement," in Shurden, *The Struggle for the Soul of the SBC*, 17. For vital statistics on Bailey Smith and his August 20, 1980, statement, see Smith Papers, inventory, box 1.

31. Shurden, *The Struggle for the Soul of the SBC*, 19–23.

32. *Baptists United News*, October 15, 1980, 3, 6; Robert M. Tenery to Bailey Smith, October 29, 1980, Smith Papers, box 1.

33. The story of the moderate movement in general is told in Shurden, *The Struggle for the Soul of the SBC*, by two of the key participants—Cecil Sherman and James Slatton. In the same work, John Hewett, who became pastor of the First Baptist Church of Asheville, North Carolina, after Cecil Sherman left that position, gives the inside story on the Forum, and Walker Knight does the same for *SBC Today*. See *The Struggle for the Soul of the SBC*, 17–92, 151–68 passim.

34. James, *The Takeover*, 9–10; Morgan, "Crusade for Truth or Bid for Power?" 331; Shurden, *The Struggle for the Soul of the SBC*, xi; *Southern Baptist Advocate*, August 1980, 1.

35. *Baptists United News*, January 15, 1981, 2–4; April 15, 1981, 1; May 25, 1981, 1–3; *Southern Baptist Advocate*, March/April 1981, 1, 14.

36. *Baptist New Mexican*, June 13, 1981, 1, 4; Hefley, *The Truth in Crisis*, 1:83; Freddie Gage to Presnall Wood, April 29, 1981, Smith Papers, box 1; *Southern Baptist Advocate*, May/June 1981, 1.

37. *Arkansas Baptist Newsmagazine*, June 18, 1981, 2–3; Charles W. Allen, "Paige Patterson: Contender for Baptist Sectarianism," *Review and Expositor* 79, no. 4 (Winter 1982): 105.

38. *Baptist Messenger*, June 3, 1982, 3.

39. Hefley, *The Truth in Crisis,* 1:88–89, 92.

40. *Annual of the SBC,* 1982, 36, 47–50, 58; *Baptist Messenger,* June 24, 1982, 2–4, 6; James T. Draper, Jr., Papers (presidential), inventory, SBHLA; Hefley, *The Truth in Crisis,* 1:90–91.

41. *Biblical Recorder,* July 10, 1982, 2, 14; July 24, 1982, 11, 15; *Florida Baptist Witness,* June 24, 1982, 4.

42. Hefley, *The Truth in Crisis,* 1:93.

43. *Southern Baptist Advocate,* June 1983, 1–2.

44. *Baptists United News,* June 6, 1983, 3.

45. *Capital Baptist,* June 9, 1983, 8; Hefley, *The Truth in Crisis,* 1:93.

46. *Annual of the SBC,* 1983, 37; *Baptist Record,* June 23, 1983, 1; *Capital Baptist,* June 9, 1983, 1, 4; Hefley, *The Truth in Crisis,* 1:93–94.

47. Warren Carr to James T. Draper, Jr., August 27, 1983, Draper Papers, box 1; Hefley, *The Truth in Crisis,* 1:99–103.

48. Bobby S. Terry to James T. Draper, Jr., May 29, 1984, Draper Papers, box 4.

49. *Baptist Standard,* June 20, 1984, 9; *Baptists United News,* June 1, 1984, 1; September 14, 1984, 1; Hefley, *The Truth in Crisis,* 1:105–6; "Interview with Paul Pressler," 23; *Indiana Baptist,* June 26, 1984, 2; *Southern Baptist Advocate,* July/August 1984, 1; Charles F. Stanley Papers (presidential), inventory, box 1, SBHLA.

50. James, *Inerrancy,* 106; James, *The Takeover,* 24.

51. *Annual of the SBC,* 1984, 29–30, 56; *Birmingham News,* June 16, 1985, C1, C4; Hefley, *The Truth in Crisis,* 1:105–6.

52. *Baptists United News,* September 14, 1984, 3; Hefley, *The Truth in Crisis,* 1:107–8.

53. Hefley, *The Truth in Crisis,* 1:107; Paul Pressler to Charles F. Stanley, July 17, 1984, Stanley Papers, box 3.

54. *Baptists United News,* September 14, 1984, 5; Roy L. Honeycutt, "SBC Takeover Must Be Averted," *Baylor Line,* November 1984, 55–56; Cothen, *What Happened to the SBC?* 188–89; Lucus material and Baptist Press release, files on the SBC controversy, SBHLA; Hefley, *The Truth in Crisis,* 1:107–8.

55. John T. Bunn to Dave Lucus, October 23, 1984, in Lucus material, files on the SBC controversy, SBHLA.

56. Baptist Press release, files on the SBC controversy, SBHLA.

57. *Arkansas Baptist Newsmagazine,* June 6, 1985; *Birmingham News,* May 10, 1985, B1; *SBC Today,* January 1985, 12.

58. Baptist Press release, February 20, 1981, 1.

4. The Second Crusade: Showdown at Dallas and the Futile Search for Peace, 1985–1987

1. *Birmingham News,* June 2, 1985, A27; Hefley, *The Truth in Crisis,* 1:113–14; *Southern Baptist Advocate,* May 1985, 1.

2. Hefley, *The Truth in Crisis,* 1:113–14.

3. Baptist Press release, June 10, 1985, 1; *Baptist Standard,* June 19, 1985, 5; Hefley, *The Truth in Crisis,* 1:119–27.

4. *Arkansas Baptist Newsmagazine,* June 20, 1985, 4; *Baptist and Reflector,* June 19, 1985, 1; *Baptist Standard,* June 19, 1985, 1; *Birmingham News,* June 12, 1985, A1, A14; June 13, 1985, A1, A12; Hefley, *The Truth in Crisis,* 1:121–28; Rosenberg, *The Southern Baptists,* 196.

5. *Birmingham News,* June 13, 1985, A1, A12; Shurden, *The Struggle for the Soul of the SBC,* 61.

6. *Arkansas Baptist Newsmagazine,* June 20, 1985, 6–7; *Baptist and Reflector,* June 19, 1985, 4; *Baptist Standard,* June 19, 1985, 4; James, *The Takeover,* 13–15.

7. *Annual of the SBC,* 1982, 54; 1984, 29, 56; *Baptists United News,* August 19, 1983, 4–5; Robert S. Crowder to James T. Draper, Jr., March 5, 1983, Draper Papers, box 1.

8. Minutes, Executive Committee of the SBC, September 16–18, 1985, addendum H.

9. *Alabama Baptist,* December 19, 1985, 6; January 9, 1986, 1; March 17, 1988, 5; August 4, 1988, 14; *Annual of the SBC,* 1986, 87–88; 1987, 77–78; 1988, 87–88; 1989, 68–69; *Baptist and Reflector,* May 28, 1986, 2; *Baptists United News,* December 19, 1985, 7; *Birmingham News,* February 18, 1986, A9; May 6, 1986, A5; May 9, 1986, B1; May 28, 1987, A2; March 11, 1988, C1; *Christian Index,* May 15, 1986, 1; minutes, Executive Committee of the SBC, September 16–18, 1985, addendum H; June 9, 1986; *Southern Baptist Convention Book of Reports,* 1986, 6–7.

10. *Alabama Baptist,* March 17, 1988, 5; *Annual of the SBC,* 1989, 68–69. Robert S. Crowder died in Birmingham, Alabama, at the age of eighty-three on October 13, 1993.

11. *Birmingham News,* April 14, 1985, C13; Hefley, *The Truth in Crisis,* 1:230; transcript of oral history interview with Wallace B. Henley by Irma R. Cruse, 1985, 15–20, in Special Collections, Samford University Library.

12. Transcript of Wallace Henley interview, 20–22.

13. *Alaska Baptist Messenger,* July 1985, 10; *Annual of the SBC,* 1985, 64–65, 77–78; *Arkansas Baptist Newsmagazine,* June 20, 1985, 8–9; *Baptist Beacon,* June 19, 1985, 1, 8; *Baptist Message,* June 20, 1985, 1; *Birmingham News,* June 11, 1985, C2; June 13, 1985, C2; Hefley, *The Truth in Crisis,* 1:128–31; James, *The Takeover,* 14; transcript of Wallace Henley interview, 23–25.

14. *Annual of the SBC,* 1986, 257.

15. *SBC Book of Reports,* 1986, 183–84.

16. *Birmingham News,* February 20, 1986, C3.

17. Hefley, *The Truth in Crisis,* 2:24–25.

18. *Birmingham News,* April 17, 1986, C1; Hefley, *The Truth in Crisis,* 2:40; *Richmond Times-Dispatch,* April 18, 1986, B4; Charles F. Stanley to Ronnie Lowery, March 18, 1986, Stanley Papers, box 1.

19. Hefley, *The Truth in Crisis,* 2:41–44.

20. *Baptist and Reflector,* May 28, 1986, 1–2; *Christian Index,* June 5, 1986, 22.

21. Joe Edward Barnhart, *The Southern Baptist Holy War* (Austin, Tex.: Texas Monthly Press, 1986), 207; Hefley, *The Truth in Crisis,* 2:39–40.

22. *Annual of the SBC,* 1986, 61; Hefley, *The Truth in Crisis,* 2:44, 66–68; *Religious Herald,* June 19, 1986, 3.

23. Hefley, *The Truth in Crisis,* 2:68–71; *Religious Herald,* June 19, 1986, 8.

24. *Christian Index,* June 19, 1986, 7; Hefley, *The Truth in Crisis,* 2:71, 74, 80; *Religious Herald,* June 19, 1986, 16.

25. Ammerman, *Baptist Battles,* 74.

26. *Annual of the SBC,* 1986, 37–39; *Baptist Message,* June 19, 1986, 4–5; Hefley, *The Truth in Crisis,* 2:69–70; *SBC Book of Reports,* 1986, 51.

27. *Birmingham News,* June 13, 1986, C1.

28. *Annual of the SBC,* 1986, 250–57; *Birmingham News,* June 10, 1986, A1, A14; Hefley, *The Truth in Crisis,* 2:71–72; Alan Neely, ed., *Being Baptist Means Freedom* (Charlotte, N.C.: Southern Baptist Alliance, Publishers, 1988), 25–30; *Richmond Times-Dispatch,* November 21, 1986, 4B; November 22, 1986, 8A; *Southern Baptist Advocate,* May 1986, 7; July 1986, 9–13.

29. Hefley, *The Truth in Crisis,* 2:189–94; *Richmond Times-Dispatch,* November 22, 1986, A8.

30. *Birmingham News,* February 22, 1987, D4; Hefley, *The Truth in Crisis,* 2:202–3; James, *The Takeover,* 55–58; interview with Mrs. Anne Neal (third president of SBA) on May 18, 1989, in Montevallo, Ala.; interview with Alan Neely (interim executive director of SBA) on August 17, 1988, at Southeastern Baptist Theological Seminary in Wake Forest, N.C.

31. *Alabama Baptist,* September 22, 1988, 8; December 8, 1988, 3, 11; *Birmingham News,* September 12, 1988, A4; minutes, Executive Committee of the SBC, February 20–21, 1978; interview with Alan Neely; interview with Anne Neal; *SBC Today,* January 1989, 1–2, 20.

32. *Alabama Baptist,* January 12, 1989, 7; March 16, 1989, 7; September 22, 1988, 8; *Birmingham News,* March 23, 1988, F1; James, *The Takeover,* 55–58; Walter B. Shurden, *The Baptist Identity: Four Fragile Freedoms* (Macon, Ga.: Smyth & Helwys Publishing, 1993), 84.

33. *Conference on Biblical Inerrancy*, 73–110 and editorial preface; James, *The Unfettered Word*, 5, 11, 184–87.

34. *Arkansas Baptist Newsmagazine*, June 4, 1987, 13; *Richmond Times-Dispatch*, May 20, 1987, B3.

35. *Birmingham News*, June 14, 1987, A7.

36. *Arkansas Baptist Newsmagazine*, June 4, 1987, 12, 14; June 25, 1987, 8.

37. *Annual of the SBC*, 1987, 33–35; *Arkansas Baptist Newsmagazine*, June 25, 1987, 6–7, 11; *Biblical Recorder*, June 27, 1987, 2–3.

38. *Annual of the SBC*, 1987, 56–57, 232–42; *Arkansas Baptist Newsmagazine*, June 25, 1987, 9–10; *Baptist Digest*, June 29, 1987, 2–3; *Biblical Recorder*, June 27, 1987, 1, 10–11; Hefley, *The Truth in Crisis*, 3:71, 82–83; *Northwest Baptist Witness*, June 9, 1987, 6; Rosenberg, *Southern Baptists*, 200–201.

39. *Arkansas Baptist Newsmagazine*, June 25, 1987, 9–10; *Birmingham News*, July 24, 1987, SC2.

40. *Alabama Baptist*, July 9, 1987, 1; *Birmingham News*, June 16, 1987, A6; June 17, 1987, A4; June 18, 1987, A9; *Folio: A Newsletter for Southern Baptist Women in Ministry*, 1987, 3; Hefley, *The Truth in Crisis*, 4:137; John W. Storey, "Religious Fundamentalism, an Elusive Phenomenon," Lamar University–Beaumont, Distinguished Faculty Lecture, October 19, 1987, 7.

5. The Second Crusade: The Moderates' Last Stand, 1988–1990

1. *The Asheville Citizen and The Asheville Times*, August 1, 1987, 13, files on the SBC controversy, SBHLA; *Birmingham News*, June 9, 1987, SC1; October 2, 1987, SC1; Hefley, *The Truth in Crisis*, 4:108; Morgan, "The Texas Connection," 59.

2. *Alabama Baptist*, November 24, 1988, 11; *The Atlanta Journal and The Atlanta Constitution*, November 15, 1987, A1, A21, files on the SBC controversy, SBHLA; *Birmingham News*, November 11, 1987, C11; Hefley, *The Conservative Resurgence*, 150–52; Hefley, *The Truth in Crisis*, 5:159.

3. *Annual of the SBC*, 1989, 69–73; *Alabama Baptist*, November 24, 1988, 11, 14; *The Bell*, July 20, 1990, 1–2; *Birmingham News*, November 6, 1990, F1; *SBC Today*, December 1988, 1–2, 4–5, 11.

4. *Alabama Baptist*, December 7, 1989, 7; November 29, 1990, 1, 3; Hefley, *The Conservative Resurgence*, 123–26.

5. *Alabama Baptist*, March 3, 1988, 6; Carl L. Kell, "They Have Seen a Great Light: Towards a Rhetoric of the Inerrancy Movement in the Southern Baptist Convention, 1970–1987," research paper submitted at Western Kentucky University, copy in the files on the SBC controversy, SBHLA. See Appendixes I and II.

6. *Alabama Baptist*, March 17, 1988, 1.

7. Hefley, *The Truth in Crisis*, 4:26, 30; Jerry Vines Papers (presidential), inventory, box 1, SBHLA.

8. *Alabama Baptist*, June 23, 1988, 1, 5; June 30, 1988, 1; *Annual of the SBC*, 1988, 61; *Baptist Courier*, June 23, 1988, 1–2, 7; *Birmingham News*, June 23, 1988, B3; Hefley, *The Truth in Crisis*, 4:78.

9. *Birmingham News*, June 29, 1988, B8.

10. *Alabama Baptist*, June 23, 1988, 3; January 5, 1989, 6; Hefley, *The Truth in Crisis*, 4:45, 57–58.

11. *Alabama Baptist*, June 23, 1988, 3; July 14, 1988, 3; *Annual of the SBC*, 1988, 68–69; *Baptist Courier*, June 23, 1988, 3; James, *The Takeover*, 50–52.

12. *Alabama Baptist*, July 14, 1988, 3.

13. Ibid., 1, 3; *Annual of the SBC*, 1988, 72–73.

14. *Alabama Baptist*, January 12, 1989, 5; Hefley, *The Truth in Crisis*, 4:43.

15. *Birmingham News*, April 29, 1989, C2; Hefley, *The Truth in Crisis*, 4:194–97, 212.

16. *Word & Way*, June 22, 1989, 4.

17. *Alabama Baptist*, March 16, 1989, 5; *Southern Baptist Advocate*, March 1989, 25–26.

18. *Southern Baptist Advocate*, March 1989, 25–26.

19. *Alabama Baptist,* June 8, 1989, 8; *Southern Baptist Advocate,* May 1989, 1, 11; Larry Holly to Jerry Vines, May 23, 1989, with attached paper by Holly entitled "How can it be? Mr. Baugh." Vines Papers, box 2.

20. *Alabama Baptist,* May 11, 1989, 3; *Annual of the SBC,* 1989, 38–39, 44–46, 58; *The California Southern Baptist,* June 22, 1989, 1; Hefley, *The Conservative Resurgence,* 87, 89; *Word & Way,* June 22, 1989, 1, 3.

21. *Alabama Baptist,* October 5, 1989, 11.

22. Ibid., January 11, 1990, 3; Hefley, *The Truth in Crisis,* 5:153–54.

23. *SBC Today,* January 1990, 20; *Southern Baptist Advocate,* February 1990, 13.

24. *Alabama Baptist,* February 15, 1990, 1, 11; March 1, 1990, 5; *Birmingham News,* February 5, 1990, B2.

25. *Alabama Baptist,* February 15, 1990, 1, 11; March 8, 1990, 1; October 4, 1990, 6; Baptist Press release, February 9, 1990, 1–3; March 15, 1990, 1–3.

26. *Alabama Baptist,* March 15, 1990, 1, 4; Baptist Press release, February 27, 1990, 1–3; March 15, 1990, 1–3.

27. Baptist Press release, May 15, 1990, 1–4; Hefley, *The Conservative Resurgence,* 150–54; *Wall Street Journal,* April 25, 1990, A1, A10.

28. *Alabama Baptist,* April 5, 1990, 9; May 3, 1990, 5; "Baptists Committed to the Southern Baptist Convention—Publication," national edition, 1990 (a tract); Baptist Press release, March 27, 1990, 1–3; May 3, 1990, 6–8; May 18, 1990, 9; *Birmingham News,* May 24, 1990, C6, C11; Hefley, *The Conservative Resurgence,* 185–86, 200, 204–5; *Southern Baptist Advocate,* February 1990, 3.

29. Hefley, *The Truth in Crisis,* 5:13; Hefley, *The Conservative Resurgence,* 191.

30. *Annual of the SBC,* 1990, 56; Baptist Press release, June 13, 1990, 1–2; *Birmingham News,* June 13, 1990, A1, A12; Hefley, *The Conservative Resurgence,* 204, 207.

31. *Alabama Baptist,* May 3, 1990, 5; June 7, 1990, 6; June 21, 1990, 7; June 28, 1990, 1; *Arkansas Baptist Newsmagazine,* June 21, 1990, 4–7; *Baptist Beacon,* June 28, 1990, 5; *Birmingham News,* May 24, 1990, 6, 11; June 13, 1990, A1, A12; *Fayetteville Observer,* August 4, 1990, A9; Hefley, *The Conservative Resurgence,* 196; *Southern Baptist Advocate,* February 1990, 1.

32. *Annual of the SBC,* 1990, 57, 63; *Arkansas Baptist Newsmagazine,* June 21, 1990, 7; *SBC Book of Reports,* 1991, 58, 64, 112, 134.

33. Baptist Press release, June 21, 1990, 1–2.

34. *Alabama Baptist,* November 15, 1990, 3; *The Bell,* July 27, 1990, 2; *Charlotte* [North Carolina] *Observer,* June 23, 1990, A13; interview with John Franklin Turner, August 9, 1990, in Clinton, N.C.

35. *Alabama Baptist,* August 9, 1990, 12; August 16, 1990, 9; August 30, 1990, 1, 3; September 13, 1990, 7; Baptist Press release, May 15, 1990, 1–3; June 21, 1990, 1–2; *The Bell,* July 27, 1990, 2; August 24, 1990, 2; August 31, 1990, 1; *Birmingham News,* July 23, 1990, A4; August 24, 1990, B1–2; August 25, 1990, B8; August 31, 1990, B1.

36. *Alabama Baptist,* August 9, 1990, 12; October 4, 1990, 11; November 1, 1990, 9.

37. Ibid., October 4, 1990, 3; October 25, 1990, 15; December 6, 1990, 3, 6; *Birmingham News,* August 25, 1990, D8; August 26, 1990, A25, A28; August 28, 1990, E2; August 31, 1990, B1–2; October 11, 1990, B4; October 12, 1990, C1; Nan S. Knight to Morris Chapman, November 13, 1990, Morris Chapman Papers (presidential), box 1, SBHLA; Hope for Reconciliation: A Dialogue, Samford University, October 11, 1990, author's notes.

6. The Fundamentalist Purges

1. Hefley, *The Truth in Crisis,* 1:91; 2:132–33; *Southern Baptist Advocate,* Fall 1982, 3.

2. *Annual of the SBC,* 1980, 194; Barnes, *The Southern Baptist Convention,* 299; Eighmy, *Churches in Cultural Captivity,* 158.

3. *Annual of the SBC,* 1986, 40, 67–68; 1987, 54, 58; *Baptist Standard,* June 20, 1984, 3; Hefley, *The Truth in Crisis,* 2:72; *SBC Today,* January 1990, 5.

4. Hefley, *The Truth in Crisis*, 2:131, 136–38; 4:171–73; James, *The Takeover*, 33–35; McKibbens, "Report to the Dunster Society," 11–12.

5. *Alabama Baptist*, March 8, 1988, 3; June 23, 1988, 6; Hefley, *The Truth in Crisis*, 4:49.

6. *SBC Today*, November 1988, 1–2.

7. Minutes (corrected), Executive Committee of the SBC, February 20–22, 1989; Hefley, *The Truth in Crisis*, 4:192–94.

8. *Alabama Baptist*, April 13, 1989, 3; Hefley, *The Truth in Crisis*, 4:198–202; 5:59–62; James, *The Takeover*, 33–35.

9. *Alabama Baptist*, March 9, 1989, 6; April 13, 1989, 3; May 4, 1989, 3, 7; Hefley, *The Conservative Resurgence*, 78–79, 82.

10. *Alabama Baptist*, August 24, 1989, 1; October 5, 1989, 1, 6, 11; *Annual of the SBC*, 1989, 76–77, 82–86; *Birmingham News*, June 10, 1989, C4.

11. *Alabama Baptist*, February 15, 1990, 11; March 1, 1990, 2–3; *Annual of the SBC*, 1990, 82–84; Baptist Press releases, February 1, 1990, 1–2, February 5, 1990, 1–4, and February 23, 1990, 1–6; Hefley, *The Conservative Resurgence*, 145.

12. Baptist Press release, April 12, 1990, 3–5.

13. *Alabama Baptist*, June 7, 1990, 6; Baptist Press release, May 18, 1990, 3–4; *Birmingham News*, June 12, 1990, E1, E4.

14. *Alabama Baptist*, June 21, 1990, 3; Baptist Press release, June 14, 1990, 1–2.

15. *Baptist Beacon*, June 28, 1990, 1; Baptist Press release, June 14, 1990, 2–3; Hefley, *The Conservative Resurgence*, 249.

16. *Alabama Baptist*, October 11, 1990, 7; March 7, 1991, 6; March 21, 1991, 6; June 13, 1991, 13; *SBC Book of Reports*, 1991, 7–8, 41–42.

17. Hefley, *The Truth in Crisis*, 2:21; James, *The Takeover*, 27–28; *The* [Raleigh, N.C.] *News and Observer*, August 1, 1987, C4; Rosenberg, *The Southern Baptists*, 204; *Wall Street Journal*, March 7, 1988, 1, 15.

18. Hefley, *The Truth in Crisis*, 1:176; 2:141–42; 4:169–70; James, *The Takeover*, 35–37.

19. Hefley, *The Truth in Crisis*, 2:152–53; James, *The Takeover*, 35–37.

20. *Alabama Baptist*, June 30, 1988, 1; September 22, 1988, 3; Hefley, *The Truth in Crisis*, 3:101–19; 4:169–70, 173–81, 185; James, *The Takeover*, 35–37.

21. Baptist Press releases, March 1, 1990, 2–3, and March 5, 1990, 1–4; James, *The Takeover*, 35–37.

22. Hefley, *The Conservative Resurgence*, 260; Hefley, *The Truth in Crisis*, 4:111.

23. *Birmingham News*, August 6, 1986, A5; Hefley, *The Truth in Crisis*, 171–72.

24. *SBC Today*, November 1988, 11.

25. Jerry D. Brown to Other Executive Committee Members, February 28, 1989; Doyle J. Collins to Jerry D. Brown, March 7, 1989; Larry Holly to Wayne L. North, May 22, 1989; Paige Patterson to Larry Holly, July 6, 1989, Baptist History File, Sunday School Board, SBHLA.

26. Larry Holly, "History of the Presidency," July 21, 1989, Baptist History File, SSB, SBHLA.

27. *Alabama Baptist*, August 17, 1989, 1; August 24, 1989, 3; Hefley, *The Conservative Resurgence*, 95–104.

28. *Alabama Baptist*, August 24, 1989, 3; September 7, 1989, 3.

29. Ibid., February 22, 1990, 3; *Birmingham News*, August 18, 1990, D8; Hefley, *The Conservative Resurgence*, 266–71.

30. Hefley, *The Conservative Resurgence*, 266–80 passim.

31. *Alabama Baptist*, January 24, 1991, 3, 7; January 31, 1991, 3; July 11, 1991, 13.

32. Ibid., March 28, 1991, 3; May 9, 1991, 3.

33. *Birmingham News*, July 16, 1990, C7; *Wall Street Journal*, March 7, 1988, 11.

34. *Biblical Recorder*, editorial, March 14, 1987, 2; *Birmingham News*, October 1, 1988, B7, 12; Hefley, *The Truth in Crisis*, 2:168–70.

35. Hefley, *The Truth in Crisis*, 2:168–70.

36. James, *The Takeover*, 46.

37. Hefley, *The Truth in Crisis*, 5:69–70.

38. *Alabama Baptist*, July 26, 1990, 1, 3; August 2, 1990, 8; Morgan, "The Texas Connection," 62–63.

39. Press conference, July 17, 1990, in Nashville, author's notes. (The author was present for the entire press conference and took full notes. He also collected a number of handouts that were distributed.)

40. Ibid.; Hefley, *The Conservative Resurgence*, 311–12.

41. *Alabama Baptist*, September 26, 1991, 3; Hefley, *The Conservative Resurgence*, 311–12.

42. *Alabama Baptist*, July 26, 1990, 1, 2, 4.

43. *Baptist Digest*, January 12, 1987, 1, 6; Rosenberg, *The Southern Baptists*, 199–200.

44. *Baptist Digest*, January 12, 1, 6.

45. *Alabama Baptist*, July 28, 1988, 1, 13; August 4, 1988, 8; *Birmingham News*, August 6, 1988, B7; James, *The Takeover*, 42–43.

46. *Alabama Baptist*, August 4, 1988, 8.

47. Ibid., July 20, 1989, 1, 6; July 27, 1989, 2–4; August 10, 1989, 3, 10.

48. Ibid. (all dates cited).

49. Ibid., November 9, 1989, 7.

50. Ibid., December 3, 1992, 6; Baptist Press releases, June 1, 1990, 1–2, and June 11, 1990, 1–3; *Birmingham News*, May 24, 1990, B3; Hefley, *The Conservative Resurgence*, 187–88.

51. *Wall Street Journal*, March 7, 1988.

7. The Impact of the New Crusades on Southern Baptist Institutions of Higher Learning

1. Marsden, *Fundamentalism*, 160.

2. *Annual of the SBC*, 1969, 58, 70–71; clipping from *Presbyterian Journal*, July 6, 1969, Owens Papers, box 4.

3. *Baptist and Reflector*, June 20, 1979, 2; Neely, *Being Baptist Means Freedom*, 62–63.

4. *Southern Baptist Advocate*, September/October 1984, 10, 20, 24; Storey, "Religious Fundamentalism," 6–7.

5. Neely, *Being Baptist Means Freedom*, 62–63; Rosenberg, *The Southern Baptists*, 80–81.

6. Barnhart, *The Southern Baptist Holy War*, 86, 202–3; W. W. Finlator, "Reclaiming the Birthright," sermon preached at Wedgewood Baptist Church, Charlotte, N.C., November 5, 1989. A copy of the sermon was given to the author by Finlator.

7. Hefley, *The Truth in Crisis*, 1:171; interview with Paige Patterson, December 30, 1992; *Southern Baptist Journal*, January 1981, 5.

8. Hefley, *The Truth in Crisis*, 2:111–17.

9. Ibid., 1:211–13.

10. *Biblical Recorder*, November 30, 1991, 1, 10.

11. *Birmingham News*, December 5, 1986, C2; Hefley, *The Truth in Crisis*, 2:117–22; James, *The Takeover*, 31–32; *Southern Baptist Advocate*, December 1986, 1, 20.

12. *Alabama Baptist*, October 26, 1989, 16; Hefley, *The Truth in Crisis*, 4:134–36.

13. Hefley, *The Conservative Resurgence*, 252–53.

14. J. Stafford Durham to the Federal Communications Commission, September 14, 1984; Harold C. Bennett to Louis Moore, September 28, 1984; Louis Moore to Harold C. Bennett, October 5, 1984, files on the SBC controversy, SBHLA.

15. Hefley, *The Truth in Crisis*, 2:48–50, 54, 110–11, 123. Although Molly Marshall-Green was a tenured faculty member at Southern Seminary, she did not last long after Roy Honeycutt's retirement. She was forced to resign by Albert Mohler, the new president, in the summer of 1994 for her "failure to relate constructively" to the Southern Baptist Convention and for her views on the Bible, God, the atonement, and universalism. It was alleged that her views were

in conflict with the seminary's "Abstract of Principles," which, as a faculty member, she had signed. See Religious News Service article in the *Birmingham News,* August 26, 1994, G1.

16. Baptist Press release, April 26, 1990, 1–4; *Alabama Baptist,* May 24, 1990, 8; "The Cover-up at Southern Seminary," by Jerry A. Johnson, files on the SBC controversy, SBHLA.

17. Baptist Press releases, April 26, 1990, 1–4, May 11, 1990, 2–4, May 18, 1990, 7–8, and May 29, 1990, 4–5.

18. *Alabama Baptist,* October 4, 1990, 3, 8. Baptist Press releases, May 18, 1990, 7–8, May 29, 1990, 4–5, and June 14, 1990, 3; Hefley, *The Conservative Resurgence,* 204, 208; *SBC Book of Reports,* 1991, 149.

19. S. Ernest Vandiver to "concerned Baptists," May 2, 1990, copy in Special Collections, Samford University Library.

20. *Alabama Baptist,* April 18, 1991, 6, 11; Hefley, *The Conservative Resurgence,* 316–17.

21. *Alabama Baptist,* March 19, 1992, 1, 7.

22. McKibbens, "Report on the SBC to the Dunster Society," 10–11.

23. David O. Beale, *S.B.C.: House on the Sand* (Greenville, S.C.: Unusual Publications, 1985), 74; *Birmingham News,* November 27, 1987, SC3; Hefley, *The Truth in Crisis,* 4:149–52; *SBC Today,* November 1988, 3.

24. *Alabama Baptist,* January 21, 1988, 1, 8; September 1, 1988, 2; Hefley, *The Truth in Crisis,* 4:157–60.

25. *Alabama Baptist,* November 10, 1998, 9; *SBC Today,* January 1989, 21.

26. *Alabama Baptist,* June 8, 1989, 6; Hefley, *The Truth in Crisis,* 4:161–62.

27. *Alabama Baptist,* March 29, 1990, 3.

28. Baptist Press release, March 16, 1990, 1–5.

29. *Alabama Baptist,* January 4, 1990, 11; July 12, 1990, 13; March 12, 1991, 8, 10; August 8, 1991, 3, 6; December 17, 1992, 10; Baptist Press release, June 29, 1990, 2; *Chronicle of Higher Education,* March 18, 1992, A16, A18–19.

30. *Alabama Baptist,* April 23, 1992, 3; May 28, 1992, 3.

31. Hefley, *The Truth in Crisis,* 3:154–55.

32. *Alabama Baptist,* September 7, 1989, 3, 8; October 26, 1989, 1, 15.

33. Ibid., March 29, 1990, 3.

34. Ibid., November 7, 1991, 7; Hefley, *The Conservative Resurgence,* 253–54; Morgan, "The Texas Connection," 67–68.

35. *Richmond Times-Dispatch,* February 14, 1987, B6.

36. Hefley, *The Truth in Crisis,* 2:183–84, 186.

37. *Alabama Baptist,* November 22, 1990, 1–3; *Birmingham News,* November 13, 1988, 25A; November 12, 1990, B1–2; August 31, 1991, D8.

38. *Birmingham News,* November 14, 1990, A1–2; November 22, 1991, E1–2.

39. Ibid., October 19, 1989, B8; October, 23, 1989, SC1.

40. Ibid., January 1, 1988, SC5.

41. Hefley, *The Truth in Crisis,* 3:191.

42. *Alabama Baptist,* April 16, 1992, 7; June 4, 1992, 6; *Baptist Courier,* November 21, 1991, 6–7; *Baylor Line,* January/February 1992, 48–49; *Biblical Recorder,* May 30, 1992, 9.

43. *Alabama Baptist,* April 16, 1992, 7; *Biblical Recorder,* May 30, 1992, 9.

44. Hefley, *The Conservative Resurgence,* 15–22.

45. *Richmond Times-Dispatch,* February 14, 1987, B6.

46. *Southern Baptist Advocate,* August 1980, 1.

47. Lucus material, files on the SBC controversy, SBHLA; Hefley, *The Conservative Resurgence,* 284–86; Hefley, *The Truth in Crisis,* 1:109–10.

48. Hefley, *The Truth in Crisis,* 2:36–39.

49. *Baylor Line,* November 1988, 17–20.

50. Ibid.

51. Ibid.

52. Ibid., March/April 1992, 38–39, 55.

53. Ibid., September 1990, 30; November 1990, 2–9.

54. Ibid., November 1990, 2–9.

55. *Alabama Baptist*, November 1, 1990, 12; *Baylor Line*, November 1990, 2–9; July/August 1991, 4–5, 47; *Birmingham News*, November 14, 1990, A6; Hefley, *The Conservative Resurgence*, 291.

56. Hefley, *The Conservative Resurgence*, 288–91, 296–97.

57. *Alabama Baptist*, July 11, 1991, 8; *Baylor Line*, January 1991, 25–26; *Birmingham News*, November 13, 1990, A2; Hefley, *The Conservative Resurgence*, 296–97.

58. *Birmingham News*, November 13, 1990, A2.

59. *Alabama Baptist*, December 13, 1990, 7; May 30, 1991, 15; July 11, 1991, 8; *Baylor Line*, January 1991, 23–24.

60. *Alabama Baptist*, August 1, 1991, 6; *Baylor Line*, September/October 1991, 6–7.

61. *Alabama Baptist*, October 10, 1991, 8; *Baylor Line*, November/December 1991, 5.

62. *Baylor Line*, September/October 1991, 5, 7.

63. *Baptist Standard*, November 21, 1991, 3, 4, 17.

64. *Baylor Line*, Fall 1992, 53.

8. Issues Other Than Inerrancy Raised by the Fundamentalist Crusades

1. Ammerman, *Baptist Battles*, 102.

2. *Annual of the SBC*, 1982, 32, 64–65; Hefley, *The Truth in Crisis*, 2:15; *West Virginia Southern Baptist*, June–July 1984, 4.

3. *Annual of the SBC*, 1986, 72, 76; Hefley, *The Truth in Crisis*, 2:148–49.

4. *Annual of the SBC*, 1989, 53–54; *Ohio Baptist Messenger*, June 5, 1986, 1.

5. Hefley, *The Conservative Resurgence*, 319.

6. *Alabama Baptist*, February 15, 1990, 11; August 1, 1991, 6.

7. Ibid., September 21, 1989, 6.

8. Ibid., November 23, 1989, 1–3, 6; January 18, 1990, 1, 3, 6; February 15, 1990, 3; March 1, 1990, 6; March 8, 1990, 3.

9. *Southern Baptist Journal*, March 1983, 7.

10. *Baptist Record*, June 23, 1983, 1, 3; *Folio: A Newsletter of Southern Baptist Women in Ministry*, Fall 1983, 3; Hefley, *The Truth in Crisis*, 1:96.

11. *Annual of the SBC*, 1984, 65; *Baptist Standard*, June 20, 1984, 4; *Folio*, Spring 1984, 7–10; James, *The Takeover*, 25; Rosenberg, *The Southern Baptists*, 143; *Wall Street Journal*, March 7, 1988, 11.

12. *Birmingham News*, October 20, 1987, E8; *Wall Street Journal*, March 7, 1988, 1, 11.

13. *Folio*, Summer 1989, 5.

14. Ibid., Autumn 1989, 1, 6.

15. Ibid., Spring 1991, 1; Summer 1992, 1.

16. *Alabama Baptist*, September 21, 1989, 1, 3; October 26, 1989, 1; *Arkansas Baptist Newsmagazine*, June 7, 1990, 5; *Birmingham News*, November 19, 1987, A5.

17. Author's notes taken at the press conference on July 17, 1990.

18. *Alabama Baptist*, March 3, 1988, 11; Lucus material, files on the SBC controversy, SBHLA.

19. *Annual of the SBC*, 1984, 81–82; *Birmingham News*, February 18, 1987, D9; Hefley, *The Truth in Crisis*, 2:170.

20. *Birmingham News*, July 17, 1990, C8. The author's notes taken at the press conference on July 17, 1990, reveal that Shackleford repeated some of the information he had stated to reporters earlier.

21. *Birmingham News*, June 30, 1990, C4; July 12, 1990, A2; July 14, 1990, A2; *Birmingham Post-Herald*, July 19, 1990, A5; Hefley, *The Truth in Crisis*, 2:47, 160–61, 165–67; *Houston Chronicle*, December 8, 1984, clipping with date but no page number, files on the SBC controversy, SBHLA; James, *The Takeover*, 44–45.

22. Ibid. (all sources cited in 21).

23. *Alabama Baptist*, August 2, 1990, 8.

24. Ibid.; author's notes taken at the press conference on July 17, 1990.

25. *Birmingham News*, September 28, 1990, B2.

26. *Alabama Baptist*, January 28, 1988, 3; February 25, 1988, 3; *Birmingham News*, October 30, 1987, SC2.

27. *Birmingham News*, October 30, 1987, SC2; Hefley, *The Truth in Crisis*, 2:167–68; James, *The Takeover*, 47–48.

28. *Birmingham News*, June 11, 1992, A8; *SBC Today*, January 1989, 24.

29. Robert C. Liebman and Robert Wuthnow, eds., *The New Christian Right* (Hawthorne, N.J.: Aldine, 1983), 119; Matthew C. Moen, *The Transformation of the Christian Right* (Tuscaloosa: University of Alabama Press, 1992), 16–19, 21–22; James A. Reichley, *Religion in American Life* (Washington, D.C.: Brookings Institution, 1985), 330; Rosenberg, *The Southern Baptists*, 182.

30. *Birmingham News*, December 10, 1986, A12; Samuel S. Hill, Jr., and Dennis E. Owen, *The New Religious Political Right in America* (Nashville: Abingdon, 1982), 51, 117–18; Allen Hunter, "In the Wings: New Right Ideology and Organization," *Radical America* 15, no. 1 (Spring 1981): 113, 117–18, 124–25; Liebman and Wuthnow, *The New Christian Right*, 25–26; Lienesch, "Right-Wing Religion: Christian Conservatism as a Political Movement," 403; Moen, *The Transformation*, 21–22; Reichley, *Religion in American Life*, 315–17, 319–27; Wade Clark Roof and William McKinney, *American Mainline Religion: Its Changing Shape and Future* (New Brunswick, N.J.: Rutgers University Press, 1987), 31; Rosenberg, *The Southern Baptists*, 183–84.

31. John H. Buchanan, "Religiously Inspired Censorship in the Public Schools," *National Forum* [the Phi Kappa Phi journal] 68, no. 1 (Winter 1988): 34.

32. Hill and Owen, *The New Religious Political Right in America*, 69–72; John D. Lofton, Jr., "Roundtable President; Ed McAteer is Music Man of the Religious Right," *Conservative Digest* 7, no. 1 (January 1981): 74–79; Moen, *The Transformation*, 16–19, 21–22, 36; Rosenberg, *The Southern Baptists*, 190–91.

33. *Annual of the SBC*, 1980, 29, 40, 56; Liebman and Wuthnow, "The New Christian Right," 33; Moen, *The Transformation*, 18–19; *Southern Baptist Advocate*, September 1980, 8–9.

34. *Biblical Recorder*, July 10, 1982, 9; July 24, 1982, 8, 15; Hefley, *The Truth in Crisis*, 2:8; Rosenberg, *The Southern Baptists*, 193.

35. Moen, *The Transformation*, 39–42; Tim LaHaye to Joe Haag, February 24, 1982; Tim La-Haye to Bailey Smith, February 24, 1982, Smith Papers, box 2, SBHLA.

36. Tim LaHaye to Bailey Smith, February 24, 1982, Smith Papers, box 2, SBHLA.

37. *SBC Today*, December 1984, 1.

38. Hefley, *The Truth in Crisis*, 4:71–75; James, *The Takeover*, 37–41; Paige Patterson to David T. Morgan, May 3, 1994.

39. Howe, "From Houston to Dallas," 41.

40. *Alabama Baptist*, June 20, 1991, 7; August 29, 1991, 3; *Annual of the SBC*, 1986, 39, 43, 75–76; 1990, 58, 63; *Birmingham News*, November 19, 1986, A6; August 31, 1991, D8; Hefley, *The Conservative Resurgence*, 109–11, 190; *Southern Baptist Advocate*, June 1990, 2–3.

41. Baptist Press releases, April 16, 1990, 1, and May 18, 1990, 1.

42. Interview with Alan Neely, August 17, 1988; Rosenberg, *The Southern Baptists*, 209.

9. After New Orleans: The Crusaders Consolidate Their Power, 1990–1991

1. Hefley, *The Conservative Resurgence*, 311.

2. *SBC Book of Reports*, 1990, table of contents and 23. The same information is found in the *Annual of the SBC*, 1990.

3. *Alabama Baptist*, September 5, 1991, 1.

4. Ibid.

5. Ibid., August 9, 1990, 12; Hefley, *The Conservative Resurgence*, 235.

6. *Alabama Baptist*, August 16, 1990, 9; August 30, 1990, 1, 3; *The Bell*, August 24, 1990, 2;

August 31, 1990, 1; *Birmingham News,* July, 23, 1990, A4; August 24, 1990, B1–2; August 25, 1990, B8; August 31, 1990, B1; Hefley, *The Conservative Resurgence,* 234–35.

7. *Alabama Baptist,* September 12, 1990, 7; Hefley, *The Conservative Resurgence,* 246–47.

8. *Alabama Baptist,* October 11, 1990, 5; *Birmingham News,* September 24, 1990, B2.

9. *Alabama Baptist,* September 27, 1990, 1, 3.

10. Ibid., May 16, 1991, 1, 11; *Birmingham News,* March 10, 1991, A21–22; July 29, 1991, A3.

11. *Alabama Baptist,* May 16, 1991, 1, 11; *Birmingham News,* May 11, 1991, C4; May 12, 1991, A6.

12. *Baylor Line,* July/August 1991, 28–29, 47.

13. *Birmingham News,* May 11, 1991, C4.

14. Hefley, *The Conservative Resurgence,* 334–35; Shurden, *The Baptist Identity,* 84.

15. *Alabama Baptist,* August 8, 1991, 12.

16. Ibid., October 3, 1991, 11; January 23, 1992, 11.

17. Ibid., January 23, 1992, 11.

18. Ibid., February 20, 1992, 3.

19. Ibid., May 7, 1992, 1, 11.

20. Ibid., November 19, 1992, 1, 11; Hefley, *The Conservative Resurgence,* 240–46, 337.

21. *Alabama Baptist,* April 4, 1991, 3; May 16, 1991, 1, 8; *Birmingham News,* May 8, 1991, D4; Jerry Vines to the BSSB Search Committee, March 29, 1991, SBC controversy file, Special Collections, Samford University Library.

22. *Alabama Baptist,* June 13, 1991, 1, 7, 8; July 11, 1991, 3.

23. *Annual of the SBC,* 1991, 35, 73–77; *Baptist Record,* June 13, 1991, 1–3; *SBC Book of Reports,* 1986, 51; 1991, 41.

24. *Alabama Baptist,* June 27, 1991, 1, 15; July 11, 1991, 8; July 25, 1991, 1, 13; May 7, 1992, 8.

25. Ibid., September 26, 1991, 3; October 24, 1991, 3.

26. Ibid., January 16, 1992, 1; February 27, 1992, 1; October 1, 1992, 1, 3, 8; *Birmingham News,* January 22, 1992, D4; February 19, 1992, A13.

27. *Alabama Baptist,* October 24, 1991, 1, 10.

28. Ibid., November 14, 1991, 3; December 5, 1991, 3, 7; January 16, 1992, 4; *Biblical Recorder,* November 30, 1991, 1, 10.

29. *Alabama Baptist,* December 12, 1991, 1, 11, 15.

30. Ibid., January 23, 1992, 7.

31. Ibid., January 16, 1992, 1, 7, 10; *Birmingham News,* January 17, 1992, B2.

32. *Alabama Baptist,* February 6, 1992, 3–4, 9; February 20, 1992, 1, 3; March 26, 1992, 1, 3; *Birmingham News,* February 15, 1992, D10.

33. *Alabama Baptist,* April 9, 1992, 5; *Birmingham News,* April 3, 1992, D1–2.

34. *Alabama Baptist,* November 14, 1991, 7.

35. Ibid., July 11, 1991, 11.

36. Ibid., December 5, 1991, 7; *Biblical Recorder,* October 26, 1991, 3, 9; *Fayetteville Observer,* November 9, 1991, A9; November 13, 1991, A1, A4; Hefley, *The Conservative Resurgence,* 322–31 passim; interview with Glen Holt at the First Baptist Church in Fayetteville, N.C., on June 1, 1992.

37. *Alabama Baptist,* September 5, 1991, 5; October 24, 1991, 6; January 23, 1992, 4; June 18, 1992, 6.

38. Ibid., May 23, 1991, 6; October 10, 1991, 3; January 9, 1992, 12; February 13, 1992, 1, 3, 8; *Birmingham News,* March 13, 1992, B3.

Epilogue

1. *Alabama Baptist,* June 18, 1992, 6; October 22, 1992, 6.

2. Ibid., February 27, 1992, 1, 3; March 12, 1992, 1, 3; March 19, 1992, 3; *Birmingham News,*

March 7, 1992, C4; June 16, 1992, C7; interview with Glen Holt, June 1, 1992. See also *Annual of the SBC*, 1993, 4.

3. *Alabama Baptist*, May 14, 1992, 6–7.

4. Ibid., June 4, 1992, 5; June 18, 1992, 5, 10; June 25, 1992, 3.

5. Ibid., June 11, 1992, 3; June 18, 1992, 1, 3, 5; *Birmingham News*, June 6, 1992, D10; June 9, 1992, A5; June 12, 1992, B3.

6. *Alabama Baptist*, January 9, 1992, 12; March 26, 1992, 1, 3; October 22, 1992, 11. In 1993 Paige Patterson and his wife Dorothy would seek a "watchcare" relationship with the Wake Forest Baptist Church. Apparently they intended to retain full membership in the First Baptist Church of Dallas. The Wake Forest church's deacons voted sixteen to one to reject their request, and they were asked to withdraw it before the church could vote on it. They did so. The Pattersons were invited to worship anytime, but they were told that if they were admitted to membership in the church (even on a watchcare basis), it would "certainly result in disruption and division in this congregation." See *Alabama Baptist*, February 11, 1993, 14.

7. Ibid., May 14, 1992, 3; November 12, 1992, 3; November 19, 1992, 7; December 10, 1992, 6; *Birmingham News*, November 18, 1992, A1–2; November 19, 1992, C1–2.

8. *Alabama Baptist*, March 17, 1994, 1–3; March 24, 1994, 1, 3, 7; March 31, 1994, 3; April 7, 1994, 6, 8; April 21, 1994, 11; May 5, 1994, 3; June 23, 1994, 13.

9. Ibid., May 12, 1994, 1, 6; *Birmingham News*, May 20, 1994, 62.

10. *Alabama Baptist*, June 9, 1994, 1; June 16, 1994, 1; June 23, 1994, 1; September 1, 1994, 1, 10.

11. Leonard, *God's Last and Only Hope*, 160.

12. *Alabama Baptist*, April 2, 1992, 8.

13. *Birmingham News*, September 14, 1994, A1, A10; *Chronicle of Higher Education*, July 13, 1994, A13–14. Besides the creation of new divinity schools at larger Baptist institutions, Gardner-Webb University (once a tiny two-year college in central North Carolina) established a divinity school in 1993. A spokesman for the institution claimed that it was conservative, but he proudly asserted that it trained students to think for themselves. One student said the school followed a middle course.

Bibliography

Primary Sources

Manuscript Collections

Morris Chapman Papers (presidential). 4 boxes, unprocessed collection. Southern
  Baptist Historical Library and Archives, Nashville, Tenn.
James T. Draper, Jr., Papers (presidential). 4 boxes. SBHLA, Nashville, Tenn.
M. O. Owens, Jr., Papers. 4 boxes. SBHLA, Nashville, Tenn.
Adrian Rogers Papers (presidential). 2 boxes. SBHLA, Nashville, Tenn.
Bailey Smith Papers (presidential). 2 boxes. SBHLA, Nashville, Tenn.
Charles F. Stanley Papers (presidential). 3 boxes. SBHLA, Nashville, Tenn.
Jerry Vines Papers (presidential). 4 boxes. SBHLA, Nashville, Tenn.

Official Records and Proceedings

Annual of the Southern Baptist Convention. Nashville: Executive Committee of the SBC,
  published annually.
Baptist Press Releases. Issued regularly and available at the SBHLA, Nashville, Tenn.
Minutes, Executive Committee of the SBC. Available at the SBHLA, Nashville, Tenn.
Proceedings of the Conference on Biblical Inerrancy, 1987. Nashville: Broadman Press,
  1987.
SBC Book of Reports. Published by the Convention and distributed to messengers at
  each SBC annual meeting.

Special Materials

Audiotape of a conference in Louisville, Kentucky, with William E. Hull, Duke
  McCall, William A. (Bill) Powell, Sr., and others in attendance. December 14,
  1973. Made available to the author by M. O. Owens, Jr., in 1993.
Baptist History File, Sunday School Board, available at the SBHLA, Nashville, Tenn.
Files on the SBC Controversy. (Consists of letters, research papers, newspaper and
  journal clippings, etc.) SBHLA, Nashville, Tenn.
Firestorm Chats with Judge Paul Pressler. Audiotape in the SBHLA, Nashville, Tenn.
Transcript of an oral history interview with Wallace B. Henley by Irma R. Cruse.
  Special Collections, Samford University Library, Birmingham, Ala.

Author's Notes Taken at Interviews, Public Debates, and Press Conferences

Hope for Reconciliation: A Dialogue held at Samford University, October 11, 1990.
  (Participants: Paul Pressler, David Montoya, Wayne Dorsett, and Randall Fields.)
Telephone interview with Bert Card (former president of the Baptist Faith and Mes-
  sage Fellowship) of Atlanta, Ga., on July 12, 1993.

Interview with Glen Holt, president of the North Carolina Baptist Convention and pastor of the First Baptist Church of Fayetteville, N.C., June 1, 1992.

Interview with William E. Hull, vice-president for academic affairs, Samford University, June 16, 1993.

Interview with Alan Neely, former professor of missions at Southeastern Baptist Theological Seminary, August 17, 1988.

Interview with Mrs. Anne Neil, third president of the Southern Baptist Alliance, May 18, 1989.

Interview with M. O. Owens, Jr., and Gerald C. Primm, former North Carolina Baptist pastors and leaders in forming the Baptist Faith and Message Fellowship, December 29, 1992.

Interview with Paige Patterson, president of Southeastern Baptist Theological Seminary and a spearhead of the second fundamentalist crusade, December 30, 1992.

Telephone interview with Lee Porter, former registration secretary of the Southern Baptist Convention, April 19, 1994.

Interview with Mrs. William A. (Betty) Powell, Sr., (wife of Bill Powell) and James A. Pate (father-in-law of Bill Powell), July 1, 1993.

Interview with John Franklin Turner, pastor of Brown Baptist Church in Clinton, N.C., August 9, 1990.

Press Conference called by Al Shackleford and Dan Martin after they were fired by the SBC Executive Committee on July 17, 1990. Author's notes and handouts by Shackleford and Martin.

Correspondence and Other Materials Sent to Author and in His Possession

Finlator, William W. (former pastor of Pullen Memorial Baptist Church, Raleigh, N.C.). One letter, a sermon entitled "Reclaiming the Birthright," and a manuscript book review of *The Southern Baptists: A Subculture in Transition*, by Ellen Rosenberg.

Owens, M. O., Jr., Ten letters [September 16, 1992, and following] and his vita.

Pate, James A. One letter [February 1993].

Patterson, Paige. Eight letters [September 23, 1992, and following], his vita, an article by him entitled "Reflections on the Atonement," and an unpublished master's thesis written at Southern Baptist Theological Seminary in 1976 by Noel A. Hollyfield, Jr., and entitled "A Sociological Analysis of the Degrees of 'Christian Orthodoxy' Among Selected Students in the Southern Baptist Theological Seminary."

Pressler, Paul. Two letters [September 30, 1992, and August 8, 1993], his vita, and a document entitled "Ancestors of Judge Paul Pressler Who Have Been Active Baptists."

Primm, Gerald C. One letter and miscellaneous material on the conservative movement in North Carolina beginning in 1969.

Journals and Newspapers

Alabama Baptist
Alaska Baptist Messenger
Arkansas Baptist Newsmagazine
Baptist Beacon

Baptist Courier
Baptist Digest
Baptist Message
Baptist Messenger
Baptist New Mexican
Baptist Record
Baptist and Reflector
Baptist Standard
Baptists United News
Baylor Line
The Bell [Congregational paper of Snyder Memorial Baptist Church, Fayetteville, N.C.]
Biblical Recorder
Birmingham [Alabama] *News*
Birmingham [Alabama] *Post-Herald*
California Southern Baptist
Capital Baptist
Charlotte [North Carolina] *Observer*
Christian Index
Christianity Today
Chronicle of Higher Education
Fayetteville [North Carolina] *Observer*
Florida Baptist Witness
Folio: A Newsletter for Southern Baptist Women in Ministry
Hawaii Baptist
Houston [Texas] *Chronicle*
Indiana Baptist
Iowa Southern Baptist
Maryland Baptist
Michigan Baptist Advocate
Minnesota-Wisconsin Southern Baptist
Montana Baptist
Montgomery [Alabama] *Advertiser*
National Forum [the Phi Kappa Phi journal]
Nevada Baptist
New England Baptist
New York Baptist
[Raleigh, N.C.] *News and Observer*
North Plains Baptist
Northwest Baptist Witness
Ohio Baptist Messenger
Penn/Jersey Baptist
Philippine Baptist
Religious Herald
Richmond [Virginia] *Times-Dispatch*
Rocky Mountain Baptist
SBC Today

Southern Baptist Advocate
Southern Baptist Journal
Sword and the Trowel
Utah-Idaho Witness—Southern Baptist
Wall Street Journal
Western Recorder
West Virginia Southern Baptist
Word & Way

Contemporary Histories and Studies

Ammerman, Nancy T. *Baptist Battles: Social Change and Religious Conflict in the South-*
ern Baptist Convention. New Brunswick and London: Rutgers University Press,
1990.
————, ed. *Southern Baptists Observed.* Knoxville: University of Tennessee Press,
1993.
Barnhart, Joe Edward. *The Southern Baptist Holy War.* Austin: Texas Monthly Press,
1986.
Beale, David O. *S.B.C.: House on the Sand.* Greenville, S.C.: Unusual Publications [of
Bob Jones University], 1985.
Cothen, Grady C. *What Happened to the Southern Baptist Convention?* Macon, Ga.:
Smyth & Helwys Publishing, 1993.
Davis, Jimmy Thomas. Organizational Ideographs: A Study of the Recent Rise of
Southern Baptist Fundamentalism. Unpublished Ph.D. dissertation, Indiana
University, 1987.
Dowler, Joanne Dailey. Fantasy Theme Analysis and Religious Movements: A Rhe-
torical Criticism of the Conservative Inerrancy Movement in the Southern Bap-
tist Convention. Unpublished master's thesis, University of New Mexico, 1992.
Farnsley, Arthur Emery, II. *Southern Baptist Politics: Authority and Power in the Restruc-*
turing of an American Denomination. University Park: Pennsylvania State Univer-
sity Press, 1994.
Hefley, James Carl. *The Conservative Resurgence in the Southern Baptist Convention.*
Hannibal, Mo.: Hannibal Books, 1991.
————. *Issues and Effects: The Controversy Between "Conservatives and Moderates" in the*
Southern Baptist Convention. Hannibal, Mo.: Hannibal Books, n.d.
————. *The Truth in Crisis.* 5 volumes. Dallas: Clarion Publications, and Hannibal,
Mo.: Hannibal Books, 1986–1990.
Hill, Samuel S., Jr., and Dennis E. Owen. *The New Religious Political Right in America*
Nashville: Abingdon, 1982.
James, Gordon. *Inerrancy and the Southern Baptist Convention.* Dallas: Southern Baptist
Heritage, 1986.
James, Robison B., ed. *The Takeover in the Southern Baptist Convention: A Brief History.*
Decatur, Ga.: *SBC Today,* 1989.
————. *The Unfettered Word: Southern Baptists Confront the Authority-Inerrancy Ques-*
tion. Waco, Tex.: Word Book Publisher, 1987.
James, Robison B., and David S. Dockery. *Beyond the Impasse? Scripture, Interpretation,*
and Theology in Baptist Life. Nashville: Broadman Press, 1992.
Kell, Carl L. They Have Seen a Great Light: Toward a Rhetoric of the Inerrancy Move-

ment in the Southern Baptist Convention, 1970–1987. Unpublished research paper produced at Western Kentucky University. Located in the SBHLA, Nashville, Tenn.

Leonard, Bill J. *God's Last and Only Hope: The Fragmentation of the Southern Baptist Convention.* Grand Rapids, Mich.: Eerdman's, 1990.

Lienesch, Michael. *Redeeming America: Piety and Politics in the New Christian Right.* Chapel Hill: University of North Carolina Press, 1993.

McNabb, Freddie, III. Inerrancy and Beyond: The Controversy in the Southern Baptist Convention. Unpublished master's thesis, University of Southern Mississippi, 1991.

Moen, Matthew C. *The Transformation of the Christian Right.* Tuscaloosa: University of Alabama Press, 1992.

Neely, Alan, ed. *Being Baptist Means Freedom.* Charlotte, N.C.: Southern Baptist Alliance, Publishers, 1988.

Paschall, Henry F. *Identity Crisis in the Church: The Southern Baptist Convention Controversy.* Nashville: Privately published, 1993.

Rosenberg, Ellen M. *The Southern Baptists: A Subculture in Transition.* Knoxville: University of Tennessee Press, 1989.

Shurden, Walter B. *The Baptist Identity: Four Fragile Freedoms.* Macon, Ga.: Smyth & Helwys Publishing, 1993.

———, ed. *The Struggle for the Soul of the SBC.* Macon, Ga.: Mercer University Press, 1993.

Wiles, Dennis Ray. Factors Contributing to the Resurgence of Fundamentalism in the Southern Baptist Convention, 1979–1990. Unpublished Ph.D. dissertation, Southwestern Baptist Theological Seminary, 1992.

Contemporary Articles and Speeches

Allen, Charles W. "Paige Patterson: Contender for Baptist Sectarianism." *Review and Expositor* 79, no. 1 (Winter 1982): 105–20.

Baker, James T. "Southern Baptists in the 70s." *Christian Century,* June 27, 1973, 699–703.

"Baptists Committed to the Southern Baptist Convention—Publication," National Edition, 1990. [A tract published by the moderate group known as Baptists Committed.]

Buchanan, John H. "Religiously Inspired Censorship in the Public Schools." *National Forum* 68, no. 1 (Winter 1988): 34–35.

Garrett, James Leo, Jr., "Who Are the Baptists?" *Baylor Line,* June 1985, 11–15.

Guth, James L. "Preachers and Politics: Varieties of Activism among Southern Baptist Ministers." In *Religion and Politics in the South,* edited by Tod A. Baker et al., 161–83. New York: Praeger, 1983.

Hastey, Stan L. "McAteer Key Figure in SBC Swing to New Right Causes." *Biblical Recorder,* July 24, 1982, 8, 15.

Hinson, E. Glenn. "Southern Baptists and the Liberal Tradition," *Baptist History and Heritage* 19, no. 3 (July 1984): 16–20.

Hobbs, Herschel H. "The Baptist Faith and Message—Anchored But Free." *Baptist History and Heritage* 13, no. 3 (July 1978): 33–40.

Honeycutt, Roy L. "SBC Takeover Must Be Averted." *Baylor Line*, November 1984, 55–56.

Howe, Claude L., Jr., "From Houston to Dallas: Recent Controversy in the Southern Baptist Convention." *Theological Educator*, 1985 special issue, 31–44.

Hunter, Allen. "In the Wings: New Right Ideology and Organization." *Radical America* 15, nos. 1–2 (Spring 1981): 113–38.

"Interview with Judge Paul Pressler." *Theological Educator*, 1985 special issue, 15–24.

"Interview with Adrian Rogers." *Theological Educator*, 1988 special issue, 3–14.

"Interview with Porter Routh." *Theological Educator*, 1985 special issue, 25–27.

Knight, Walker. "Pressler: Politicizing the SBC." *SBC Today*, February 1, 1987, 3.

Leonard, Bill J. "The Origin and Character of Fundamentalism." *Review and Expositor* 79, 1 (Winter 1982): 5–16.

———. "Southern Baptists in Search of a Century." *Christian Century*, July 24, 1985, 683–84.

———. "Southern Baptists and the Separation of Church and State." *Review and Expositor* 83, no. 2 (Spring 1986): 195–208.

———. "Unity, Diversity, or Schism: The SBC at the Crossroads." *Baptist History and Heritage* 16, no. 2 (April 1981): 2–8.

Lienesch, Michael. "Right-Wing Religion: Christian Conservatism as a Political Movement." *Political Science Quarterly* 97, no. 3 (Fall 1982): 403–25.

Lofton, John D., Jr., "Roundtable President: Ed McAteer is Music Man of the Religious Right." *Conservative Digest*, January 1981, 74–79.

Lyles, Jean Caffey. "Creeping Creedalism in the Southern Baptist Convention." *Christian Century*, July 9, 1980, 691–92.

Marty, Martin E. "Fundamentalism as a Social Phenomenon." *Review and Expositor* 79, no. 1 (Winter 1982): 19–29.

May, Lynn E., Jr., "The Southern Baptist Convention, 1979–1993: What Happened and Why?" *Baptist History and Heritage* 28, no. 4 (October 1993): 2–35. [Along with the editorial by May are articles by Stan Hastey, James C. Hefley, Richard D. Land, and Bill J. Leonard.]

McBeth, Leon. "Fundamentalism in the Southern Baptist Convention in Recent Years." *Review and Expositor* 79, no. 1 (Winter 1982): 85–104.

McKibbens, Thomas R. "Report on the SBC to the Dunster Society." Speech delivered on October 20, 1987. In the Files on the SBC Controversy, SBHLA, Nashville, Tenn.

Morgan, David T. "The Great Awakening in North Carolina, 1740–1775: The Baptist Phase." *North Carolina Historical Review* 45, no. 3 (Summer 1968): 267–83.

———. "Upheaval in the Southern Baptist Convention, 1979–1990: Crusade for Truth or Bid for Power?" *Journal of Religious History* 17, no. 3 (June 1993): 321–35.

———. "Upheaval in the Southern Baptist Convention, 1979–1990: The Texas Connection." *Perspectives in Religious Studies* 19, no. 1 (Spring 1992): 53–71.

Neely, Alan. "Where Do We Go from Here?" A speech delivered to the SBC Forum on June 11, 1988, in San Antonio, Texas. Published by the Southern Baptist Alliance.

Patterson, Paige. "Evidences." Circulated by Paige Patterson with a rebuttal from Fisher Humphreys. In possession of Fisher Humphreys and made available to the author.

——. "Paige Patterson to Friends, May 2, 1980." With an attachment called "A Reply of Concern." In possession of Fisher Humphreys and made available to the author.

Plowman, Edward E. "Conservative Network Puts Its Stamp on the Southern Baptist Convention." *Christianity Today,* July 18, 1980, 844–45.

Reavis, Dick J. "The Politics of Armageddon." *SBC Today,* December 1984 and January 1985, 3.

"Report of the President's Task Force on the Denominational Crisis." *Religious Herald,* November 3, 1988, 1–2.

Sherman, Cecil. "The New Baptists." *Baylor Line,* September 1985, 20–23.

Shurden, Walter B. "The Erosion of Denominationalism: The Current State of the Southern Baptist Convention." A speech delivered at the annual meeting of the South Carolina Baptist Historical Society, November 12, 1984. In the SBC Controversy File, Special Collections, Samford University Library, Birmingham, Ala.

——. "The Inerrancy Debate: A Comparative Study of Southern Baptist Controversies." *Baptist History and Heritage* 16 (April 1981): 12–19.

——. "The Southern Baptist Synthesis: Is It Cracking?" *Baptist History and Heritage* 16 (April 1981): 2–11.

Soderburg, Kema. "Conservatives Hail Inerrancy Decision." In the [Raleigh, N.C.] *News and Observer,* August 1, 1987, C4.

Storey, John W. "Religious Fundamentalism, an Elusive Phenomenon." Lamar University, Beaumont, Tex., Distinguished Faculty Lecture, October 19, 1987.

Waldman, Peter. "Holy War: Fundamentalists Fight to Capture the Soul of Southern Baptists." *Wall Street Journal,* March 7, 1988, 1.

Yance, Norman A. "Religion Southern Style: Southern Baptists and Society in Historical Perspective." *Perspectives in Religious Studies.* Special Studies Series 4. Danville, Va., 1978.

Secondary Works

Reference Works

Encyclopedia of Southern Baptists. 4 vols. to date. Nashville: Broadman Press, 1958–1993.

Hill, Samuel S., ed. *Encyclopedia of Religion in the South.* Macon, Ga.: Mercer University Press, 1984.

Monographs and Special Studies

Baker, Robert A. *The Southern Baptist Convention and Its People, 1607–1972.* Nashville: Broadman Press, 1974.

Barnes, William W. *The Southern Baptist Convention, 1845–1953.* Nashville: Broadman Press, 1954.

Beale, David O. *In Pursuit of Purity: American Fundamentalism Since 1850.* Greenville, S.C.: Unusual Publications [of Bob Jones University], 1986.

Berger, Peter. *The Heretical Imperative.* New York: Doubleday Anchor, 1979.

Black, Earl, and Merle Black. *Politics and Society in the South.* Cambridge: Harvard University Press, 1987.

D'Antonio, Michael. *Fall from Grace: The Failed Crusade of the Christian Right*. New York: Farrar, Straus, and Giroux, 1989.

Dworkin, Andrea. *Right-Wing Women*. New York: Perigee Books, 1983.

Eighmy, John Lee. *Churches in Cultural Captivity: A History of the Social Attitudes of Southern Baptists*. Knoxville: University of Tennessee Press, 1989.

Ericson, Edward L. *American Freedom and the Radical Right*. New York: Ungar, 1982.

Furniss, Norman. *The Fundamentalist Controversy, 1918–1931*. Hamden, Conn.: Archon, 1963. (Originally published in 1954.)

Garrett, James Leo, Jr., E. Glenn Hinson, and James E. Tull. *Are Southern Baptists Evangelicals?* Macon, Ga.: Mercer University Press, 1983.

Hunter, James Davison. *American Evangelicalism: Conservative Religion and the Quandary of Modernity*. New Brunswick, N.J.: Rutgers University Press, 1983.

Liebman, Robert C., and Robert Wuthnow, eds. *The New Christian Right*. Hawthorne, N.Y.: Aldine, 1983.

Marsden, George. *Fundamentalism and American Culture*. New York: Oxford University Press, 1980.

———. *Reforming Fundamentalism: Fuller Seminary and the New Evangelicalism*. Grand Rapids, Mich.: Eerdman's, 1987.

———. *Understanding Fundamentalism and Evangelicalism*. Grand Rapids, Mich.: Eerdman's, 1991.

McBeth, H. Leon. *The Baptist Heritage*. Nashville: Broadman Press, 1987.

Reichley, James A. *Religion in American Life*. Washington, D.C.: Brookings Institution, 1985.

Roof, Wade C., and William McKinney. *American Mainline Religion: Its Changing Shape and Future*. New Brunswick, N.J.: Rutgers University Press, 1987.

Sandeen, Ernest R. *The Roots of Fundamentalism: British and American Millenarianism, 1800–1930*. Chicago: University of Chicago Press, 1970.

Shurden, Walter B. *The Life of Baptists in the Life of the World*. Nashville: Broadman Press, 1985.

Thompson, James J., Jr., *Tried as by Fire: Southern Baptists and the Religious Controversies of the Twenties*. Macon, Ga.: Mercer University Press, 1982.

Young, Percy Deane. *God's Bullies*. New York: Holt, Rinehart, and Winston, 1982.

Index

Abington Township v. Schempp, U.S. Supreme Court case, 8
Abortion: fight over at SBC annual meetings, 51, 59; resolution against at Kansas City, 65; condemned by Southwestern Seminary's board of trustees, 141; as a serious issue among Southern Baptists, 152–55; *mentioned*, 62, 113, 114, 115, 116, 136, 164, 178
Abstracts and Principles, doctrinal statement signed by Southern Seminary faculty members, 135
Alabama, University of, 29
Alabama Baptist, 120, 124, 178
Alabama Baptist Convention: consensus politics of are threatened, 188–89; *mentioned*, 74, 95, 143, 155, 157, 166, 170
Alabama Baptists for Life, prolife group: calls for political action, 154–55
Aldridge, Marlon, South Carolina pastor: grows tired of fighting the fundamentalists, 172
Alien immersion, 12
Allen, Jimmy, former SBC president: chairs meeting in Atlanta, 172; attends meeting called by Walter Shurden, 186
Allen, Loyd, faculty member at Southern Seminary: resigns to go to Mississippi [Baptist] College, 137
Alliance of Baptists. *See* Southern Baptist Alliance
Allred amendment: offered by Thurmond Allred, pastor from Concord, N. C., 25
American Association of University Professors: says academic freedom in peril at Southeastern Seminary, 139
American Baptist Seminary Commission, an SBC commission, 11
American Bible Society, an organization with which the SBC associates, 11
American Coalition of Traditional Values: headed by Tim LaHaye, 165
American Revolution, 1, 2
Ammerman, Nancy, sociologist and author

of book on the SBC Controversy: surveys Southern Baptists on the inerrancy issue, 80, 192; on abortion, 153; member of Baptist Center for Ethics' board, 175
Annual of the Southern Baptist Convention, 42
Annuity Board, one of the major SBC boards, 11, 105, 154, 172
Antimissionary Baptists: hold hyper-Calvinist views, 1–2
Arminius, Jacob, Dutch theologian, 1
Ashcraft, Morris, academic dean at Southeastern Baptist Theological Seminary: resigns after fundamentalists gain control, 138
Associated Baptist Press: founding of announced, 123, 160–61; *mentioned*, 176, 190
Associated Church Press, 159
Association of Theological Schools: Southeastern Seminary's accrediting problems with, 138–40; reaccredits Southwestern Seminary, 188
Atlanta Constitution: defends Mercer University, 144
Atlanta convention of the SBC (1986): 40,000 messengers attend, 79–82
Autographs, original manuscripts of the biblical texts: the only inerrant ones according to fundamentalists, 45–46

Baggett, Hudson, editor of the *Alabama Baptist*: calls Dan Martin and Al Shackleford casualties in a civil war, 24; criticizes FMB for rejecting Greg and Katrina Pennington, 126
Bagley, George, retired executive secretary-treasurer of the Alabama Baptist Convention: disappointed at success of fundamentalists, 170
Bailey, Robert W., Alabama pastor: disappointed upon leaving the SBC meeting in Atlanta (1986), 81
Baker, Douglas, South Carolina pastor: moderate candidate elected president of the South Carolina Baptist Convention, 90